A DEVIL WENT DOWN TO GEORGIA

RACE, POWER, PRIVILEGE, AND THE MURDER OF LITA McCLINTON

DEB MILLER LANDAU

PEGASUS BOOKS
NEW YORK LONDON

A DEVIL WENT DOWN TO GEORGIA

Pegasus Books, Ltd.
148 West 37th Street, 13th Floor
New York, NY 10018

First Pegasus Books cloth edition August 2024

Interior design by Maria Fernandez

Library of Congress Cataloging-in-Publication Data is available.

ISBN: 978-1-63936-683-5

10 9 8 7 6 5 4 3 2 1

Printed in the United States of America
Distributed by Simon & Schuster
www.pegasusbooks.com

To my boys

❖

"My wish for you
Is that you continue
Continue
To be who and how you are
To astonish a mean world
With your acts of kindness"

—*Maya Angelou*

CONTENTS

PROLOGUE

'm sitting in a rented Pacifica minivan in a desolate parking lot at City Lake Park in Albemarle, North Carolina, waiting to meet a man recently released from prison for orchestrating a murder. For decades, newspaper headlines across the country called him "The Hitman"—*Hitman Found, Suspected Hitman Charged in Killing of Buckhead Socialite, Hitman Released*. I spent months hunting him down before he finally called me—I was at the grocery store buying milk—and we've talked and emailed several times since.

"While it would be refreshing to have the opportunity to meet with someone that is all about learning the truth and printing it," he said, "I'm not sure if you have the resources to do the things that I would require of you." I had looked over my shoulder in a fit of nonsensical panic—is anyone seeing this?—but it was an opening, even though I had no idea what he was talking about.

He knows I'm coming, but he's ghosted me for the past couple of weeks, and now I fear I've made the trip for nothing. I've taken a redeye to Charlotte from my home in Oregon, achieved only a couple of hours of neck-jerking airplane sleep, and now find myself in a tiny town in the middle of nowhere—for what?

I first wrote a retrospective about the brutal 1987 murder of Lita McClinton Sullivan for *Atlanta* magazine in 2004. It was a case that shook the city, later the country, and still later the world. A Black socialite from a politically powerful Atlanta family, gunned down in broad daylight in one of the most upscale, whitest neighborhoods in Georgia. For a decade, the case went cold, unnervingly frigid. It became fodder for newspapers and magazines, was featured on television shows like Dominick Dunne's *Power, Privilege, and Justice*, CBS's *48 Hours*, *Extra!*, *FBI: Most Wanted*, and many others. Journalists like me followed it for years, lawyers didn't sleep, cops took it to their graves, and Lita's family pushed and bent till they almost broke.

I'd been a writer for a decade when I got the Atlanta magazine assignment, but this was the first true crime story I'd ever covered—and I fell into it, hard. I got pulled in by reading police reports, news stories, and endless court documents, but what really climbed under my skin was the humanity and depravity of it all. What makes people become who they are? What leads us to the choices we make?

The story impacted me so much, I still had the banker's box full of files upon whose lid I'd scrawled *Sullivan* with a black Sharpie decades prior. The box survived several moves, a flooded basement, a storage locker, my divorce, neglect. In it were yellowing court documents, hand-scrawled notes, business cards of long-retired police detectives, and a photo of Lita given to me by her parents; it's the same one that graces the cover of this book. I'd periodically pull out that photo and wonder what she was thinking in that moment, what she thought in so many moments before and after. I kept in loose touch with the McClinton family lawyers and their private investigator. Sometimes I'd google James Sullivan. Every time I thought about pitching the box, I'd put the lid on and shove it back on a shelf, sensing there was more story left inside it.

Then, as the world was in lockdown in May of 2020, George Floyd was murdered by police in Minneapolis, and something in me shifted. Just a few years prior, I had joined millions of women who'd taken to the streets wearing homemade pink "pussyhats" to fight against misogyny and protect the rights of women. Then, brave women took to the highways of social media as the #MeToo movement shone light in the faces of miscreant men and demanded a change in the power imbalance of Hollywood and beyond. Now, I joined other outraged protestors who flooded the streets shouting about how Black lives mattered only to be teargassed and harangued as angry mobs.

In the eye-stinging haze of pepper spray and the reverb that followed that summer, I began thinking about Lita and the McClinton family in this new day of reckoning. How clearly had I seen Lita the first time I wrote this story? I felt increasingly called to reexamine not only Lita's life and death, but my own exploration of it too.

Around this time, I reached out to my old *Atlanta* magazine editor, and we talked for hours. Finally, around the middle of the call, he said in his slow Georgia accent, "Well, sounds like maybe it's time to write a book."

There it was, the reason I'd carried that box around all these years. The responsibility of reopening it felt both essential and monumental. As I sifted through the papers, I began to slowly realize the story I thought I knew wasn't the whole story. I've spent the past few years drowning in court documents, grasping to get my hands on information that evaporated years ago, clinging to the fading memories of retired cops, investigators, reporters, family members, and attorneys. Many people are no longer alive. Others don't return my calls. Still others can't or don't want to remember; it's still too painful. My walls are decorated with sticky notes that keep falling to the floor. The more I learn, it seems, the less I know.

So here I am, rubbing crusty bits of sleep from the tender crannies of my eyeballs, in a rented minivan in a tiny town in the middle of nowhere, trying to talk to a hitman.

If North Carolina is the rough shape of a revolver pointing west, Albemarle, the Stanly County seat, is just north of the trigger. I've driven all around, past junkyards with broken cars and rusted washing machines, past the "Home of Kellie Pickler" sign in the courthouse square celebrating the *American Idol* contestant who escaped this town, past the colonial homes, deserted textile mills, and unabashed cemeteries on the side of the road. And I've done some googling. This little agricultural town about an hour east of Charlotte grew up around the production and manufacturing of cotton. For decades, everyone worked at "the mill"—bagging sacks of raw cotton, spinning fiber into yarn, attaching toes to socks at the hosiery mills. Since the textile mills closed in the 1980s, the town has grappled to redefine itself. A lot of families here struggle to make ends meet.

It's January 13, 2023, and unseasonably cold. No one is out, save for a couple of weathered souls walking into the forest playing disc golf. I check my phone again. Still no text from the hitman. I feel a mix of relief and disappointment. I'm not entirely sure what I'm hoping he'll tell me, other than his side of the story.

I sigh, scroll to the "Lita" album in the photos app on my phone, and look at her pensive, beautiful face. Whatever happens today, it's a good reminder: it all starts and ends with Lita McClinton Sullivan.

I decide not to wait any longer and dial his number. To my surprise, he answers right away.

"Where you at?" he asks in his big booming voice. No pleasantries, no small talk.

"In Albemarle," I say.

"Yeah, I *know*," he says like I'm stupid. "Where?"

I tell him I'm at the park, but before I can suggest a coffee shop, somewhere warm, safe, and public with people around, he interrupts and says he's on his way.

Click.

I panic, looking around the empty parking lot, the quiet lake. I wonder briefly if there are bodies in that water, what would happen if the cops found my empty minivan. This isn't how it's supposed to go. Literally no one knows where I am. I turn on location sharing and shoot a text to my friend in Atlanta: "Meeting hitman in 5!" She sends back a wide-eyed emoji and, even though it's freezing, I begin to sweat.

I take a deep breath, look at Lita one last time, and think, *OK, let's do this.*

❖

Three days later, I'm visiting the home of Lita's parents, Jo Ann and Emory McClinton. I first met the McClintons two decades ago when I was a writer at *Atlanta* magazine. Back then, they lived in a giant neoclassical colonial home that would later become a Landmark Building on Atlanta's Registry for Historic Places. The ranch home they live in today, on a generous swath of property on the outskirts of Atlanta, is more navigable for two people approaching their nineties. It's surrounded by pine trees, the ground splendid with the burnt orange of pine straw. There's a wheelchair on the stoop, some garden gnomes beside the driveway, a few Christmas ornaments still decorating the yard.

It's January 16, the federal holiday celebrating Martin Luther King Jr.'s birth. Had he lived, the civil rights leader would be ninety-four. It's also thirty-six years to the day since Lita McClinton Sullivan's murder. I comment on this anniversary to Lita's mother, Jo Ann, assuming we should acknowledge the weight of it, but Jo Ann just shrugs. Her grief isn't particular on this day; the pain of losing her eldest daughter has long since settled into her bones. It ebbs and flows, but it's always there.

Jo Ann, who spent more than twelve years as a representative on the Georgia General Assembly, has barely aged since I first met her. She's a little shorter but still glamorous. She's wearing a brown velour pantsuit, her hair curled and set, makeup flawless. Her gold jewelry clicks and jangles when she moves. She doesn't remember meeting me back in 2004—she's spoken to so many reporters over the years—but she's warm and welcoming. It took some time for us to get to this place; understandably, the family had some resistance to reopening this deep wound. It took several emails and calls, plus a vote of confidence from Patrick McKenna, the investigator who worked tirelessly on behalf of the family for decades, before Jo Ann agreed to meet with me. She understood why I wanted to write the only comprehensive book about Lita's murder, why retelling it now felt important, but she needed to know I wouldn't be reckless with the story. She said she'd participate, but only if I wrote a nonsensational account, a balanced look at all that went down.

We settle in a formal dining room as I pull a recorder, pen, and notebook out of my backpack. I see the legs and shadow of a man sitting on a couch in another room, where the TV's on, barely audible. Jo Ann tells me her husband, Emory McClinton, also eighty-nine, is riddled with cancer and suffering from dementia. It's hard to reconcile this with the man I met back in 2004. I remember being struck by his height and the intensity with which he held eye contact when he shook my hand—a man who didn't suffer fools.

Jo Ann smiles and looks down at her hands, twirls the wedding ring that's been on her finger for more than seventy years. Jo Ann and Emory met at Catholic school when they were in the fourth grade. They married as high school seniors and have been together ever since. They had their first child, Lita, when they were just nineteen. Two more babies came quickly after that. The young family lived with Jo Ann's mother, who helped with the bills and the babies while Emory took the bus each week from Atlanta to Tuskegee University in Alabama to study engineering. Georgia Tech would become the first white people-only university in the South to admit Black students without a court order, but not until 1961.

"So," I say once Jo Ann and I settle into upholstered dining room chairs. I've thought about this moment for months. This time feels precious, like a thing I need to handle with utmost care. I don't want to say anything offensive, or make assumptions, or overstay my welcome. I have so many questions, but I don't know if I'll have ten minutes or two hours. Will she tire and decide this conversation isn't worth it? I take a deep breath. "Tell me all about Lita."

CHAPTER 1

THE DOORBELL RINGS
(JANUARY 16, 1987)

I t's the Friday before the long weekend—the second-ever Martin Luther King Day is on Monday—and it's overcast and drizzly, one of those cold midwinter days after the holidays when brittle pine needles from the Christmas tree still linger in the carpet. Usually a late sleeper, Lita has been awake since dawn, unable to sleep, puttering about in her white satin dressing gown. She's nervous about this afternoon; what happens today will change everything.

In a few short hours, a judge will make a major decision on the division of assets in her divorce, a near-final step in the long and arduous death march of her ten-year marriage. Just a few days past her thirty-fifth birthday, Lita longs for it all to be over. Though she's tried to put on a brave face for her family and friends, Lita is jumpy and uneasy, not her usual composed and joyful self. There's been some strange things happening lately—an early banging on the door a few days ago, the tingling creep up her spine when she feels like she's being followed around town. Maybe it's all nothing, a paranoia borne of the divorce stress, but she's a little spooked.

It's around 8:15 A.M. when the doorbell rings. Lita wonders who it could be so early in the morning. She tightens her robe and heads downstairs to answer the door.

❖

Half an hour earlier, less than a mile from Lita's townhouse, Randall Benson opens the Botany Bay Florist on Peachtree Street in Buckhead, an affluent commercial and residential district of Atlanta. Randall, twenty-six, fastidious and tidy, wears a neat mint-blue linen suit and bowtie. He is running late, which is unusual for him. The shop is supposed to open at 8 A.M. but by the time he turns on the lights, unlocks the front door, and retrieves the register cash hidden in the walk-in cooler in the back, it's about 8:05 A.M. He chastises himself for having to rush. He is a contractor for several florists around town, and reputation is everything. He'd been hired by Botany to help through the holidays and into January; he's only been working there about a month. Given the dreary morning, he expects a slow day, so he's surprised when the bell jingles.

"Helloo!" he sings from behind the counter. The flower shop was built inside an old filling station, so there is a drive-up curb and a wall of windows where the garage doors used to be. As Randall takes in the customer walking toward the counter, he hesitates, heat suddenly creeping up the back of his neck, an alert ringing in his belly. The man looks nothing like the usual upscale Buckhead business crowd that comes in to buy flowers on the way to or from work. This guy is rough and grubby, with no hint of a smile. He wears green work pants and a faded flannel shirt. Randall pegs him as in his mid-thirties, around six feet tall with curly hair and an unruly beard.

"I need a dozen roses," the man says, not making eye contact. "In a box."

Randall, a lifelong Georgia boy, detects an accent different from his own but can't quite pin it. "Well, that sounds lovely," Randall says, working hard to ignore the prickling in his ears. "What color are we looking for?"

"It don't matter. Just a dozen roses."

Randall swallows hard. "Well, is there a special occasion? If it's for your wife or your girlfriend, you'll want red. But if it's for an anniversary, you'll want yellow and . . ."

"Listen, I told you it don't matter," says the man. "Just hurry."

"Of course," says Randall, mentally working out what he should do. Is something happening here, or is he imagining it? Regardless, he wants the interaction to be over so he can finish opening the store and get on with the day. He glances out the store's front windows and notes a dirty white Toyota car with a blue pinstripe parked diagonally, so that Randall is looking at the passenger side. He makes out the shadowy profile of a man waiting in the driver's seat. Exhaust from the tailpipe tells him the engine's still running. Randall chooses pale pink roses because they are the freshest and begins quickly wiring the buds. He's wired five when the man tells him not to bother with the others.

"Are you sure? If we don't wire them, the heads will droop," explains Randall. Seeing the man's confusion he adds, "And then they won't last as long." Again, the man insists it doesn't matter.

Randall gently lays the flowers on a bed of green tissue paper in a long white box and belts it with a pink satin ribbon. He is about to affix the shop sticker when the man tells him not to and says he doesn't need a card.

"I see," says Randall, anxious to be rid of the man. "That'll be $28.15."

The guy searches his pockets and pulls out several crinkled bills, but it becomes clear he doesn't have enough cash.

"Hang on a minute," he says, leaving the box on the counter while he goes out to the car. Randall braces himself, deciding if this is a robbery, he'll simply hand over the cash and let the man take whatever he wants. But if it's a robbery, why order flowers? Randall watches the man open the passenger door and say something to the driver. The driver turns to rummage around in the back seat, which is full of what looks to Randall like rolled sleeping bags.

Finally, the man returns. He dumps $30 in cash on the counter, takes the flowers, and says, "Keep the change."

Randall watches the car drive away, noting the North Carolina plates. He breathes a sigh of relief, feeling like he's dodged some sort of bullet.

CHAPTER 2
LITA: BACK TO THE BEGINNING (1952–1976)

L ita McClinton is born on January 7, 1952, at a time when Atlanta is on the brink of the civil rights cultural revolution. In her lifetime, she'll see the birth of the Southern Christian Leadership Conference (SCLC), formed in 1957 to coordinate nonviolent civil disobedience and organize voter registration drives. She'll watch Morehouse College students orchestrate sit-ins to oppose segregation (1960); she'll experience the aftershock of Brown v. Board of Education, the landmark case that led to the desegregation of schools. Thurgood Marshall, the lead attorney behind the case, who will later become the first Black justice on the Supreme Court, is a McClinton acquaintance. Family friends include Maynard Jackson, who will become the first Black mayor of Atlanta, and Andrew Young, who will follow Jackson as mayor and later become the US ambassador to the United Nations. While Lita's a tween, she'll witness the passing of the Civil Rights Act (1964) and the Voting Rights Act of 1965. She'll see the dismantling of laws that criminalized marriage and sexual relations between white people and Black people, and she'll ride into adulthood during the *Black is Beautiful* movement—a cultural turning point in the outward celebration of Afrocentric pride, heritage, and aesthetic. She'll grow up with a stellar education, part of an affluent, politically powerful Black family.

But at the time of her birth, Atlanta's not there yet. Jim Crow laws man-
dating racial segregation in all public facilities mean restaurants carry signs
saying "Whites Only," bus stations have "Colored" waiting rooms, markets
have separate doors for "White" and "Colored," bars proclaim "No Beer for
Indians," and Black passengers must ride in the back of the bus. But the
city is changing, thanks in part to the highly educated lawyers, doctors, and
preachers coming out of the Atlanta University Center, the world's oldest
and largest consortium of Historically Black Colleges and Universities
(HBCUs), including Morehouse College, Morehouse School of Medicine,
Clark Atlanta University (formerly Clark College), and Spelman College.
These HBCUs, concentrated in the heart of the city, give young Black
students education, opportunity, and an incredible sense of community.

Lita and her siblings grow up in a brick split-level rancher in Cascade
Heights, a westside neighborhood that had morphed from white to Black
in the "white flight" of the 1950s and '60s, when segregationists fled for the
suburbs in protest of racial integration. It and nearby Collier Heights are
some of the first neighborhoods in a major metropolitan city where Black
doctors, lawyers, and politicians have built their own homes, designed
by Black architects and built by Black-owned construction companies.
Baseball legend Hank Aaron lives down the road from the McClintons,
as does civil rights leader John Lewis and many doctors, administrators,
and educators. The affluent community bustles with picnics, parties, PTA
meetings, and stimulating conversation. Lita's parents sip sweet tea at the
dining room tables of other prosperous families, discussing such heady
topics as desegregation, the economy, and what exactly it means to have
"civil rights" anyway. Emory becomes head of the regional civil rights office
for the U.S. Department of Transportation, and Jo Ann is a community
organizer, active in Democratic politics and the NAACP.

The McClintons are mannered practitioners of Southern etiquette,
staunch believers in decorum, and very protective of their children. Lita,
Valencia, and Emory Jr. always dress impeccably, the girls in hats and
gloves, little Emory in suspenders. Any time they go shopping, their mother
forces them to use the toilet and hydrate before they leave home so they

won't have to suffer the humiliation of using inferior restrooms or drinking from "colored" water fountains.

With her middle name a nod to her father's favorite jazz singer, Sarah Vaughan, Lita LaVaughn McClinton is herself like an upbeat jazz tune—lively, fun, and magnetic, easily attracting friends who want to swing in her groove. She loves to get dressed up, dance around the house, and pick wildflowers on her way to and from school.

The McClintons are Catholic and send their kids to Catholic schools because they believe deeply in the value of a good education, despite a lifelong struggle to square racial inequities with Catholic convictions. If God is above everything and all living beings are equal, they wonder, why would the archaic rules of segregation exist? While the Supreme Court's 1954 decision declared segregated schools inherently unequal, desegregation is slow to take hold in Atlanta, especially in private schools. Lita goes to Drexel High, the all-Black Catholic school near their neighborhood. In 1967, when she is sixteen, the archdiocese closes the school in the name of desegregation. Most kids have no choice but to bus downtown to St. Joseph's, but Jo Ann doesn't want her children going to what she deems an inferior school, so she lobbies to send them to all-white St. Pius X Catholic High School. She eventually succeeds, and Lita and Valencia are among the first Black students to integrate at St. Pius. But it isn't easy. When Martin Luther King Jr. is assassinated in 1968, some of the white kids at school laugh and joke about it. Lita and her sister grip each other's hands and hold their heads high. Their parents have taught them ignorance is borne of fear. Those kids came from families threatened by King's power. The McClinton kids have learned that hate never serves. The only choice is to love others, even when the others don't love you back. Jo Ann and Emory buckle down and help plan Dr. King's funeral.

While the battle for civil rights wages in the background of Lita's childhood, PR people rebrand Atlanta "The City Too Busy to Hate" because of the way residents mix across a checkerboard of white and Black. The McClintons' lives intermingle with white friends and work acquaintances, but their world is still decidedly segregated.

Every evening the family eats together; on football Sundays they eat at halftime so Emory Sr. and Jr. won't miss the game. Dinnertime conversations are robust and cerebral. Everyone is expected to contribute; there is nowhere to hide. Once, when Valencia comes home with a rare "C" on her report card, she shares the news at the dinner table. Her father hits the roof. "But the sisters say a C is average," Valencia says.

"No," says Jo Ann. "You cannot afford to be average." Jo Ann tells her children that Black women especially are already burdened with prejudices they must work extra hard to overcome. People will see the color of their skin and make assumptions—about their intelligence, sophistication, value. The next day Jo Ann marches into school and tells the nuns, "Don't ever tell my child C is average; I expect more of them and they expect more of themselves."

❖

After high school, Lita goes to Spelman College and thrives, easily making friends and joining in campus activities. She studies political science with the idea of one day becoming a lawyer—something her politically active parents encourage. She is slender, five feet seven, with a huge welcoming smile and a way of making strangers instantly at ease. In her second year, Lita meets Poppy Finley, another poli-sci major and "city student" who, like Lita, lives at home instead of on campus. Poppy has a car and gives Lita rides to and from school. Where Poppy is shy and quiet, the calm in a storm, Lita is outgoing and social, the spark that ignites a room. Poppy's the yin to Lita's yang, and they become fast friends.

Lita loves being around smart, well-educated Black women who embrace their history and culture with pride and confidence. On weekends, Lita and her sister shop for big belts and lowrider bell-bottoms at the Snooty Hooty boutique in Phipps Plaza mall and go disco dancing at the gay clubs in Buckhead. Black people and white people commingle on the dance floor; the gay men are fun to dance with and make the girls feel safe. When Lita's dad announces he disapproves of the girls going dancing alone, it is decided that Jo Ann will go with them. She settles into a nook beside a fireplace, chats with the regulars, and watches while her daughters boogie the night away.

Throughout college Lita dates a boy she'd met in high school. He's gorgeous and smart, a relative of Maynard Jackson, so his family travels in similar circles as the McClintons. He goes to Howard University in DC, but despite the long distance, the couple manages to date for about three years. He's Lita's first love and she adores him. But one Christmas she learns that he'd come to Atlanta without calling her. She's doesn't understand what happened. Later, she learns that he'd come out as gay but didn't have the nerve to tell her. It's a time in the South when no one knows yet how to talk about homosexuality, so they simply break up and never really speak again. Lita is devastated and slow to move on.

When Lita graduates on the dean's list in 1974, it's clear to everyone that she isn't going to be a lawyer. While her parents hoped to see their daughter thrive in the legal or political arena, it's just not in her personality to battle in a courtroom. She's smart enough, savvy enough, but the thing that really lights her up is fashion—the feel of fabrics, the combining of seemingly disparate patterns, the knowing of what works and what doesn't. She devours fashion magazines, spends hours pulling together new looks and helping friends pick outfits.

By early 1976, Lita is working at T. Edwards, a high-end boutique in the Lenox Square Mall, where she's learned about merchandising, managing inventory, and how to share her ideas with customers. She's twenty-five, forging a career path, about to start training as a clothing buyer at Rich's department store, when James Vincent Sullivan strolls into the boutique and laser-beams his sights on her. He's a quirky white guy, lean, about five foot ten—and a good decade older than she is. He's wearing polyester pants and thick horn-rimmed glasses and has a mop of curly brown hair. He says he's here to buy a gift for a girlfriend, so she shows him some ideas—maybe a scarf, or a soft sweater—but they're both too distracted by his flirting. He is taken with her, it's clear. There's something about him—his charming New England accent, the way his eyes crinkle when he smirks, the absoluteness of his attention. It's like she's walked into a ray of sunlight after a long, dreary rain. It feels good, this warmth, this light.

CHAPTER 3
JIM
(1941–1976)

By all accounts, James Vincent Sullivan is smart, savvy, a fastidious keeper of records, a decent tennis player, and a man who will stop at nothing to get what he wants.

His ambitions started early.

Born on April 5, 1941, in Dorchester, a working-class suburb on the south side of Boston, Massachusetts, Jim Sullivan grows up surrounded by love, a blue-collar belief in hard work, and the unrelenting rules of the Catholic church. His father is a typesetter at the Hearst-owned local newspaper, his mother a devout Catholic homemaker devoted to her three children: Jim, Francis, and baby Rosemary. The kids go to parochial school for elementary, and it's evident early that Jim is observant and smart. In high school, Jim wins acceptance into the Boston Latin School, a prestigious, academically rigorous prep school. Good grades come easily to him, and while most subjects bore him, math is different. In it, he sees possibility. Even as a teenager, he knows the world runs on money, and the key to money is math. He's witnessed his father struggling to make ends meet and vows he won't get locked in the same cage.

"Sully" is an active, social kid, a hall monitor, a member of the golf team, part of the gun club. He's on the staff of both the school magazine and the yearbook. He is an altar boy and, at seventeen, notices Catherine "Cappy" Murray singing in the church choir. They start dating and soon become inseparable. Jim accompanies Cappy's family on summer trips to Nantasket Beach on the Massachusetts shore. Cappy's father is a broody drinker, and it's easy for the teens to swipe booze to sip under the docks. Under graying wooden planks, with the sounds of waves lapping the shoreline, Jim tells Cappy his plans: he's already won a scholarship to attend the College of the Holy Cross in Worcester, where he'll study economics, marry Cappy, and start building his fortune. Cappy hangs on Jim's every word—she fell for him the moment they met, and he knows it. He graduates from high school in 1958. The yearbook photo of him with tousled curls is captioned with, "May his future be as glorious as his past."

Catherine goes to nursing school while Jim works hard at Holy Cross. They see each other on weekends and at Christmas and school holidays. When he earns his economics degree in 1962, he sets to work launching his career. He gets a job in the accounting department of Jordan Marsh, a large department store in Boston, then climbs the ladder at Peat Marwick, the accounting firm. At night, he takes graduate classes in business management at Boston University.

Jim and Catherine marry in a large church wedding in 1965—he is twenty-four, she's twenty-three. Soon after, Cappy gets pregnant. Then again, and again, and again.

At thirty, Jim finds himself with four little mouths to feed, a wife busy with the children, and a plodding job that bores him. By all measures, he's living a full if unremarkable life. He provides for his family, his wife seems happy enough, and he has community through church and the neighborhood. He's smart, nice-looking, and affable—everyone says so. But he can feel the plan of his youth fading away, and it terrifies him. It's not enough. He wants more, bigger, better.

And then, Uncle Frank calls.

Frank Bienert founded Crown Beverages in 1962 and grew it into a successful wholesale liquor distributorship in Macon, Georgia, eighty miles southeast of Atlanta and worlds away from Boston. In 1974, Frank, at sixty-four, is married but has no children of his own and needs a succession plan, someone he can trust, a family member he can mold to one day take over the business. Jim, now thirty-three, is a likable family man who's reportedly excellent with numbers—maybe he's the guy?

Catherine has no desire to move to some random town in the middle of Georgia, but Jim just uses her dissatisfaction as leverage. He tells Uncle Frank that he'll uproot his family to Macon only if he receives a growing percentage of the business and is listed as the sole owner of the company upon Uncle Frank's death. Frank, taken aback by his nephew's demands but impressed with his gumption, appraises his nephew. If he is this good at negotiating his own terms, thinks Uncle Frank, then surely he'll be the same dog-on-a-bone when it comes to effectively running the company.

Jim and Catherine move to Macon, but it doesn't take long before the arrangement is fraught with tension. Catherine hates the heat and struggles to connect with the social nuances of the conservative Southern town. She resents Jim for dragging her and the children away from their home and, as he gets busier trying to take over Crown Beverages, she grows distant and more disgruntled.

It's not going great for Jim at work either. While some of the employees find his manner refreshing, if a little brash, others think him egotistical, argumentative, and difficult to work with. Jim wants to change the company's structure and sets to work dismantling the good-ole-boy ways of doing business. In doing so, he alienates customers who disapprove of his impetuous attempts to disrupt the conventions they'd grown accustomed to. Nothings rubs Southerners rawer than unchecked superiority—especially from a Northerner. Behind his back it is well known Jim will never be accepted here. Jim either doesn't notice or doesn't care; he believes so deeply in his ambitions that he can't see beyond them.

But Uncle Frank sees right through. In just ten months of working with his nephew, he is ready to call the succession plan quits. It's simply not working out, and the constant conflict is wrecking everything he built. While Jim and the family spend Christmas in Boston in 1974, Frank instructs his lawyers to draw up termination paperwork and remove Jim from his will. As the year wanes, he writes a damning statement he means to give Jim when he returns to Macon in January. In it, he writes, "You haven't carried your weight, earned your keep . . . or made our lives easier, better or happier for your coming here. On the contrary, you have made things harder for just about everyone . . . and have put a serious and undue strain upon me and my family's well-being." He says Jim has sown chaos, and that his management style is "the worst I've ever experienced."

But Uncle Frank never gets the chance to fire his nephew. In early January, just after Jim returns from Boston, healthy, robust Uncle Frank suddenly and mysteriously drops dead.

Jim has his uncle's body sent back to Boston for burial the next day.

"Why Jim was in such a rush to dispose of Uncle Frank's remains, and why there was no investigation into the puzzling death, have never been fully explained," wrote author Marion Collins, adding that Uncle Frank was strong and healthy and had never taken a sick day in his life.

Rumors fly in Macon and back in Massachusetts that Jim must've had something to do with Uncle Frank's death, but the death is ruled cardiac arrest, and no autopsy is performed before Frank's burial.

Because the lawyers never got the chance to complete the paperwork, Jim becomes the sole heir to Crown Beverages and Uncle Frank's fortune. He'll enjoy his newfound wealth alone, however. Just ten days after her husband becomes a millionaire, Catherine, staring down the barrel of a life in Macon with a man she's grown to despise, announces she's leaving. Jim has changed. Gone is the pious and frugal man she married, replaced by a money-hungry tyrant who has lost interest in his wife and family. She packs the kids into the station wagon, collects their few belongings, and drives back to Boston with the parting words, "Money doesn't make you happy."

Jim, now a very wealthy man, is so bitter at his wife's departure that he grants her a measly $10,000 lump sum, the old family car, and full custody of the kids. Catherine, now taking care of all expenses and the rearing of their four children, gets just $1,000 per month in child support. Though Jim experienced the privilege of a private school education, he tells Catherine if she wants their kids to go to private school, she'll have to pay for it herself.

Now the boss at Crown, Jim suddenly has influence. He is, after all, white and newly rich—attributes that afford him easier entry into the echelons of power in conservative Macon. He joins the chamber of commerce, donates to charities, and attends cocktail parties and social events where he's free to embellish his history and openly flirt with the women.

He often drives to Atlanta to meet with company lawyers and indulge in the spoils of being single in an exotic city. Less than a year after Catherine left him, Jim walks into a boutique in one of Atlanta's upscale malls. There, in a moment that would change their lives forever, he notices the shop clerk and the pilot light in his heart ignites.

"Hello," she says, with her wide, beautiful smile. "How can I help you?"

CHAPTER 4
THE WEDDING (1976)

The romance between Lita and Jim is as intense as it is unlikely. She's a former debutante who went to private schools and cotillions, Southern, well-educated, and sheltered by the embrace of her family and friends. She's twenty-five, just beginning her adult life, and he's thirty-five, a Northerner who's already lived a full life, but Lita doesn't learn about that till later. She knows little about him, only that he's a successful businessman, having inherited his uncle's business in Macon. And he's charming, unlike anyone she's ever encountered.

Aside from age and upbringing, the biggest difference is the color of their skin. It's 1976 and mixed-race couples are still an unusual sight in the South. After all, Georgia's anti-miscegenation laws, which criminalized marriage between white people and Black people, had been repealed only a few years earlier. In neighboring Alabama, mixed-race marriages won't be legal until 2000.

But after that day at the boutique, the couple is gripped by exhilaration and desire. He asks Lita to coffee, later to the movies and basketball games—chaperoned by family friends on the insistence of her father. They move on to dinner and dancing, private evenings together where he showers her with gifts. His attention is intoxicating, a drug. Soon, they spend all their time together. Lita gets busy updating Jim's wardrobe, teaches him how to fix his hair, and convinces him to ditch the glasses for contact lenses. He adores everything Lita does and says, tells her she's gorgeous, that he can't wait to show her the world.

To Lita's friends and family, it seems an odd union. Jo Ann believes Lita is still smarting from her breakup with the Howard boy and that Jim is just a 180-degree rebound, a distraction they hope will simply burn out and fade away. The McClintons find Jim boastful and arrogant, not at all what they want for their daughter. Just eight years younger than they are, he's closer to their age than he is to Lita's. Emory is especially suspicious of Jim's self-aggrandizing and the flippant way he dodges questions about his past, as though it's none of their business. They sweat it out, hoping the novelty will wear off. But it doesn't. Instead, Lita falls deeper in love with Jim, even though her family can't stand him.

Lita still lives with her parents, and conversation at the dinner table now revolves around their disapproval of Jim. But the more Emory pushes, the more tears Lita sheds. The McClintons are horrified when, just a few months after Jim entered their lives, Lita announces he has proposed. Not only is it sudden and shocking, but Jim's neglected to show Emory the respect of asking for his daughter's hand—a slight that rankles Emory for decades to come.

Macon, where Jim lives, is a conservative town built on the backs of enslaved laborers. Progress is slow to come to rural Georgia, and the McClintons know how tough it will be for their daughter to be in a mixed-race marriage there. After all, Macon has a terrible reputation in dealing with integration. But Jo Ann worries that if they disapprove too strongly, it could backfire and push Jim and Lita closer together or, worse, push Lita away from them. They reluctantly go through the motions of preparing for a wedding, one so very different from the one they'd envisioned for their firstborn daughter.

❖

"Hello," says Jo Ann, picking up the phone in their Macon hotel room. They are here a few days before the wedding, helping Lita prepare. "Hello?"

she says again. She can hear a soft whimper on the other end. "Lita? Lita, sweet baby, what's wrong?"

"I . . ." Lita begins in a calm, tight voice, a couple octaves above her normal range. "I have to tell you something."

"OK," says Jo Ann, her mind whirling. Is it the flowers? Did the caterer mess up? Is something wrong with her dress?

"Just listen and don't panic," says Lita softly. Clearly, she's been crying.

"My goodness, Lita! What is it?" Jo Ann motions Emory to come over to sit on the bed and listen in. They lean into the receiver as they hear Lita take a deep breath.

"Jim was married before," she announces quickly, flatly. "He's divorced."

"Excuse me?" says Jo Ann. She and Emory exchange panicked glances. "He's what?"

Lita explains that not only does he have an ex-wife, but he also has children—four of them, all living in Boston. Lita knows the explosive power of this news. Jim's one saving grace with her parents is that he's Catholic, but even that is falling apart.

Tears rush to Jo Ann's eyes and she thinks she might faint. She hands the phone to Emory, who struggles to contain his disappointment, his rage. Divorce is a major no-no in the Roman Catholic Church. In 1976, the divorce rate for Americans is about 20 percent, but dips to less than 5 percent for Catholic couples. And remarriage is flatly forbidden based on Jesus's dictum, "What God has joined together, let no man put asunder." In other words, once you marry, you remain so until death.

Emory takes the phone and demands to speak to Jim. Jo Ann goes numb as her husband drills Jim, questioning his motives, blasting him for the secrecy and mistrust.

"How? How could you keep this from us?" Emory asks. He rests his elbows on his knees, holds his head in his hand as Jim talks on the other end. Finally, Emory hangs up the phone and looks at his wife, a woman he's known since he was a boy, the woman he's vowed to have and to hold forever. "God help us," he says. "They're going to go through with it."

❖

The night before the wedding, Jim hands Lita a piece of paper and asks her to sign it.

"What's this?" she says, distractedly ticking the final items off her to-do list.

"Just a formality," says Jim. "Some paperwork."

Lita looks at the document and sees the words *Prenuptial Agreement*. She freezes—she's still reeling from the news of Catherine and the kids, and now this? How on earth will she tell her parents? The guests are coming, everything is set; there's simply no backing out now. She's dizzy in love, naive, and desperate to just get on with their life together. "OK," she says, kissing him. "I trust you." She signs the paper without reading the details.

On December 29, 1976, on what Lita's mother would later call the worst day of her life, Lita and Jim get married in a small wedding on Uncle Frank's twelve-acre Macon estate, a property Jim inherited upon his uncle's untimely death. Another repercussion of Frank's unrevised will is that Frank's widow, Agnes, did not inherit her own home—but is allowed to live there until her death.

No one from Jim's family in Boston, including his children, come to the wedding. He tells the McClintons he's estranged from his siblings, that his mother can't travel, but the truth is, he hasn't told his family about Lita at all.

"The wedding was one of the most miserable and disappointing days of my life. I tried not to show it, Emory and I went through the act," Jo Ann told writer Marion Collins. "Later I found a photograph of myself sitting at a window looking so dejected, so bad, that I tore it up. I saw all of the pain on my face, and I just couldn't keep it."

CHAPTER 5

MACON
(1976-1983)

For the first eighteen months of their marriage, Lita commutes to Atlanta during the week, working as an assistant buyer in the fur department at Rich's department store in Atlanta. She drives the eighty miles down I-85 to Macon on weekends. At first, the couple lives on the estate with Uncle Frank's widow, Agnes, but it's an unromantic and untenable situation. Lita wants to be with her husband, set up a home, and enjoy the glow of newlywed bliss, not under the watchful eye of his grieving aunt. But Jim's in no rush for Lita to move permanently to Macon. At first, he doesn't even tell people he got remarried—not his employees, his associates, or even his ex-wife or children, who occasionally come for visits. Once, the children went back to Boston and reportedly told their mother that their dad was sleeping with the maid.

Finally in 1978, Lita quits her job and the Sullivans buy an expansive $350,000 columned mansion on Nottingham Drive in Macon's prosperous Shirley Hills neighborhood. The home is surrounded by forest and has a pool overlooking the Ocmulgee River. Lita gets a thrill decorating the house with antique furniture, paintings, and sculptures, buying Baccarat crystal and Gorham silver flatware. Jim indulges his bride and gets a kick out of the fairy tale they're creating together. Shirley Hills residents, spread out on acreage of their own but highly attuned to the comings and goings of their neighbors, are almost entirely white.

❖

PRESENT DAY

Knowing that the machinations of power in Macon tip unapologetically away from Black people, I wanted to learn what life would've been like for Lita in Macon in the late 1970s and early 1980s. I reach out to Scott Freeman, author of *Otis! The Otis Redding Story* and *Midnight Riders: The Story of the Allman Brothers Band*, and later my editor at *Atlanta* magazine. Around the time Jim and Lita moved to Macon and for a long time after, Scott was a reporter for the *Macon Telegraph*. He knows what makes Macon tick, what shakes it up, and what lurks in the hairy shade of its armpits. And he knows the ins and outs of the Lita-Jim story.

Today, he lives in a cottage by the Chattahoochee River near Carrollton, Georgia. It's only an hour from Atlanta, but worlds away in terms of culture. Confederate flags fly from farmhouses on large parcels of land. Tiny nondescript BBQ joints serve the best ribs you'll ever eat. The open sky makes it easier to breathe. It's like living off the grid—but with good Wi-Fi. When I go to visit Scott for the first time in fifteen years, I follow a series of back roads that turn to dirt roads before dead-ending at the property he shares with a celebrated author and playwright. It's gorgeous, peaceful. Scott greets me as though it were yesterday, not twenty years ago, when he first assigned me this story for *Atlanta* magazine.

He leads me inside the wooden cabin he's turned into a home. Shelves sag under the weight of books—so many books! Music memorabilia, old playbills, and concert photographs decorate the walls. Hundreds of lanyards carrying decades of press credentials hang from a lamp. Seven guitar cases sit stacked in the corner. Everywhere are relics from his recently discovered lineage—turns out Scott, a native Georgian, has Muscogee/Creek ancestry. On the wall hangs a black-and-white Edward S. Curtis photograph of an

Indigenous woman, and a large arrowhead rests on a bookshelf. Scott tells me the Creeks were the first tribe that was "whitened" in America. The awareness of this lineage and what it means to be both Indigenous and "the white man" has given Scott the opportunity to step outside the culture he was raised in and see it from an entirely new perspective.

We sit in his living room, he in a worn recliner, me on a couch littered with books and sheet music. When he was a reporter in Macon, the daily print newspaper covered mostly stories about white Maconites despite Black people accounting for 45 percent of the population.

"Macon is an island," he tells me. "It's not near any other major cities, which sort of allowed it to evolve into its own very unique place."

Known for its antebellum architecture, musical history, and the 300,000 Yoshino Cherry Trees that burst open each March, Macon was once a major shipping crossroads for the cotton industry. Like in other Southern cities, trading enslaved people became an integral part of Macon's economy and, although enslavement was abolished in 1865, the roots run deep. White supremacy reigned and, in many cases, still does today.

"White people tolerated people of other colors as long as they embraced white culture and toed the line," said Scott, who is white. "White people didn't care about Blacks unless they put a problem on their doorstep." Once, Scott dated a Black woman, and they were both shunned—he for dating outside his race, she for thinking herself too good for her own kind. Laws and declarations be damned; for a long time, segregation persisted.

We move to the kitchen as Scott begins to prep dinner. The aroma of ginger and garlic fills the house as he tells me about Macon's musical history. For a time, he says, Macon was one of the hottest music cities in America, with a soul train of performers chugging through on their way to stardom, including hometown hero Otis Redding, James Brown, and Little Richard. Phil Walden, who managed Otis Redding until the star's death in 1967, founded Capricorn Records in Macon in 1969 and launched The Allman Brothers Band and other groups that would define the Southern Rock sound. But by the time the Sullivans settled in to make Macon their home in the late 1970s, Black culture had been once again buried underground, and the once thriving "Black downtown" was boarded up and falling into disrepair.

When Lita moved to conservative, white Macon, interracial couples were still a generally unwelcome anomaly, and unchecked racism was rampant. A scenario, Scott says, that would've been more than daunting. Not only does this brash Northerner move down and take over a good ole Southern business, now he has the gall to bring a Black wife to Shirley Hills? Scott says it would've been almost unimaginable.

❖

Yvette Miller was in her second year of law school in 1979 when a cousin encouraged her to enter the Miss Macon pageant. Yvette was a high-achieving student, not a pageant kind of girl, but she thought it might be fun. Yvette had been the first Black student to attend her middle school in Macon, she was the only Black woman in her law class, and she would go on to become the first (and still only) Black female judge to preside over the Georgia Court of Appeals when she was elected twenty-five years ago.

"You don't live in Georgia as a Black woman and not learn how to stand up and fight for your rights," she told me recently.

Yvette met Lita and Jim when they became her sponsors in the pageant. Lita, always quick to volunteer in her community, wanted to help Black girls in Macon believe they could win a contest that, to date, had only ever been won by white girls. As sponsors, the Sullivans helped Yvette financially, and Lita guided her in everything from how to carry herself, to what to wear for the evening gown and swimsuit competitions. Lita shared with Yvette what her own mother taught her: to be pretty, you must suffer a little. In other words, smile—and don't ever let them see you sweat.

Yvette thought the Sullivans were a charming interracial couple, something extremely rare in Macon. Yvette was only a few years younger than Lita, but Lita seemed so much more sophisticated. "She was a standout Spelman graduate, someone who was just really poised and eloquent," says Yvette. "She was so worldly, and I was from Macon, she was from Atlanta.

She was already married. I felt like she knew just about everything. I was just enamored with her and loved her."

She liked Jim too. "At first, I saw a strong husband who was truly in love with his wife," she says. Lita and Jim seemed comfortable together. "They were a great couple."

Like Yvette, Lita had grown up around intelligent, educated people, and she learned quickly that not everyone in Macon was cultured or open-minded. Yvette says moving to Macon as the Black part of an interracial couple "Would've been very, very difficult" for Lita. "It was something that people looked down on. A lot of people wouldn't come over to their house, to their affairs and things."

On more than one occasion, the Sullivans awoke to their yard strewn with garbage; Lita was *tsk-tsked* at the grocery store, and society women froze her out of social events. Lita—the girl who'd pushed through the doors at all-white St. Pius X high school, who'd excelled at Spelman, who had a politically aware upbringing, who could seemingly make friends anywhere—used her formidable determination to shove it all aside.

❖

1978

For a while Jim and Lita thrive amid the challenges of their unconventional union and, in fact, it seems to bring them closer together. They host dinner parties for friends from Atlanta, travel to Europe and the Caribbean. They both love dogs and fawn over their two Irish wolfhounds. They like having a home they can show off to friends and acquaintances. While Jim runs Crown Beverages, Lita volunteers with the American Heart Association, counsels unwed mothers, and helps Yvette prepare for the Miss Macon pageant. Jim's newfound wealth garners the couple invitations to fundraisers and charitable events, and they get busy breaking into Macon's upper echelons—a major feat for a Black woman and a Northerner. Southerners are slow to welcome outsiders and tend to be sticklers for social norms.

Lita manages to make friends, including Jan Marlow, who lives half a mile down the road with her husband Clyde and a houseful of kids. Jim's own children come for brief visits in the summer and swim in the pool, while Lita buys their favorite snacks and cares for them while Jim's at work. The kids accept Lita, but she's more like a fun aunt than a stepparent. Jim makes a point of being busy at work when they visit; the kids hardly know or see their father. Jan and Clyde frequently enjoy happy hours and dinner parties with Jim and Lita, along with another couple, Fran and Ed Wheeler. Both white couples are open and accepting of the interracial marriage but certainly aware that some of their neighbors are not.

"You probably couldn't pick a much worse town than Macon to have a Black wife," Ed Wheeler told writer Marion Collins. "I remember one story Jim told. He said he had this vision of owning a home in the South and pulling up in his yard and having a little Black boy come out and park the car for him. Then he said, 'Little did I know that the Black boy might be my son.' And Lita roared with laughter; we all did . . . They put on a brave face."

For his part, Jim seems to revel in the novelty of having a controversial marriage and the attention it brings. Later, when he talks to reporter John Connolly about why he married Lita and brought her to Macon when he must've known how difficult it would be, Jim said, "It was hubris. I wanted to show them I could get away with anything."

❖

To the outsider, the marriage seems happy at first, but inside the house on Nottingham, among the shiny objects and fine furnishings, a power imbalance has begun to tip the scales. The generosity Jim first showed Lita wanes as he spends more and more time at work or traveling on business. The man who shined his spotlight on her in the beginning simply shuts it off, and she is left scrambling in cold shadows. She feels increasingly alone, panicked that she's done something wrong, that she is wrong.

Jim grows grouchy, impatient, and frugal. He doesn't want Lita to work but insists she pay for everything out of a paltry allowance he doles out each week as though she's an employee. With it, she must buy all the groceries, her clothes, trips to the salon, accoutrements for entertaining, gas, dog food, and any personal items. When Jim buys something he deems a "household expense"—whether it's a $.59 ginger ale, a $1.50 carton of milk, or $10 for dog food—he tracks it on a notepad and docks it from Lita's weekly allowance. When Lita—who is technically entitled to half their shared assets—indulges her desire to have new speakers installed in her car, Jim deducts it from her allowance for months until it's paid off.

Jan sees Lita buckling under the pressure of his increasing control. Jim's inconsistency is confusing to her too. When guests visit, Jim takes everyone out to dinner and orders expensive wines, but at home, he penny-pinches on daily necessities. He buys tailored suits but wears his dead uncle's underwear and frayed, yellowing shirts around the house. He swipes condiment packages from restaurants, reuses paper towels, saves the plastic sheathes from the dry-cleaning to use as Saran Wrap, and complains when Lita wants to run the air conditioning in the hot Georgia summers. They both drive a Mercedes-Benz, but the cars seem to always be on empty and Lita must use her allowance to fill them.

Lita and Yvette become close friends, despite their four-year age difference. When the white winner of the 1978 Miss Macon pageant gets called up to compete for Miss Georgia, Yvette, the runner-up, becomes the first Black woman to be crowned Miss Macon. It's momentous for the time, and the friends are proud of their work together. They tool around town in Lita's Mercedes, taking long lunches or meeting for drinks. Lita is always well-dressed and put together, but Yvette senses there are cracks in the facade. While the Sullivans appear to be the picture of affluence, Lita seems lonely and rarely has any cash. Lita is embarrassed when the bill comes and she must once again put her share on a credit card.

Yvette begins to see Jim's dark side. Once, when Yvette was at the house, Jim told Lita to stop eating so much, seeming more concerned about her weight than slender Lita ever was. She also sees how he flirts with attractive women, and it strikes her that Jim will not be someone Lita will be able to depend on in her old age. Yvette aches for her friend but sees she is trapped.

"She was like a battered wife, but she didn't appear to be battered," Yvette tells me later. "But her soul, I think, was battered."

Lita steeps in shame at the way she's treated but keeps most of it to herself. The last thing she wants is to tell her parents they were right about Jim, that she's failing as a wife, that the pressures of fitting into a white world are finally wearing her down.

Lita and Jim's vigorous sex life dwindles, and for Lita there's no colder freeze. When his attention drifts, when he starts spending long evenings away from home, she tries to playfully bring him back by arranging special dinners, wearing lingerie, and surprising him at work. It only serves to annoy him—why is she spending money on frivolous things? Why is she coming to the office when she knows how busy he is? When Lita outright asks him if he's having an affair, he becomes enraged and vehemently denies it. Then he buys her jewelry and soaks her with attention for a while, convinces her it's all in her imagination. But it doesn't take long before he turns his attention away again and she's left alone in the dark.

Today, this cycle of gaslighting, ridicule, and control would trigger the red flags of domestic violence, but in the early 1980s this kind of mistreatment was dismissed as a "private matter."

Jim flirts with other women—it's excused as his charming Irish American way—but his increasingly solicitous behavior only intensifies Lita's suspicions he's seeing other women. Little does she know to what extent.

❖

Back in 1977, just a few months after Jim and Lita's wedding, Tanya Tanksley had just walked out of a convenience store when Jim pulled up beside her in his Mercedes and asked for her phone number. At the time, Tanya was eighteen, Jim thirty-six. Surprised, she jotted down her number and left, thinking little of it. But then he called her, kept calling her. Finally, after a month, she agreed to go out with him. Jim dusted off his moves,

shining his beam upon her, buying her gifts and telling her he couldn't wait
to feel her Black skin against his, that she was the most stunning woman
he'd ever seen. It was an eerily familiar playbook; today, we'd call it love-
bombing. Tanya, young and naive, had never felt so much shine. She began
sleeping with him. She even introduced him to other women—some white,
some Black—with whom he'd also have sex, often at the Nottingham house
while Lita was in Atlanta.

"He cheated on Lita all the time," an employee at Crown told Marion
Collins. "I heard the name Tanya, and there was a woman who was married. One husband punched Jim out. He broke a tooth and had to go to
the dentist. He never wanted any of his women to know he had money, so
he would borrow my car—I had a Pontiac Grand Prix then—to go meet
with them, and then give me his Mercedes."

While his employees know that he's constantly cheating on Lita, no one
has the nerve to tell her. Lita occasionally comes by the distributorship
office to examine his phone records and scan his daily journal to see who
he's meeting. She knows he's a detailed notetaker, but the random jottings
are often cryptic—initials or weird symbols—and it's difficult to tell what's
work-related and what isn't. But one name keeps appearing out of the sea
of hieroglyphs: Tanya. Lita has no way of finding out who this is—these
are the days before Google or Facebook—but she makes a mental note.

One day, Lita is at home in her bedroom when she finds a blond hair in
the en suite bathroom sink. She pulls the hair out, lays it on a tissue, and
stares at it, as though it might come to life. When Jim comes home, she
presents him with the tissue.

"What?" he asks, barely glancing. He throws his keys on the side table
and bends to greet the dogs.

"Whose is this?" says Lita, pointing at the long blond hair.

"I have no idea," says Jim, annoyed. "Why are you showing me garbage?"

"Well obviously, this isn't mine. And it's not yours," says Lita, her voice
starting to shake. "I'll ask again, whose is it?"

Jim pushes past her, saying he doesn't appreciate the accusation. Then
he mutters something about maybe it belongs to their maid. She knows as

well as he does that the blond hair doesn't belong to the maid—the maid is Black.

"I need to get out of here," says Lita, hands shaking as she collects her purse and keys. "I'm going to Atlanta. I'll be at my parents'."

Jim stands, mouth agape, as his wife drives away. "Suit yourself," he mutters under his breath.

Surrounded by her parents' rock-solid marriage, Lita finally admits to her mother that she suspects Jim is cheating, but she doesn't tell her the extent of what's happening. Jo Ann listens to her daughter, and they discuss how marriage is hard sometimes, that there needs to be room for trust and forgiveness. After a few days, Jim calls, profusely apologizing, and convinces Lita to come back home. When she arrives back in Macon, he gives her a $28,000 diamond ring and promises they'll go to marriage counseling. Another time it's a tennis bracelet, another a mink coat. The high of these little hits of dopamine doesn't last long, but it's a pattern repeated, again and again.

"Over time Lita changed completely, beginning from the day she found that first strand of blond hair," said Jo Ann later. "You wouldn't know it if you didn't know her, but she became filled with mistrust and disillusion." Sunny, bubbly Lita, who gave up her budding career, left her hometown, and wreaked havoc on her family, felt trapped.

Lita and Jim never did go to marriage counseling.

❖

By 1981, after the Sullivans have been married for five years, Jim has grown bored of running the distributorship, and ever-shrinking, ever-gossipy Macon has lost its charm. He begins quietly looking for a buyer for Crown Beverages but doesn't tell anyone, including Lita. He takes a few furtive trips down to Florida, where he's fallen in love with Palm Beach, a place straight out of *Lifestyles of the Rich and Famous*. He begins secretly putting the money together to purchase a $2 million beachfront mansion—another tidbit he keeps from his wife. He churns through considerable negotiations with the banks and the home's two sellers to come up with creative ways to finance it.

A co-seller of the house, a woman named Joyce, knows Jim is married and finds it strange that the wife never comes to look at the home her husband is desperate to buy.

"I'm so curious to meet Mrs. Sullivan," drops Joyce one day, after Jim has visited several times alone. It's a massive home, and she's incredulous that the wife wouldn't want to be part of its purchase. "Isn't she anxious to see her new home?"

"Oh, she's so busy in politics and things," replies Jim. "She's excited. She'll love it." But Lita doesn't know anything about it. When Jim's gone, she assumes he's away on business; he says nothing about buying a mansion. But she's also distracted. Desperately wanting to have children of her own, Lita has thus far been unable to get pregnant. She drives to and from Atlanta for appointments with specialists at Emory University. Finally, after reams of tests, doctors determine that she'll be unable to conceive. These are the days before in vitro fertilization, and solutions are few and far between. Devastated, Lita, at thirty, gets a hysterectomy—her hopes of having her own children gone. Jim, already neglectful of the four children he does have, seems relieved. For a while, the anguish of not having children consumes Lita, and she and Jim live in a sort of codependent status quo. Things get tolerable for a while, until inevitably she accuses him of philandering again. He denies, they fight, and he begs forgiveness with expensive jewelry that he gives her but keeps under lock and key until he wants her to wear it.

❖

In December 1982, Lita finds a Christmas card addressed to Jim. *Missing your kisses at Christmas. Love Tanya.* Tanya, the name in the day planner. That Jim's mistress feels bold enough to send a card to their home incenses Lita. She drives to the return address on the envelope, parks, and waits.

When a young Black woman pulls up to the home, Lita is at first surprised. This certainly isn't the owner of the blond hair that Lita was expecting. She gets out of her car and walks over to the young woman. "Are you Tanya?"

"Yes, ma'am," says Tanya, at first calm, friendly. But Lita sees the flicker of recognition harden the young woman's eyes, watches her demeanor shift from defense to offense.

"Did you send this to my husband?" Lita demands, shaking the card.

"Excuse me," Tanya says, now hurrying past Lita. The affair has been going on for years—it isn't her problem if Lita is too blind to see it.

Fuming, Lita drives home and packs as many clothes and belongings as she can into the back of her Mercedes. In tears, she drives straight to her parents' house in Atlanta. When Jim calls, his voice is full of both apology and impatience.

"Let me speak to Lita, please," Jim says when Jo Ann answers the phone.

"I'm sorry, she's indisposed."

"Please," says Jim, sighing. He doesn't have time for this.

"My daughter does not wish to speak to you right now," says Jo Ann and hangs up.

That week, Lita talks to a lawyer, but Jim catches wind of it and decides to call her bluff by having his own lawyer serve Lita with divorce papers. One thing he knows about Lita is that she doesn't want to be a person who fails at marriage. She comes from a Catholic home where family values and loyalty mean everything—she's witnessed her parents' loving, enduring marriage and wants that so acutely she can't see straight. He knows she'll never actually leave him; it's what lets him get away with everything. And Jim, not wanting to be twice divorced, agrees they should make the marriage work.

Jim's attorney suggests the couple sign a postnuptial agreement, one that will supersede the prenup and give Lita more financial leeway and some security should the marriage dissolve. The new agreement has her on a bigger allowance—now $300 a week instead of $150—plus $30,000 per year for three years if they ever divorce. It's certainly better than the pittance she'd get with the original prenup, but Lita doesn't actually own anything. Jim's made sure that all their assets belong only to him. Still, Lita returns to Macon. One night after they've reconciled in bed, he slides over the papers and once again she signs without absorbing the details.

A few months later, in October of 1983, Jim sells the liquor distributorship for $5 million, plus he'll keep control of the company pension fund and will receive $20,833 a month in a non-compete agreement. None of the postnup reflects this newfound wealth, but Lita doesn't realize it because she's blindsided with the news that he's sold the company, and the even bigger headline: start packing, we're moving to Florida.

CHAPTER 6
PALM BEACH
(1983-1985)

P alm Beach stretches along a skinny barrier island flanked by the Atlantic Ocean on one side and the Intracoastal Waterway on the other. Three bridges cross the Intracoastal to the mainland of West Palm Beach, the working side of town, where the downtown office buildings and high-rises peter out as you head west.

Palm Beach grew largely out of the aspirations of industrialist oil tycoon Henry Flagler, who envisioned the town as an exclusive metropolis for sun lovers and beachgoers. Flagler was a major developer on the Atlantic coast in the late 1800s and responsible for building the railroad that would bring the wealthy down from New England to winter in Palm Beach.

Some two thousand Black laborers built several of the island's architectural masterpieces, including the opulent thousand-room Royal Poinsettia Hotel (which shuttered in the 1930s) and The Breakers, a bustling Mediterranean-style resort that's still the center of the island's life today. The Black workers lived in an area called The Styx, named for the river that forms the boundary between Earth and the Underworld in Greek mythology. While they worked on luxurious buildings by day, they slept in tents and shacks, with no electricity or running water. Still, they forged a community and called the place home. When Flagler wanted to develop the Styx land, the story goes, he invited Styx residents to a party in West Palm Beach and while they were gone, he burned their shacks and shanties to the ground. The now-homeless Black community moved over the bridge to rebuild their lives in West Palm Beach's Pleasant City neighborhood. The eviction, or exodus (depending on who you talk to), sent a message to Black folks: this isn't yours, nor will it ever be.

Today, Palm Beach is its own world. It has its own police force, municipal government, and city council, which has historically weighed in on everything—the allowable decibel of leaf blowers, whether male joggers should be permitted to run shirtless, the suitable height of hedges, and how big a flag you can fly. At one point, municipal workers scented the sewage with lilac and honeysuckle so residents wouldn't have to whiff their own excrement. All of it aims to protect the town's tanned, gleaming-toothed residents from the plebeian masses, to help bolster the elitist narrative that only the chosen ones live here.

"Their big fear is that people will come to the island who don't live there," says Frank Cerabino, a longtime columnist at the *Palm Beach Post*. He says that when Neiman Marcus wanted to open a store on the glitzy Worth Avenue, for example, the town council agreed but with the proviso they would only advertise in the town's newspaper, and not in publications circulated to shoppers who didn't live on the island.

I recently asked Cerabino what it would've been like for Lita in Palm Beach in 1983. "Well, it would've been horrible," he said bluntly. "Even today, it's a really rough place for an interracial couple."

Life in Palm Beach revolves around the social scene, much of which plays out at exclusive golf, tennis, and yacht clubs peppered along the island. The clubs often have decades-long waiting lists, enormous initiation fees, and steep annual dues, but pride themselves on offering their guests privacy, security, and exclusivity. It's a world of handshake deals and gossip-filled lunches, conversations with like-minded name-droppers who care deeply if someone went to boarding school at Andover, rowed for Yale, or spent summers in the Hamptons. This red carpet of elitism rolls out for white people with wealth and pedigree; historically, if you weren't white, you could forget about becoming a member.

Two years after the Sullivans arrived in Palm Beach, Cerabino and his colleagues at the *Miami Herald* wrote a three-part series on the private clubs in South Florida, specifically calling out the "guest rule," which stated members couldn't bring guests that wouldn't be considered suitable as members. While most clubs claimed they were non-discriminatory, the guest rule served as a coded way of saying Jews, Black people, and Hispanics were not welcome. Members who violated the guest rule could face fines, letters of reprimand, or temporary suspensions. Once, Cerabino tells me, at the Palm Beach Everglades Club—an exclusive golf and social club that's been obliging members with last names like Vanderbilt, Dodge, Pillsbury, and Pulitzer since 1919—a socialite was reprimanded for bringing a "cosmetics empress" to lunch because the guest's father was Jewish. That guest turned out to be Estée Lauder, the founder of the namesake cosmetics company, who would later be the only woman on *Time* magazine's list of the most influential business geniuses of the twentieth century. Sammy Davis Jr., at the height of his career as a world-famous entertainer, was escorted out of the Everglades for the double whammy of being Jewish and Black.

In the *Herald*'s reporting, a Miami Beach surgeon was quoted as saying, "At the hospital where I work the Black doctors are intellectually fine and wonderful people, but they aren't able to handle the cosmopolitan aspects of circulating in society. Until we get some erudite cosmopolitan Blacks in the area, we're going to have that problem."

This is two years *after* the Sullivans' arrival. When they pull up to their new home in 1983, less than 0.1 percent of the town's 9,729 year-round residents are Black—most likely live-in nannies or maids.

❖

When Lita sees Casa Eleda for the first time, she can't help but be dazzled. The mansion, known locally as the "ham-and-cheese house" for the alternating layers of red brick and pink coral coquina, is 17,000 square feet of opulence on one of the most affluent stretches of roadway in the United States. The home was built in 1928 for financier Mortimer Schiff, who later served as president of the Boy Scouts of America. He named the Italianate villa Casa Eleda for his wife Adele, (Eleda is Adele backward). Designated a historic landmark by the Palm Beach Landmarks Preservation Commission, the home was designed by Swiss architect Maurice Fatio, the creative engine behind several mansions and public buildings in Palm Beach.

Like many of the mansions off highway A1A, the coastal byway that runs alongside the ocean, Casa Eleda overlooks the Atlantic and includes 165 feet of private beachfront property, accessible by a private tunnel running under the road. Lita gets lost exploring the home's nine bedrooms and ten bathrooms. She follows endless hallways that connect rooms via archways under hand-painted ceilings. French doors lead to three covered loggias that overlook the courtyard, pool, and fountain. The house has five fireplaces, a "breakfast porch," and a butler's pantry that connects the dining room to the kitchen, plus staff quarters, a guest wing, and a massive master suite that overlooks the ocean. In the basement, there's a games room and a temperature-controlled wine room.

For Jim, living on this exclusive strip of land known for its history of obscenely wealthy and deviant residents (including Bernie Madoff, Jeffrey Epstein, and Donald Trump) is a dream come true, a marker that he's made it to the big leagues. Amid the billionaires and bad behavior, Jim can reinvent himself, shake off Macon, finally shed his working-class skin, and slide into a shinier version of himself.

For Lita, the move to Palm Beach is like entering a different universe. At first, she too is awed by the glitz and glamour of Palm Beach and notices how happy it makes Jim. With suddenly no business to run, the profits from the sale, and a hefty monthly income, he seems more relaxed, less grouchy, friendly again. She grows optimistic that maybe this move will patch Jim's roving eye, pull him back to her, and do them both some good.

The couple stays up late and sleeps late. They spend their days getting lost in the nooks and crannies of their new home. The mansion needs work and Jim dives into the renovations, giving Lita free rein to decorate its many rooms. This activity and shopping frenzy invigorates their relationship for a while. They host friends from Macon and Atlanta, with Jim generously doling out wine and cigars and giving long-winded tours of his precious new palace.

They try to make friends and immerse themselves in the Palm Beach social scene. Lita volunteers at Planned Parenthood and other organizations across the bridge in West Palm Beach. Jim joins the Palm Beach Tennis Association and donates to charities, which earns him invites to black-tie cocktail parties at The Breakers, lunches at the Everglades, and schmoozy gallery openings.

But it doesn't take long for them to realize that the color of Lita's skin is a big problem for Jim's long game, a serious kink in the wobbly rope ladder that leads to his social aspirations. While Lita had certainly experienced discrimination in Macon, the overt and unapologetic racism in Palm Beach is almost unbearable, and now she's far from her friends and family, feeling truly trapped on an island. People openly stare as they pass her on the street, shooting her looks that say, *Why are you here?* She goes to the parties with Jim, but no one approaches her—or they flash her fake smiles before whispering to their neighbor. She witnesses the way people lean in to her husband but physically lean away from her. It's so unfamiliar and humiliating for Lita, who grew up going to cotillions, meeting politicians and influential leaders—both white and Black.

Once, when Jo Ann was visiting at Casa Eleda, a young Black repairman assumed they were the hired help. He apologized profusely when Jo Ann set him straight, but they all knew how unusual it was for a Black woman to live in a place like Palm Beach, let alone be the lady of the house.

"There still is a feeling here that it's alright if your gardener is Black, but you are not going to have him over for cocktails," a neighbor told a reporter, expressing a common sentiment among Palm Beach residents.

Jim once again begins distancing himself from Lita. At one cocktail party, Jim's arousal meter spikes at the sight of Korean-born Hyo-Sook "Suki" Rogers, the gorgeous wife of investment adviser Leonard Rogers. Jim introduces himself to Suki, telling her stories, lavishing her with compliments, and charming her with his peculiar New England accent. When Lita finally ventures over to join them, he introduces her as Lita Sullivan. It's only later, when Suki comments on the coincidence of their shared last name, that she realizes Lita is Jim's wife.

❖

Outwardly, Jim is charming and generous, a gracious host when their friends come down from Georgia. But at home, he stresses about the endless renovation costs and blames Lita for not fitting in. While he thinks nothing of spending hundreds of dollars on wine or wooing new acquaintances out on the town, he complains about every penny Lita spends. He resumes deducting everything from lightbulbs to toilet paper from Lita's allowance.

Lita's pal Jan Marlow comes down from Macon for frequent visits, often for a week at a time, but finds the hot air in the house suffocating. She asks Jim to please turn the air conditioning on in the evenings so she can sleep. Jim begrudgingly turns it on in the guest wing, but it's never cool enough in the huge house.

One morning, Jan and Lita are in the kitchen cleaning up from the night before when Jan notices a crumpled paper towel on the roll, as though it's been used. She goes to toss it, but Lita tells her not to.

"Jim will get mad. Just leave it alone," says Lita. "That's the one he uses to wipe his hands."

Jim is now driving a Rolls-Royce that is frequently out of gas, so he takes Lita's Mercedes and gives it back to her on empty, forcing her to refill it using her allowance.

By day Jim scolds the maids for wasting cleaning supplies, and by evening he's telling his new acquaintances that he's an heir to the Hearst newspaper fortune, that he graduated from Harvard, that he is related to the pope. None of which is true.

"I remember one night sitting in the parlor at the front of the house overlooking the ocean and we were sitting talking after dinner," Jo Ann told writer Marion Collins. "Jim told me that as a child, when his family came to Florida on vacation, they had driven by the Casa Eleda. 'This is the house I always wanted,' he said, puffing on a cigar and drinking. I found out later that the family never even went to Florida on vacation."

It's as though Jim thinks that, if his stories are convincing enough, he might embody them, fully become who he's desperate to be. He gains more clout in Palm Beach by throwing himself into the fundraising efforts of Yvelyne "Deedy" Marix, Palm Beach's first woman mayor, who is seeking reelection. Marix, the daughter of a French count and English aristocrat, runs a successful travel business with her husband and is a beloved stickler for the Palm Beach town ordinances. Jim throws a fundraiser party for her in early 1985 and, after she wins reelection, she rewards his support with a much-coveted appointment to the town's Landmarks Preservation Commission. Now, Jim has a say in anyone's property or home renovations, and this semblance of power makes him a popular lunch or tennis guest at the very clubs he longs to join, the very clubs where Lita is not welcome.

❖

When her friends and family leave after their short visits, Lita plummets into isolation and loneliness. She begins to make frequent trips to Atlanta, stretching long weekends and finding any excuse not to go back to Florida. Her best friend Poppy and her husband Marvin Marable now have a baby—Lita and Jim are little Ingrid's godparents. Lita would've loved to be changing diapers and shopping for baby outfits alongside Poppy, but her infertility and resulting hysterectomy—not to mention the lack of love between her and Jim—make it clear there will be no nursery, no babies, no small kids running around the giant Florida house. Poppy's daughter is a light in Lita's life, and she wants to spend as much time with her best friend and goddaughter as possible.

Under the sparkly Florida sun, Jim takes advantage of Lita's absence. Behind her back and the averted eyes of the maid, Jim entertains an array of overnight guests, including Tanya Tanksley, who was apparently undeterred by Lita's confrontation. He buys her plane tickets over the phone, which she picks up at the Macon airport whenever he beckons, eager to spend the weekend in Jim's mansion.

Lita suspects Jim's cheating again—he certainly flirts with every attractive woman he meets—but she's losing her will to fight after a tumultuous eight years of marriage. She hates Palm Beach, feels neglected and unloved by her husband. She feels more like herself in Atlanta, surrounded by family and old friends. Eventually, Lita convinces Jim to buy a 4,000-square-foot condo in The Coaches, a cul-de-sac of nine luxury townhouses in Buckhead, an affluent Atlanta neighborhood. Jim relents because Lita has become an albatross around his neck. If she spends more time in Atlanta, it's easier for him to carry on with his philandering. Jim continually reminds Lita that, like Casa Eleda and their home in Macon, their cars, and all their other assets, the deed on the Buckhead condo is in his name only. But Lita is happy to have a place in Atlanta that isn't her parents' house, where she can go when she needs a break from the increasingly insufferable Casa Eleda.

On one of Lita's trips back to Palm Beach, she finds lacy red lingerie in the sheets of the master bed, and all the humiliation and shame comes flooding back to her. It's the bra that broke the camel's back, and what follows the tears and rage and self-pity is a simple and crystalline clarity: it's time to get out.

In August 1985, while Jim is out of town, Lita rents a U-Haul, packs it with her clothes, the few pieces of jewelry not locked in the safe, her favorite shampoo, and a few household items, and hitches it to her Mercedes. She picks up Ashley Wilkes, her little terrier, named for the indecisive Southern gentleman in Margaret Mitchell's *Gone with the Wind*, wipes her mascara-smudged eyes, and takes one last look at the house she never wanted. After nine years of marriage, thirty-three-year-old Lita gets behind the wheel and drives north to Atlanta—this time for good.

CHAPTER 7

COMING HOME
(1985–1986)

When Lita finally pulls up to the Slaton Drive townhouse after driving nearly six hundred miles towing a U-Haul, she breathes a sigh of relief so deep she feels like she's been holding her breath for years. She's finally coming home; Atlanta is in her heart and in her bones, and like her, the city is finding its true self. Everywhere you look are signs of growth. The winding pretzel of freeway known forever as Spaghetti Junction (or Malfunction Junction, depending on the day) is almost complete, ensuring decades of suburban sprawl. Ted Turner's Atlanta-based CNN runs the world's first twenty-four-hour television news network. Mayor Andrew Young, a former aide to Martin Luther King Jr., is prepping to host the 1988 Democratic National Convention—a major event in the conservative South. At night, the clubs are throbbing with hip-hop, rhythmic rap, and offshoots of Southern gospel and Motown R&B. Midtown is a debaucherous land of vice and liberation, with bars, clubs, and sex shops freely celebrating the '80s vibe, interrupted only by the cruel reality of AIDS. The city is still recovering from the terrifying chill of the Atlanta child murders, where twenty-nine Black children and teens were murdered over three years, from 1979 to 1981. The sense of escalated worry and vigilance still sits like a brick on the chest of every Black mother in town.

While Atlanta constantly reckons with its past and prejudices, the city is growing in defining ways. Planted in the fertile soil among the concrete, steel, and glass skyscrapers are hopes and dreams, visions of a future full of equity, character, and freedom.

Lita looks up at her European-style white brick townhouse. The Coaches is like a gated community without the gate—the only way in or out is via a driveway that leads to an asphalt courtyard surrounded by nine townhouses—some attached, some detached.

She's the only Black person living anywhere near this luxury community, but she feels safe here. Her neighbors include the president of the Atlanta Falcons football team, several lawyers, and members of Atlanta's influential social elite. They know Lita—she's been partially living in and decorating the townhouse for a year. They see her good Southern upbringing, the way she goes out of her way to say hello or stop for a chat. They've met Jim; they know only that this is the couple's second home, but Lita spends a lot of time here, alone.

Poppy lives with her husband and baby in nearby Sandy Springs. Lita's sister Valencia and husband Jeff are there too. Her parents are twenty minutes away, her brother nearby. The elegant campus of the Atlanta History Center and the stately governor's mansion are just a stone's throw, and it's a quick drive to Phipps Plaza, the mall where she and her sister shopped for bell-bottoms and miniskirts in college.

Sitting parked in front of the Slaton Drive townhouse where she will now live fully alone, she takes another deep breath and contemplates leaving the air-conditioned car and facing the work of unloading the trailer in the summer heat. She pats Ashley Wilkes on the head and wonders what Jim will do when he discovers she's gone. Burning a hole in her purse is one of Jim's monthly $20,833 checks from Crown Beverages that she'd intercepted in the mail. She knows she's going to need it. Tomorrow, she'll cash it and clean out their joint checking account. Then she'll call him and tell him she's never, ever coming back.

❖

Richard Schiffman is a young divorce attorney with just a few years of practice under his belt when he meets Lita through Democratic party friends of the McClintons, but he quickly sees the inequity in Lita's situation. He's taken with her immediately.

"She was very charming, a striking-looking woman. You did a double-take and noticed her because she was attractive," he said later, describing Lita. "She was always very nicely dressed, and she was just very, very sweet. Anybody who came into contact with her in my office liked her. The courthouse staff liked her a great deal because she was just a very pleasant person to be around."

Lita hires him to help her fight what she knows will be a drawn-out battle with Jim. To start, Schiffman knows how important it is for Lita to file for divorce first so the case will be tried in Georgia, which is the only state left in the country that allows a jury to decide the division of assets in a divorce trial.

"We wanted a jury trial because a lot of what we felt were the inequities of the case were the strongest part of our action," Schiffman told writer Marion Collins, suggesting a jury could be more lenient than a judge; judges tend to look at paper, where juries tend to look at people. "She was accusing her husband of being unfaithful and of treating her very poorly," he says. He believes a jury will agree.

Schiffman also believes the postnuptial agreement Lita signed before the multimillion-dollar windfall from the sale of Crown Beverages will be deemed "unconscionable" because it "benefited one party over another."

"It left Lita with virtually nothing," he said of the postnup. "It provided that in the event of a divorce she would receive the sum of $2,500 a month for a period of thirty-six months," he explained, a total of about $90,000. "There would be basically no equitable division of property," meaning that of the three homes the Sullivans own—the house in Macon, Casa Eleda, and the Buckhead townhouse—Lita will get nothing. Everything, including the houses, the cars, Lita's jewelry, her fur coats, and the furniture, is in Jim's name. If the postnup is enforced, Lita will have little to show for almost a decade of marriage.

She files for divorce in Atlanta's Fulton County on August 14, 1985.

Jim is livid. He immediately contacts his lawyers and begins fighting the issue of jurisdiction. He believes a judge in his beloved Palm Beach will decide in his favor. He certainly doesn't want a jury in Georgia deciding his fate. That's when things get messy. He stops paying the mortgage on the townhouse, cuts off the power, and revokes the insurance on her car. Jim files motion after motion arguing that Lita isn't a resident of Georgia, even though she's spent much of the last two years in Atlanta and lived in Macon prior to that. Though his lawyers advise him to start paying the $2,500 in alimony per the postnup he's fighting to enforce, he stops sending checks. He refuses to disclose his financial statements (for which he is held in contempt of court twice) and doesn't pay his or Lita's legal bills.

Though he tries every way possible, he loses the fight to litigate the divorce in Florida. He gets another blow when a judge orders him to pay Lita $7,000 a month in temporary alimony. Jim must also pay Lita's attorney's fees and the delinquent pre-alimony payments, plus grant her use of the Mercedes, the townhouse, and the contents within. It's a huge win for Lita, what she and her lawyers believe is a foreshadowing of the win she can expect in court.

❖

While I comb through court documents and testimonies and media reports, I find myself a little judgmental over the petty scrapping of rich people bickering over money. Sell a couple houses, pawn some jewelry, and sell your extravagant wine collection, I think. Get a job, stop buying expensive things, sell the damn Rolls-Royce for chrissakes. What about Jim's kids? At this point, Jim, it seems, has largely forgotten about his children—even though he claims all four of them as dependents on his tax returns. I go through all these ruminations when I look at the details of Jim and Lita's divorce, but then I remind myself that Lita, in addition to enjoying the spoils of wealth—and who wouldn't?—has also lived a hellish existence with a controlling, cheating man who has a seemingly blatant disregard for her and his children. So, why did she stay with him? Why did she suffer through the humiliations of his philandering? Did her Catholic convictions make divorce seem impossible? Was it too unbearable to admit her parents were right about Jim?

It's easy to blame the victim.

What's also true is that Jim and Lita had stretches of happiness. They traveled to Europe, the Caribbean, and Asia. They had moments when they were in love, excited to see each other, laughing at inside jokes. But they were also human and flawed and driven by the same desires we all have—the need to be loved, seen, accepted.

Like most couples who get to this point, Jim and Lita have lost sight of the early days when their stomachs tied in knots at the sight of each other. Jim's scorn for her now is as sharp and overwhelming as his need for her was then. Now, they are both driven by a force much greater than love: fear. Jim is afraid of losing everything, Lita of losing herself.

She told her friend Jan, "I've been living in such a life of deprivation for so long that I feel like I deserve to order a magazine if I want to." For nearly a decade, Lita has had to account for every dime she's spent, sneak salon visits, beg her husband to let her wear the jewelry he'd supposedly bought for her. Friends remember her having a seven-carat diamond ring, a diamond tennis bracelet, and an exquisite ruby necklace she'd wear periodically in Macon. But most of the jewelry was kept in the safe—and Jim was the only one with access, another lever of control.

"My husband had consistently used money as a weapon against me and would cut off all of my financial resources whenever he became angry," Lita said in a divorce affidavit.

Jim once told a friend he liked to underfeed his dogs, keep them skinny by withholding treats or extra food so they'd stay lean and remain thankful for what they got. Lita, it seemed, endured a similar existence. Sure, Lita had nice things, but almost none belonged to her.

What Lita petitions for in the divorce breaks down like this: she wants the townhouse, the furnishings within, $200,000 in cash, some jewelry, and her twelve-year-old car. It totals around $1 million. Because Jim is so shady with his assets, complains of being cash poor, withholds his financial statements, and is a creative accountant, no one really knows how much money he has. Only later, once the forensic accountants excavate the quagmire of his accounts, do we learn that Jim, at the time, was worth about $8 million. After almost a decade of marriage, Lita is asking for about 12.5 percent of their wealth. By today's standards, where a 50/50 split of assets is the norm, Lita's ask seems more than fair.

❖

Attorney Ed Wheeler and his wife Fran were close to both Jim and Lita when they all lived in Macon. The Wheelers now live in Atlanta—Ed teaches at Emory University—and spend a lot of time with Lita now that she's back. Ed struggles with his split loyalties. He wants to support both of his friends and feels ever more torn as the divorce progresses. To him, Jim has always been a generous and smart guy, and Ed is incredulous that he's fighting so hard against Lita. He thinks, why not settle the matter, and simply move on?

In the spring of 1996, when Jim comes to Atlanta to meet with his lawyers, Ed offers to pick him up and drive him to his meeting—a chance for them to catch up and an opportunity for Ed to extend an olive branch. Months earlier, Jim had asked Ed to give a statement that would bolster his argument that Lita was a resident of Florida, not Georgia, and Ed had refused, not wanting to get in the middle of things. Jim was disappointed, and their friendship had cooled.

Ed pulls up to the Ritz-Carlton in Buckhead. It's sunny and humid, but not yet unbearably hot, still a hint of breeze. Jim gets in, freshly showered, wearing khaki pants and a blue sport coat, looking spry and fit, tanned from the Florida sun. He seems genuinely happy to see Ed. They talk of the weather, Jim's flight up, the Atlanta traffic. While Jim meets with his lawyers, Ed runs errands and thinks about what he'll say to Jim. He wants to talk with him not as an attorney, but as a friend. He sees what the whole thing is doing to Lita, and he feels he must do something.

After his meeting, Jim gets back in the car, visibly agitated. He mutters about the lawyers' fees and phone charges, how it's bleeding him dry.

Ed finally gets the nerve to speak.

"Listen, Jim. I'm saying this as your friend," says Ed, pulling away from the curb and easing into Atlanta traffic. "I don't know what you're hearing from your lawyers, but I think Lita's got a pretty good shot of prevailing in the division of property. I think she'll get an equitable division of the assets, and I think that's . . . well, I think it's right."

His words hang in the air as though he didn't say them. He glances over at Jim, who's looking out the window, jaw clenched, a vein twitching at his temple. Ed feels for the guy—Jim has worked hard for his money. Once, he went to Crown to meet Jim for lunch and saw him sweating while loading cases of liquor onto trucks. He's a mathematical whiz, always churning through numbers, always calculating. Ed knows how much it pains his friend to part with money but—isn't it just money?

"I mean, it seems fair what she's asking for," Ed presses. "If I were a member of the jury, I would probably vote in favor of Lita on this issue."

Jim sits silent for a while, eyes clocking cars out the window, seeing but not seeing them as his mind boils. Finally, he turns to Ed and levels his gaze. "Well, if that all happens," he says, "then we'll see some scorched-earth tactics."

Ed, uncomfortable with conflict, knows from twenty years in the military that "scorched earth" means you'd destroy everything just to make sure your enemy got nothing. But he can't imagine Jim scuttling his own assets just to keep Lita from getting some cash and a house he doesn't even want.

After he drops Jim back at the hotel, he thinks about Jim's words, making a mental note to tell Lita. He's said his piece, but Jim obviously doesn't want to hear it. Some people just need to fight.

❖

Now living in Atlanta and separated from Jim, Lita is a flower finally being watered. The brown spots on her petals begin to disappear, her wilted disposition resuscitated by the sunlight of family and friends. She rekindles her friendships with her Spelman College pals, jumps into volunteering for charitable causes, and spends a lot of time with Poppy and her toddler, Ingrid. Lita and Jim stood for the baby's blessing at the Ebenezer Baptist Church when she was just six months old. Now, the three-year-old calls her "Mama Lita," and Lita cherishes her little goddaughter.

It's the mid-1980s and divorce rates are peaking across the country. As it happens, Poppy's own marriage is beginning to crumble, as is Jan's down in Macon. The three friends find solace in each other's company, often socializing or taking trips together. Lita spends evenings out dancing or hosting small dinner parties. She goes on dates, buoyed by the attention of men after years of being virtually ignored. These are the days before Tinder or Bumble; she meets men the old-fashioned way, through friends or by scribbling her phone number on a pack of matches after a night of dancing.

While Lita enjoys her newfound freedom, Jim's endless stream of legal acrobatics and accusations leaves her simmering with anxiety. The qualities she first admired in Jim—his ambition, tenacity, and clever mind—are now coming at her sideways.

And, it turns out, Poppy's husband is coming at her too.

Marvin Marable, a former New York state trooper turned Atlanta businessman, had met Poppy through Lita's family—he'd been a friend of Lita's cousin. He moved to Atlanta to invest in real estate and was introduced to Poppy because she was both a friend of Lita's and an insurance agent who could help secure his investments. They married in 1982—Lita was Poppy's maid of honor—and had Ingrid the following year. But by 1985, things had begun to sour between them.

When Lita moves back to Atlanta that summer, the tension between the Marables intensifies. Marvin doesn't like how much time his wife spends with her old friend, believing Lita's pending divorce is influencing Poppy's diminishing love for him. He liked it better when Lita was with Jim and the four of them socialized. Lita and Poppy would while away hours chatting while he and Jim drank cognac and smoked cigars.

In December, growing more suspicious of Poppy's activities, Marvin goes to Radio Shack and buys a wiretap device to place on their home phone. Every day he switches out the little cassette tape and spends evenings in his den listening to what will total more than three hundred hours of his wife's private conversations. He hides the tapes in a case in the trunk of his car, a place he knows Poppy will never look.

Like they did in college, Poppy and Lita talk on the phone for hours, chatting about the new friends they're meeting, commiserating about their decaying marriages, sharing their deepest, most private thoughts and dreams.

Marvin listens. And listens. And listens . . .

After months of eavesdropping and the realization that his own marriage is likely doomed, Marvin has an idea: why not see if he can make a buck by sharing this dirt with Jim Sullivan?

CHAPTER 8
FREE & UNEASY
(1985-1986)

O fficially separated from Lita, Jim is like a college kid on spring break—unencumbered and insatiable. He doubles down on climbing the Palm Beach social ladder and leans into his new role on the town's Landmarks Preservation Commission. The gig, though unpaid, gives him power and status in the community.

Jim, a fastidious and detailed notetaker, jots down every detail of his daily activities in his calendar—every meeting and the requisite follow-ups, to-dos, anything he's purchased, and notes pertaining to the whereabouts of one Hyo-Sook "Suki" Rogers.

Ever since they met at that cocktail party where he begrudgingly introduced her to Lita, he's been thinking about Suki's petite, sexy body and the thrill of flirting with her. Suki is, after all, drop-dead gorgeous. The Korean socialite is currently married—for the second time to the same man, Palm Beach businessman Leonard Rogers, a friend of Jim's. Born in South Korea in 1952, Suki came to the United States on a student visa in 1974, though she never really went to school. Instead, she began marrying rich men. Her first marriage was brief—only about a year—to a finance guy in Chicago. She divorced him shortly after they moved to Palm Beach, where she quickly realized the fish had much fatter wallets. When she met and married Rogers the first time, in 1980, she was twenty-eight and he was fifty-one. He was a successful businessman and lavished Suki with jewelry and gifts, anything to hang on to her. Their first marriage lasted a tumultuous eighteen months before fizzling in divorce. Though split, the couple continued to live together, which compelled them to remarry each other in 1982. They regularly appeared in photos and news bites in the "Shiny Sheet," the colloquial name for the *Palm Beach Daily News*, which covered the who's who of the Palm Beach social scene.

But by the time she meets Jim in 1985, Suki is thirty-four and bored. Leonard frequently travels out of town on business, so Suki spends her days shopping, playing tennis, and figuring out what dress to wear next. She takes a few art classes at Palm Beach Community College but stops going when the early mornings interfere with her social life. Later described by her own lawyer as "functionally illiterate," Suki can't read beyond second-grade English, but her stilted English seems to fluctuate, depending on the situation; sometimes she's shrewd and articulate, other times she conveniently feigns foreigner ignorance.

She can tell that Jim is slack-jaw smitten with her, and she finds the fact that he has money and never seems to work ideal. She knows he dates other women, including a Chinese friend of hers who slept with Jim inside Casa Eleda. Suki knows of the house because her brother admired it on a visit once. When he returned for a visit a month after she met Jim, she took her brother and knocked on Jim's door. Thrilled at the idea of Suki in his house, Jim gave them an extravagant tour, offering architectural tidbits and drinks. It marks the beginning of Jim and Suki's steamy affair.

❖

It doesn't take long before Leonard catches on to the fact that his wife is sleeping with his pal Jim. He hires a private investigator, who easily captures photos of Suki and Jim spending overnights together—sometimes at his place, sometimes at hers when Leonard's out of town. One night the investigator reports seeing Suki pull Leonard's car out of the garage and park it on the street so Jim could stow his Rolls in the garage. In the morning, Suki wouldn't let the maid inside because Jim was there. The investigator captures it all on film, including the maid pacing the sidewalk waiting to get in.

It doesn't take long before Leonard has the same private investigator serve Suki with divorce papers—for the second time. At their divorce trial, the maid testifies, "The ashtrays were filled up by someone who smokes a cigar, liquor glasses and everything was all over the kitchen," and that, after Jim stayed over, Suki would insist on washing the sheets herself.

After being kicked out of her marital home, Suki buys an apartment in West Palm Beach but doesn't like living on the working-class side of the Intracoastal Waterway. She regroups, refocuses her strategy, and begins spending more and more time at Casa Eleda with Jim.

One day, in February 1986, Jim gets a call from Marvin Marable.

"Jim," says Marvin. "I have some information that may help you in your divorce."

"Go on, then," says Jim.

Marvin tells him about the tapes, how they prove Lita is dating several different men, their wives go dancing and party all the time, that they're out drinking and dabbling with drugs. Marvin says he knows what they spend while shopping, when and where they go on trips, details about Lita's lawyer's divorce strategy, all of it.

Jim's heart pounds—this is exactly what he needs.

"I have enough," says Marvin. "I'm going to remove the device before someone finds it. But I wanted to let you know."

"No. No. No. You can't do that," says Jim. "I need this." He tells Marvin that he thinks the courts in Atlanta are going to be more lenient to Lita than the courts in Florida. They won't honor his postnup and he'll lose in court. "Please. Keep recording," says Jim. "Get me everything you can . . . And send me the tapes."

Marvin couriers the tapes to Jim and, over the next few weeks, the men speak more than twenty times. Suki hears Jim listening to the tapes, shut away in his office for hours; sometimes he'll call her in to listen. He takes copious notes, occasionally cursing before firing off a memo to his lawyer.

Jim pays to have Marvin fly down under a fake name to stay overnight at Casa Eleda and share everything he knows. They come to an agreement: Jim will pay Marvin $30,000 if the information he provides saves Jim from paying anything above his postnuptial agreement. In other words, if the judge decides the postnup is valid, Marvin will make some money.

When Marvin returns home from Florida, he trots down to the basement to retrieve the latest tape and discovers the recording device gone. Panicked, he runs upstairs to the living room, where Poppy's playing the piano. He sees her eyes are red and puffy, like she's been crying.

"I believe you have something that belongs to me," says Marvin calmly. Poppy keeps playing. Marvin waits, trying to figure out what to say next. He walks closer, cautious as though he's approaching an angry cat. Suddenly her hands stop, hovering above the keys. She turns to look at her husband and says simply, "I want a divorce."

She files the next day, using Richard Schiffman, Lita's divorce lawyer. Lita then calls the police. She explains in detail how she and Poppy deduced through hearing clicking sounds on the phone that Marvin had been taping their conversations, for months, without consent, which is illegal in Georgia.

When Marvin catches wind the Fulton County District Attorney's office is going to indict him on criminal charges for invasion of privacy, he gets rid of the tapes, discarding them in a dumpster behind a DeKalb County shopping mall. He pleads guilty to the invasion-of-privacy charges and gets two years' probation.

For his troubles, he never receives a penny from Jim.

❖

As 1986 progresses, the legal fees mount, and Jim gets desperate for the divorce to be over. From behind his big walnut desk, Jim looks out the window of his beloved Casa Eleda but doesn't see the view of the ocean;

instead, his eyes zero in on the paint chipping inside the window frame. He clenches his jaw; the familiar wave of anxiety grips his chest. The entire house needs paint and plaster and a thousand other costly things that leave him struggling to breathe. He constantly looks for ways to cut costs—not running the air conditioning, scolding the help when they leave lights on—while making sure his neighbors never notice his struggles.

Although he had sold Crown Beverages for $5 million just three years prior, the zeros on his dollar signs are fading fast. He put almost a million down on Casa Eleda—much of which he had "borrowed" from the Crown Beverages employees' pension fund. Add to that the costly renovations, a $20,000 monthly mortgage, the Atlanta townhouse, the house in Macon, club memberships, living expenses, house staff, the pool boy, legal fees, and the escalating cost of dating Suki. It makes his blood boil that he's court-ordered to pay Lita $7,000 a month in temporary alimony. He gets $20,833 each month from the sale of Crown Beverages, plus returns on his various investments, but he needs the bleeding to stop. He tried to get a jumbo loan that would buy him some time—borrow from Peter to pay Paul type of thing—but he got caught fudging the loan application form. On it, he'd listed himself as single, but when clever bank officials checked it against his tax returns and discovered he was still married, they told him they'd require Lita's signature in accordance with Florida law. On the advice of her lawyers, Lita had refused to sign.

He thinks about Suki's soft supple skin, the latest bottle of Beaujolais nouveau added to the wine collection in the basement, the cool lines of his convertible Rolls-Royce Corniche . . . He's earned this dream, has pulled himself upward rung by rung, and he's not going to let go of any of it. Over his goddamn dead body.

ʙᴏᴠᴇ: Lita at her prom with her date. ʙᴇʟᴏᴡ: Lita as a teenager at her parent's house. *Photos courtesy ⸰ the McClinton family.*

Ms. Lita McClinton (left) and Ms. Popp
Finley (below) in the 1974 Spelman Col
lege yearbook. *Photos courtesy of Spelman
College Archival Collection.*

TOP LEFT: Lita in her late teens. TOP
RIGHT: Always a lover of dogs, Lita visits
her parents house in the early 1980s.
BOTTOM: Always experimenting with
fashion, Lita on her way to school in the
1970s. *Photos courtesy of the McClinton
family.*

Lita (left) with her mother Jo Ann (middle) and her sister Valencia (right), on Lita's wedding day in 1976. *Photo courtesy of the McClinton family.*

ABOVE: Lita at the airport heading on vacation with Jim, early 1980s. RIGHT: Jim, Lita, Poppy, and Marvin. *Photos courtesy of the McClinton family.*

Lita (on right) with her siblings Valencia and Emory Jr. *Photo courtesy of the McClinton family.*

ABOVE: An investigator points out a discarded bullet shell found in Lita's backyard. BELOW: Investigators found the unopened flower box at the bottom of the stairs. *Photos courtesy of the Georgia Bureau of Investigation.*

Lita's townhouse at The Coaches in Buckhead. *Photo courtesy of the Georgia Bureau of Investigation*

ABOVE: Jim Sullivan (left), early 1990s. Suki Sullivan (right) became Jim's third wife just eight months after Lita's murder. BELOW: Jim Sullivan's mug shot after his arrest for weapons possession in Palm Beach, Florida. *Photos courtesy of the Georgia Bureau of Investigation.*

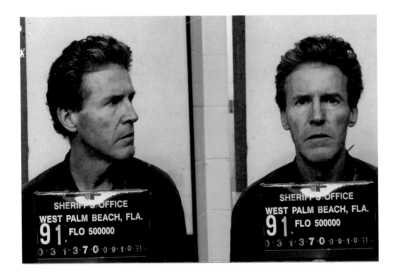

FBI special agent John Kingston played an integral role in the early investigation. *Photo courtesy of John Kingston.*

FBI special agent Todd Letcher led the raid of Jim Sullivan's Palm Beach mansion. *Photo courtesy of Todd Letcher.*

TOP: GBI special agent John Lang and APD detective Steve Balkcom standing in front of Casa Eleda in 1998. *Photo courtesy of John Lang.* BOTTOM LEFT: Private investigator Patrick McKenna worked tirelessly with the McClinton family lawyers to bring Lita's killer to justice. *Photo courtesy of Patrick McKenna.* BOTTOM RIGHT: GBI special agent John Lang. *Photo courtesy of John Lang.*

TOP: Phillip Anthony "Tony" Harwood on th[e] day of his arrest, April 19, 1998 in Albemarl[e,] North Carolina. CENTER: A young Tony Ha[r]wood. *Photos courtesy of Georgia Bureau of Inve[s]tigation.* BOTTOM: Tony Harwood around th[e] time he's released from prison in 2018. *Courtes[y] of WSBTV news report.*

ABOVE: Tony Harwood in a physical lineup soon after his arrest in 1998 (third from left). *Photo courtesy of Georgia Bureau of Investigation.* RIGHT: Phillip Anthony Harwood checked into the Atlanta Howard Johnson under the false name Johnny Furr; the discovery of the registration card was a major clue in the early investigation. *Evidence photograph courtesy of John Kingston.*

UNLAWFUL FLIGHT TO AVOID PROSECUTION - MURDER

WANTED BY FBI

FBI No.
684964MA6

Aliases: James V. Sullivan and James Sullivan

JAMES VINCENT SULLIVAN

Photograph taken September 10, 1991

Date of Birth :	April 5, 1941	Eyes:	Hazel
Place of Birth :	Massachusetts	Complexion:	Medium
Height:	5' 9"	Sex:	Male
Weight:	140 to 145 pounds	Race:	White
Build:	Thin	Nationality:	American
Hair:	Brown		

Scars and Marks: Unknown
Occupations: Owner of liquor business
Remarks: Subject is a multimillionaire and may have access to a large amount of money/funds through offshore and foreign bank accounts.
Social Security Number Used: ███████
Passport Number(s): 04141279 (U.S.); M867686 (Ireland)

CRIMINAL RECORD

December 11, 1990- Perjury
September 10, 1991- Possession of a Firearm

NCIC: 23AA0610102053031312

23	L	1	A	II	10
	L	1	R	III	

FEDERAL PROCESS

A federal warrant was issued on April 29, 1998, in the Northern District of Georgia, Atlanta, Georgia, charging JAMES VINCENT SULLIVAN in violation of Title 18, United States Code, Section 1073, Unlawful Flight to Avoid Prosecution- Murder.

IF YOU HAVE ANY INFORMATION CONCERNING THIS PERSON, PLEASE CONTACT YOUR LOCAL FBI OFFICE OR THE NEAREST U.S. EMBASSY OR CONSULATE. TELEPHONE NUMBERS AND ADDRESSES OF ALL FBI OFFICES ARE LISTED ON BACK.

Identification Order 5342
January 19, 2001
OO:AT

CAUTION

SHOULD BE CONSIDERED ARMED AND DANGEROUS

James Freeh

DIRECTOR
FEDERAL BUREAU OF INVESTIGATION
WASHINGTON, D.C. 20535

This "Wanted by FBI" poster appeared in post offices, police stations, at border patrols, and FBI offices as authorities scoured the globe searching for Jim Sullivan. *Courtesy of Patrick McKenna.*

Defense attorney Don Samuel (top left), former Fulton County executive district attorney Clint Rucker (top right), and Belinda Trahan (left center). *Photos courtesy of Court TV.*

James Vincent Sullivan in 2022, at the Augusta State Medical Prison, where he is serving a life sentence without the possibility of parole. *Photo courtesy of the Georgia Department of Corrections.*

Duo. A bronze sculpture and plaque honoring Lita at the McClinton family plot at Atlanta's Oakland Cemetery. *Photo by Deb Miller Landau.*

CHAPTER 9

TONY & BELINDA
(1986)

When long-haul trucker Tony Harwood gets a delivery job from Macon, Georgia, to Palm Beach, Florida, his girlfriend Belinda refuses to go with him. They've been fighting and she needs a break from the long boring hours in the truck, the paperwork he enlists her to handle. Tony takes the job alone. It's just an "overflow"—the stuff left behind when someone moves—and includes a huge heavy area rug, a couple of side tables, some wall sconces, and a massive grand piano. Tony hires some laborers to load the truck in Macon, throws the latch on the back door, and begins the eight-hour trip to Palm Beach.

When he rolls his rig into the horseshoe driveway at 920 South Ocean Blvd. on November 24, 1986, Tony gives a low whistle. From the truck's cab, he looks out at the Atlantic Ocean, scratches his head, and watches sailboats bobbing in the waves, the sun glinting off whitecaps like diamonds. Consuming a corner lot decorated with palm trees and bougainvillea, the house is almost too big to comprehend—like chunks of a castle connected with smooth, sandy putty. The arched windows alone probably cost more than any home Tony's ever lived in. His eyes dazzle with dollar signs.

A man comes outside and waves his hands, motioning that Tony's crew of laborers should move in and out of the side door. Tony, who prides himself on being a good judge of character, surveys the man, presumably the homeowner. He's a couple inches shorter and a good forty pounds lighter than Tony, scrawny, with curly red-brown hair and pale skin. He wears khaki shorts, brown sandals with white socks, and a flowered shirt. Tony slides out of the truck, introduces himself, and notes that the impatient little man with a funny Yankee accent doesn't bother to look him in the eye. While the man coaches the movers on where to bring the furniture, Tony leans against the shade-side of the truck, lights a cigarette, and takes it all in. The man watches the movers like a hawk.

"Hard to get good help these days," says Tony, nodding toward the sweating laborers.

"Huh?" says the man.

"I say it's hard to get good help."

"You're telling me," says the man.

"Nice place to spend the holidays," says Tony. Thanksgiving is just a couple of days out. The man only grunts in response. Always easy shooting shit, Tony talks about the drive down, feigns interest in the piano. Slowly, the man reveals that the furniture is the last of his stuff in Macon, that he must get it in one place because his soon-to-be ex-wife is trying to take him for everything he has. Tony's a natural talker, the kind of guy people tell their problems to, and this man is no different. In Tony, Jim likely sees a thug, someone uneducated and clearly inferior. Someone who doesn't matter. But Tony has been around the block. He knows what it's like to be underestimated.

❖

Tony—"Phillip Anthony Dick" on his birth certificate—arrived kicking and screaming into the world thirty-five years earlier on March 7, 1951, in Mecklenburg County, North Carolina. His unmarried mother, Mary, was twenty when Tony was born, his father a mythical creature Tony never knew. He'd heard a story that his biological father had every intention of killing his mama while she was pregnant, but maybe that was never true.

His whole life, everyone around him was a liar.

Tony's last name became Harwood when Mary wed Hurley Harwood, a man who never let Tony forget he was a bastard. Mary and Hurley went on to have four more children: Linda, Joey, Matthew, and Randy—some of whom, like Tony, lived in mobile homes on the family's compound in Finger, a dirt patch on the outskirts of Albemarle, North Carolina. "There weren't but two dirt roads in Albemarle," Tony once said. "And we lived on one of 'em."

Tony was a rambunctious child nicknamed "Cowboy," partly because he dressed like one, but partly because he was a wild horse impossible to tame. His mother had a photo of young Tony sitting on a pinto pony in downtown Albemarle. He might've been six or eight. In it, he wore shorts, a vest, cheap faux-leather chaps, and cowboy boots, squinting into the camera like he was ready for a gun fight. Mary adored that photo, wore it down with her touch, likely remembering the time when her little cowboy shot only plastic pellets from his toy guns. In second grade, Tony developed a hard crush on a girl named Vickie. He followed her to school, found excuses to hang out at her house, and had a photo of her taped to his notebook. When Vickie refused his Valentine's candy, he got so mad that he spent the afternoon throwing rocks at the glass window of her grandfather's barbershop, until the man came out and threatened to whoop his ass. In fifth grade, Tony pulled a hawkbill knife on his teacher after she tried to choke him to get him under control. Tony wasn't going to let some woman teacher strangle him. While other kids cowered at the back of the room, Tony struggled to break free from the teacher's grip. He ran his hands up between hers and knocked her hands off his neck. When he finally broke free, panting from the adrenaline and still holding the weapon, the principal ran into the classroom and threatened to hit Tony. "Not while I have this knife you ain't," Tony told him. Tony's stepfather, Hurley, came roaring into the school from his job at the cotton mill and saw the red finger indents on his stepson's neck. Hurley told the teacher to keep her hands off his kid.

To the principal he said, "You ain't touching my boy." That was one of the few times the man Tony called his father had stood up for him.

"I was a stepchild, and my daddy was an alcoholic," Tony later told me. "He was good to everyone else but his family." Once, Hurley beat Tony with an extension cord, and the blood-red welts were so bad Tony couldn't go to school for three days.

For Tony, love showed up in complicated ways.

Tony quit school in ninth grade and solidified his reputation as a bully and troublemaker. While he was no stranger to police, he wasn't considered harmful per se. "He would bully you if you'd let him," a schoolmate once said. "He could rob a store or steal your lawn mower," but he didn't go around actively hurting people.

At seventeen, he was arrested for a handful of burglary-related offenses, and though he was still a minor, he was sentenced as an adult. This was likely a major turning point in Tony's life. Tony was a wild animal that needed to be tamed, but an incarcerated teenager tends to fight when he's put in a cage. Prison made him harder, only serving to feed the beast that was growing inside him. He did his time at the Stanly County Correctional Center in Albemarle, attempted escape twice—in 1970 and '71, which added time to his sentence—and was finally released on October 29, 1975, at the age of twenty-four. For the entire seven years of his incarceration, his mother Mary was his only visitor.

Sometime after his release from prison, he married and had a daughter. But Tony was a wild stallion, and the thought of settling down hogtied his soul. The marriage didn't last, and Tony never had much of a relationship with his kid.

At six foot one, Tony was built like volcanic rock—hard, impossible to push over, and always on the verge of eruption. With thick sandy blond hair, ripped muscles, and a booming Sam Elliott-esque voice, his presence powered a room like electricity returning after a storm. He had a tattoo of the grim reaper on his left shoulder, thick fingers, and a heart he never learned how to wrangle. He became a long-haul truck driver, on the road for long stretches, sleeping in the cab, and eating at truck stops. He drank a little, smoked pot, snorted and injected cocaine. He'd hang out with guys he met in prison, crash on whoever's couch. He'd pick up women at strip clubs, get them high, party all night, then roll out for a long trip, hauling whatever needed hauling. He liked working because he liked money.

In the early 1980s, he met Belinda Trahan during a short stint living in Houston. She was an attractive blond who had recently moved to Houston to work as a secretary for her father, a man she hardly knew. She was twenty-five and liked to party but knew few people in town. A new friend invited her to come and get high over at Tony's place—an apartment in the same complex. At first, she didn't like Tony; he seemed like a self-absorbed, mannerless brute. But as the weeks went by, he kept coming around, asking how he could get in her good graces. He installed a ceiling fan in her apartment, a tactic to woo women he would hone for the rest of his life: do some odd jobs, fix things, and women tended to be grateful.

Belinda and Tony started hanging out, friends at first but they were young, horny, and often high. They had an intense, fiery relationship where they'd have massive blowout fights, followed by passionate reconciliations. In 1985, Tony packed up his van to move home to North Carolina, but he only made it halfway before coming back to Belinda. They lived a tumultuous existence crammed in her apartment. Belinda was stressed all the time—trying to deal with Tony, working for a stranger of a father. Days hopped up on coke swerved into boozy blackouts and, in a short span, she overdosed on cocaine, then attempted suicide by pills. She says she would've succeeded if Tony hadn't found her and rushed her to the hospital.

Soon after that, Tony left Texas and over the next few months pressed Belinda to come live with him in Albemarle. She finally relented in 1986, and she and her son Jimmy moved into a trailer on his parents' thirty acres in Finger, North Carolina.

Tony worked for North American Van Lines and enlisted Belinda to help with the paperwork, wrap the furniture, and occasionally move boxes. The company only hired husband-and-wife teams, so they pretended to be married—listing her as Belinda Harwood—so she could go along. She'd leave Jimmy behind with Tony's mom while she and Tony hauled loads up and down the East Coast. They made good money, but they only got paid when they were on the road working. For a time, they had fun, rolling along listening to music, getting high, camping in little towns, but the lifestyle began to wear on Belinda. It was often cold, and long, and boring. They lived in the cab of the truck; she sewed curtains to make it homier, but they'd get on each other's nerves in the small space. It wasn't the life she wanted, and when things got rough, she threatened to take Jimmy and leave Tony for good.

"I worshipped the ground she walked on," Tony said later. "Belinda was everything I'd ever dreamed of . . . kind, considerate, a kid at heart, beautiful, a good mother. She'd make any man proud." He loved Jimmy too. Jimmy spent all of seventh grade living with Belinda and Tony. Tony and his brothers taught the tween how to fish and hunt deer, shoot guns, and ride the moped Tony bought him. It was an idyllic situation for a twelve-year-old longing for a father figure. Jimmy called Tony "Daddy," and Tony thought of him as a son. But there were moments of darkness too. Even though Tony was an ox and Belinda a kitten, they could fight like wild dogs. The screaming matches were regular; Jimmy would run out of the trailer and hide somewhere on the property until things calmed down. Everything would simmer for a while until some next spark lit a fire and the whole thing would explode again. At one point, in the fall of 1986, Belinda and Tony got into such a brawl.

"She whacked me pretty good with her purse," Tony said later, recalling the incident. "So, I popped her upside the head with an open hand. And I said, 'So you wanna hit?' and grabbed her by the throat." Scared and fearing this time was worse than ever before, Jimmy sprinted to the big house and grabbed Hurley's 410 shotgun then ran back to the trailer. He pointed the gun square at Tony and screamed, "Let her go!"

Tony laughed at the boy with the gun but let go of Belinda. Jimmy, shaking and scared, led his mom to Tony's mother's house, where he hid under the table while Belinda called the cops.

Later, when things simmered down again, Tony scolded his stepfather for having a loaded gun with kids around.

❖

Inside the mansion under the Florida sun, Tony is amused by the fastidious little Yankee complaining about his wife. He notes a nice-looking Asian woman step out from the hallway and into the foyer, turn around, and go back inside.

"I probably know someone who could take care of your problem," says Tony, lowering his booming voice. He's partly joking but he's no dummy. He understands what is happening here: this man has a hot new woman and wants the old one out of his hair. "Look," Tony says, looking over his shoulder. "If you want to get this problem taken care of, you're probably looking at $25,000. And you'd need to pay half up front." The man levels his gaze at Tony, thinks for a beat, then grabs a pen. The next thing Tony knows, the man is drawing a map to a condo in some swanky neighborhood in Atlanta. On it, he writes his phone number.

While all this is happening, the movers struggle with the piano and, while wrangling it through the foyer, scratch the brownish-red terracotta floor tiles. The man becomes irate. Tony tries to calm him, assuring him he'll take care of it because drivers are responsible for any damages incurred in a move. He retrieves a claim form from the truck, writes down his personal phone number and address. Tony hopes the guy, like most customers, will forget about it and never file the claim. The man did later file a claim but by then, Tony had quit North American.

Tony leaves Palm Beach and makes his way back to Albemarle.

To Belinda, Tony acts strange when he returns—nervous and antsy like he's hiding something. He starts barhopping with a guy he refers to only as "The Bartender," which is out of the ordinary because Tony doesn't drink much. When she asks him what he's up to, he tells her the less she knows the better. She pushes. Eventually, he lets it slip that some rich white guy in Florida wants him to "take care" of his Black wife in Atlanta.

"What do you mean 'take care' of her?" Belinda asks.

Tony just looks at her and says, "You know, *take care of her*. Get rid of her."

Belinda thinks it's bullshit, his way of covering up that he's cheating on her, going to strip bars, or hooking up with another woman somewhere along the road.

"Whatever," she says. She's getting tired of him anyway. "Do whatever you want to do."

Not long after, two certified checks totaling $12,500 arrive in a plain, unmarked envelope in the mail at their humble mobile home. *Well lookie here*, thinks Tony. *It's an early Christmas present.*

CHAPTER 10

THREE DAYS BEFORE (JANUARY 13, 1987)

Tuesday, January 13, 1987, should be an ordinary day—cold, uneventful. The holidays are over, decorations droop and need to be put away. But this is no ordinary Tuesday, and no one will know until it's much too late. In the world of Lita and Jim, some notable things happen:

6 A.M.: A sudden pounding on Lita's door. Ashley Wilkes barks like crazy. Lita looks out the upstairs guest room window and sees a man in a ball cap standing on her doorstep. A small dark car with tinted windows is parked out front. She quickly closes the curtain, hurries back to her bedroom at the back of the house, crawls under her covers, and tries to go back to sleep. But the knocking has startled her so much, she can't find her way back to slumber. She finally gets up, makes coffee and, at 7:30 A.M., calls Jan in Macon.

"Lita, what is it?" asks Jan, surprised to hear her friend's voice so early.

"I'm sorry to call at this hour," says Lita. "A man was here, banging on the door, around six this morning."

"Oh, my goodness. What?" Jan asks. Jim has been trying to subpoena Jan to testify on his behalf in the divorce, but for the past couple of weeks she's successfully evaded the process server.

But maybe they've learned Jan is going to be visiting Lita in Atlanta later that day? "Did you answer?"

"Of course not," says Lita. "No one in Atlanta is going to open their door to strangers at six o'clock in the morning."

7:24 A.M.: Three people driving a car with North Carolina plates check into the Howard Johnson motel on Roswell Road, about six miles from Lita's townhouse.

7:44 A.M.: Southern Bell records reveal that a call is made from room 518 at the Howard Johnson to Jim Sullivan's mansion in Florida. The call lasts two minutes.

8 A.M.: Marvin Marable gets a voicemail message. "Marvin, this is Jim. Call me as soon as possible. It's urgent." Jim is nervous, desperate sounding, unlike his usual self. The two men haven't spoken since the wiretap debacle several months ago.

Marvin calls him back right away. "Jim, it's Marvin, returning your call."

"I need some information. It's very important, critical," pleads Jim. "Do you know if Lita is still living in the same place, in the townhouse? Do you know if she has the same car? Do you know if anyone is staying with her? Or just any information you might have."

"I have no idea, Jim," says Marvin, perplexed. "Poppy and I got divorced a month ago. I haven't been over there. I really don't know."

8:58 A.M.: Jim leaves a message for Lita's next-door neighbor Bob Christenson at the law offices of Fisher and Phillips, where he practices labor and employment law.

9:29 A.M.: Jim leaves another message for Bob. When Bob's secretary relays the two calls, Bob frowns. Bob represented Jim in an employee dispute at Crown a few years earlier and, while they are friendly enough, they haven't spoken in a year.

10:33 A.M.: Jim calls the Howard Johnson's, room 518.

10:38 A.M.: Bob finally calls Jim back. "Thanks for getting back to me, Bob," Jim says, as though it's a regular thing for him to be calling. "Say, have you seen any suspicious activity around Lita's house?"

"Um, no," says Bob, confused. "What do you mean?" He finds the call peculiar; he knows the Sullivans are embroiled in a contentious divorce. Why is Jim calling out of the blue?

"Listen," says Jim. "I need Lita's phone number. Can you give it to me?"

Bob knows Lita's number is unlisted. "I'm sorry, Jim. I can't do that. I could maybe ask her to call you, but I can't give you her unlisted number."

Jim grumbles and hangs up the phone.

Later, FBI agents will find an entry in Jim's day planner on the next day, January 14. In his tiny handwriting it says: "Get flowers."

CHAPTER 11

FOR WHOM THE DOORBELL TOLLS (JANUARY 16, 1987, AGAIN)

L ita's usually a late sleeper, but she's up early today to prepare for court. She can hear Poppy in the shower, her young daughter Ingrid likely still asleep in bed. She is so thankful they have slept over to lend moral support before the hearing.

Just a few days past her thirty-fifth birthday, Lita is tired of bracing for Jim's unceasing arrows that he slings through his lawyers with impunity. He's called her a jewelry thief and a drug abuser—she even had to shamefully pee in a cup to prove she was clean. He's even had the gall to claim she had multiple extramarital affairs—which is rich, given his own sordid history of infidelity. She knows through the grapevine that Jim is now running around Palm Beach with Suki Rogers, was sleeping with her even while Suki was still married to Leonard. It's embarrassing, humiliating. She's heard that he's even introduced Suki to his parents in Boston, which cuts deep, a final twist of the knife. Lita never met his parents; Jim always made excuses.

At 2 P.M. today, a judge will determine whether to enforce Jim's unfair postnuptial agreement or let a jury decide on what's a fair and equitable distribution of the couple's assets. Lita's lawyer says it's a good sign that the judge has already calendared a jury trial date, just ten days away. He wouldn't have done so if he planned to enforce the postnup. Of course, if the judge decides in Jim's favor, Lita could appeal, but that could drag on forever—months, even years.

But Lita has already moved on from Jim. Before Christmas, she relaxed over a long weekend in Hilton Head with Poppy and Jan then came home to throw an intimate Christmas dinner party for family and a few friends, including Ed and Fran Wheeler. After dinner, she asked Ed to be a character witness in the upcoming divorce trial, and he told her he'd talk to Jim first and get back to her. She had a busy holiday, helping organize the New Year's Eve Crescendo Ball, a major fundraiser for the Cystic Fibrosis Association—a cause she has worked tirelessly to support. The foundation president would later describe Lita as "an outstanding young Black lady that took an active interest in a white man's disease," because, he said, 99.9 percent of patients who suffer from the genetic disorder are white.

Lita's fellow event volunteers are coming over for a party to celebrate the event's success tomorrow night. Prepping and planning for it has been a good distraction. But she is tired, ready to restart her life without constant calls from her lawyer detailing all the new ways Jim is trying to hurt her. In addition to the nerves about court, she's jumpy because some strange things have been happening lately: a knock in the early morning a few days ago, the creeping suspicion she's being followed, and that odd phone call yesterday.

Lita was in the kitchen getting sodas for her mother and sister, who had stopped by on their way to go shopping for baby furniture. Valencia is four months pregnant with the McClintons' first grandchild, and everyone is excited for the baby's arrival.

"That's strange," Lita said, returning with the tray of drinks. "Jim's canceled the videotaping tomorrow." Jim's lawyers had hired a videographer to inventory the contents of the townhouse—an attempt to show Lita didn't need Jim's money because she was already living in luxury. On the advice of her lawyer, Lita had agreed to give the photographer access on Friday morning, before she left for court. They knew from Ed Wheeler about Jim's "scorched-earth" strategy, so it was odd for him to cancel something that could sway a jury in his favor.

"Maybe he's realized how petty it looks," Valencia suggested.

"Maybe," said Lita, not convinced.

Lita told her mother and sister about the early morning knock on the door, how she'd looked out to see a stranger on the stoop. Valencia and Jo Ann exchanged worried glances.

"Oh baby," said Jo Ann. "Don't answer your door."

"Of course not, I didn't," said Lita, seeing the alarm on her mother's face.

"Why don't you stay with your father and I tonight?" Jo Ann suggested. "I don't want you staying here alone."

"Don't worry," said Lita, trying to lighten things up. "I'm fine. I'm going to have dinner with Bob and then Poppy's going to stay over. We'll be fine." She wanted to change the subject, so she turned to her sister. "So, what store are you going to first?"

It's around 8:15 A.M. when the doorbell rings. Unbeknownst to Lita, a man carrying a long white flower box is standing on her doorstep. Lita tightens her robe and heads downstairs to answer the door.

The townhouses at The Coaches surround a courtyard. Each home has a garage and parking strip, but visitors can also pull into and park in the courtyard. The property is protected by a big retaining wall at the back and surrounded by leafy trees. The only way in and out is off Slaton Drive, via an ungated driveway. Lita's townhouse (#4) is part of a pair of attached townhouses; she shares a wall with lawyer Bob Christenson (#3). If you are standing at Lita's front door about to knock, Bob's townhouse is on the right.

Homer Deakins, another lawyer, lives across the courtyard, in the middle of three attached townhomes. On that Friday morning, he sips coffee in his breakfast nook overlooking the courtyard. He inhales the first sip as the steam briefly clouds his eyeglasses. Through the mist he looks out and notices a scroungy guy approaching Lita's doorstep carrying a flower box. Curious, he watches the man ring the doorbell and figures it must be an ordinary delivery. People come in and out of the complex all the time. He looks down at the day's *Atlanta Journal-Constitution* and reads the headline, UNREST ERODES KING LEGACY OF NON-VIOLENCE IN AFRICA.

Next door, Bob Christenson clicks his automatic garage door opener and walks through the garage on his way to dump the trash in a garbage bin hidden behind a half wall on the left side of his house. He drives to work with his wife, and he is always ready before she is, so he's used to accomplishing little chores while he waits.

As he emerges from the garage, Bob looks to his right and notices a man with a flower box standing on Lita's doorstep. He doesn't think much of it, other than it seems kind of early for a flower delivery. Bob drops the trash in the bin and crosses the open garage to pick up his newspaper from his front stoop. He gets a closer look at the delivery man, clocking him as a white guy in his late forties, a little rough-looking, around six feet tall, wiry but strong. He wears a light green jacket and has dirty blond hair pushed back off his forehead, like it's greasy. He wears no hat, no eyeglasses. The man wears casual street shoes—not sneakers or dress shoes.

Like all the neighbors, Bob feels protective of Lita, partially because she lives alone but also because he knows she's going through a dreadful divorce from Jim. He feels a sense of fatherly tenderness toward his gracious neighbor. He cares about her, wants to protect her. So Bob watches carefully as the delivery man steps off Lita's stoop, looks at Lita's upstairs windows, and then shoots a glance at Bob, catching Bob watching. They lock eyes and begin to walk toward each other, like you do when you reluctantly have to chat with someone, but some deep instinct tells Bob to retreat.

Feeling the follicles on his head prickle, Bob, in his early fifties, has the same lurch in his gut he'd get when he was a combat soldier in Vietnam, a visceral response, an internal alarm sounding deep inside him. It's one of those instinctual things you only really comprehend with clarity later, after whatever bad thing has already happened. He turns around and goes inside his open garage, leans against his red Porsche 911, and glances at the newspaper. The front-page story is about how Atlanta mayor Andrew Young is in Botswana, where on the eve of the second-ever federal holiday honoring Martin Luther King Jr., King's vision of nonviolence is proving a hard sell in the south African country. Bob turns the page and notes pre–Super Bowl sales for color TVs, and Tiffany & Co. has a "return to romance" sale. He looks up again and sees the flower man still waiting at the door.

❖

The doorbell rings again. Upstairs, Poppy gets out of the guest bathroom shower and hears Lita pitter-patter downstairs to answer the door. She catches her friend say an uplifting "Good morning" to the stranger at the door.

❖

"Good morning," Lita says to the man carrying a flower box with a pink bow.

"Delivery," he says, stepping over the threshold while shoving the box into her hands, causing her to back up while he pulls the door slightly closed behind him.

Before anyone would have time to think of anything, the man reaches into his jacket pocket, pulls out a gun, and fires. The first bullet misses Lita, ripping through a curtain and into the dining room wall behind her. She tries to scramble away, holding up the box of flowers to shield her face. The second bullet shoots straight through the box, hitting the left side of Lita's head near the temple before exiting through her right ear. She crumples to the floor.

Upstairs, Poppy hears the gunshots and a distinct thump. Instinctively, she pulls Ingrid out of bed and hurries her into the closet, covering her with a blanket. "Be quiet," she whispers. "Quiet as a mouse." She waits behind the closet door, paralyzed, terrified, wondering what's happening.

Bob hears the shots from his garage and runs for cover behind the half wall at the side of his house, thinking the man will come for him next. He peeks over the wall and watches the delivery guy sprint out of The Coaches, so fast that he's slipping sideways on the asphalt, still slick from earlier rain.

Homer Deakins, across the courtyard, hears the two sounds—"like steel hitting steel"—but it doesn't occur to him that it might be gunshots. He stands up in his breakfast room in time to see the flower delivery guy running hard out of the complex. Homer hurries to the back of his house, which overlooks Slaton Drive, to see if he can see the guy emerge out of the complex, but a short barrier wall and trees block his view.

Bob needs to decide in a split second: run after the guy or go to Lita? He chooses Lita. Her door is ajar, so he pushes it open and steps into the foyer, his heart racing. What he sees will stay with him for the rest of his life. In the middle of the sparkling marble floor, sweet Lita lies face-up in her silky white robe, a black hole of blood pooling beneath her head. Bob kneels beside her and discerns she's unconscious but still breathing. He sprints into the kitchen and calls 911. He grabs a hand towel and folds it into a pillow to lay under her head. Panicked, he runs outside to intercept the ambulance.

The blood-spattered coffin of pink roses lies unopened on the floor beside her.

❖

Officer Eberett Thrall, a Buckhead officer with the Atlanta Police Department, is driving solo in his patrol car when he hears a "Signal 50" over the radio, indicating someone's been shot. It takes him less than two minutes to get to 3085 Slaton Drive. He sees Bob Christenson waving wildly. He stops quickly, leaving the lights flashing and door open as he follows Bob to Lita's white brick townhouse, barely tracking Bob's flurry of words about a delivery man, flowers, gunshots. Thrall enters the foyer to find Lita struggling to stay alive, one side of her face collapsed and already swelling from the bullet wound. Blood blooms like spilled ink under her head. An ambulance has already been dispatched; all he can do now is wait. Officer Thrall kneels on the floor and holds Lita's hand, telling her softly, calmly that everything will be OK. Again and again, he tells her: *hold on, it's OK. Everything's OK. Hold on, hold on, just breathe.* She is unconscious, her eyes closed. His heart flips when she squeezes his hand, her unconscious attempt to comfort him as much as he comforts her.

After hearing the sirens and voices downstairs, Poppy peeks out of the guest room. From the top of the stairs, she can see Lita's legs not moving on the foyer floor. Officer Thrall, surprised someone else is in the house, demands, "What are you doing up there?"

"I'm, I'm hiding. With my daughter," Poppy replies in a small, scared voice. "Is . . . is Lita OK?"

He swallows hard, telling Poppy to remain upstairs. "She's alive," he says, followed by a whispered, "barely."

❖

Jo Ann is getting ready to visit her mother in the hospital when the phone rings. Emory's already left for work.

"Hello," she answers.

She hears sobbing, rustling, too much noise. It's like she's overhearing someone else's phone call, one not meant for her. Poppy sobs into the phone, unable to find words, unable to breathe. Finally, it bursts out of her like a cannon: "It's Lita. It's Lita," Poppy cries. "Lita's been shot!"

"What?? What's happening??" Jo Ann screams, but Poppy is unable to say anything else or Jo Ann is unable to absorb it. She hangs up the phone and calls her husband as she grabs her purse and car keys. She tells him what Poppy said and he hangs up so fast, she knows he's already en route to Lita's with the tunnel vision of a father. While she drives, she wonders,

Was it a robbery? Does Lita have a gun in the house? But Lita hates guns . . .
Was she shot in the arm? Her leg? Whatever it is, she'll be OK. This too shall
pass. This too shall pass. This. Too. Shall. Pass.

❖

Detective Welcome Harris of the Atlanta Police Department's homicide
division is sipping coffee at the midtown station when he gets the call. He
jumps in the car with his partner, Detective George Jackson, and arrives
arrives at 3085 Slaton Drive at around 8:45 A.M., roughly twenty-five minutes after shots were fired. They find a busy scene: several EMTs attend to
a woman—Black female, mid-thirties, gunshot victim—in an ambulance.
She is still alive, about to be transported to Piedmont Hospital, but it
doesn't look good—which is why the homicide detectives got the call in
the first place. A shaken Officer Thrall, streaked with blood, paces with
another patrolman. There are firemen, paramedics. Neighbors have
emerged from the safety of their townhomes, stunned and in disbelief.
Bob Christenson, trembling and still in shock, tries to direct the human
traffic and restore some order amid the devastation.

Jo Ann arrives just as the ambulance is leaving The Coaches, followed
by Emory's car. She flips her car around and follows them to Piedmont
Hospital, the place Lita was born.

Most of it is a blur.

The ambulance arrives at Piedmont at 9:11 A.M. A nurse directs Jo Ann
and Emory to sit down in an empty exam room to wait, panicked, unable
to think. At 9:39 A.M., a blank-faced doctor comes in and says, "I'm sorry,"
and Jo Ann's ears fill with a raw void as though she's submerged underwater.
She doesn't hear anything else the doctor says; nothing else matters. This
news, that their beloved Lita, their firstborn, the light of their family, is . . .
gone is impossible to comprehend. The doctor asks if they want to see Lita's
body and Jo Ann says no. The thought that their lively daughter is now a
"body" instead of their baby is more than she can bear.

CHAPTER 12

THE AFTERMATH
(1987)

At forty-two, Welcome Harris has been a homicide detective for more than a decade and knows his way around a crime scene. For decades, Atlanta's murder rate has ranked among the top five for US cities. They are only halfway into January, and this is the ninety-third homicide of the year—the majority are gang-related clashes in specific pockets of the city. This daytime shooting of a woman in the wealthy Buckhead suburb is both jarring and incredibly rare.

He surveys the scene, trying to get his head around how and why a woman was gunned down in broad daylight. He notes the nose of a bullet lying in the walkway. He stands in the entryway and takes in the layout of the townhouse. There's a big foyer with arched passageways to other rooms. On the left is a formal dining room and kitchen. Opposite it, the library. The living room at the back of the foyer has French doors leading to an outdoor patio. In the center of the foyer, amid the blood and discarded gauze, Harris spots a shell casing, and another casing toward the back of the foyer. A blood-spattered flower box with a big pink bow sits at the bottom of a stairway that leads to the bedrooms.

That the victim was a Black woman is curious to Harris who, along with his partner, is also Black. This is the richest, whitest neighborhood in all of Atlanta. The place is filled with ornate antique furniture, heavy floral drapes tied in gold silk cord, trinkets worth more than his annual salary. He takes in the highfalutin design of the place, the whiteness of the neighborhood, and wonders: what's going on here?

❖

Shattered and hollowed, the McClintons drive in their separate cars back to Lita's house as though they are unfamiliar characters converging in a terrible, unforgivable movie. They arrive to chaos; the townhouse, now wrapped in police tape, is crawling with cops. Detectives interview neighbors and the shivering Poppy, clinging to her toddler while trying to recount the doorbell ringing and the sound of her best friend greeting the stranger at the door.

Maybe if she can get the details just right, she'll be able to change history.

Having heard the call on the police scanner, news outlets send vans carrying reporters and photographers and, as the news spreads, friends, acquaintances, and passing-by looky-loos show up, so now it's a mess of people. A container uncontained. There are too many people, except the one person who should be here.

Jo Ann walks to the threshold of her daughter's townhome and freezes. Lita's well-appointed foyer looks like a war zone. Dark blood splotches look like freakish Rorschach tests over Lita's usually gleaming floor, and incoherent red-brown spatters now blemish the walls. Forensic experts come and go, delicately sidestepping Jo Ann as they dust for fingerprints, snap photos of bullets and casings, drop metal bits into little evidence bags, and place numbered plastic tents over every suspicious inch. A man measures the exact location of Lita's now-gone body. Her feet were here. Her torso here. Her head here, in the middle of a lake of inky blood, getting thicker and darker by the minute.

Emory joins Jo Ann in the doorway and together they notice Valencia's husband trying to shield his broken in-laws from the fact that he's picking up brain tissue off the foyer floor. For a moment Jo Ann's eyes meet his, but he looks quickly away, agonized that his mother-in-law is seeing this. Why he's here makes no sense; he's not a cop, not a forensics expert. It's further proof the scene is out of control.

Incapable of comprehending anything, numb and in shock, Jo Ann goes upstairs to lie down in Lita's bedroom. While she closes her eyes to hide from this new reality, Emory sits slumped at the end of the bed, unable to speak. They are in their mid-fifties but have grown ancient, burdened by the incomprehensible weight of a murdered daughter. When Jo Ann opens her eyes to see a photographer climbing over the retaining wall at the back of the house, she screams.

"I don't know who I asked for a cigarette," she told me later, recounting the day. "But I started smoking after that."

❖

Detective Harris and the investigative team spend the entire day at Lita's condo interviewing witnesses and collecting evidence. There are no signs of burglary or sexual assault, leading the police to believe it must be some sort of orchestrated hit.

Harris examines the two shell casings in the foyer—the casing is a bullet's cylindrical container—and notes that one stands straight up about three inches from the front door, and another one rests on its side near the back wall. The distinct grooves on the casings tell the cops the shooter used a 9mm Smith & Wesson and that he likely shot once from the doorway, and a second time farther inside the foyer. They conclude the first bullet ripped through the curtains framing the living room doorway before piercing the back door with enough force that a piece of copper jacket (the outer casing of a bullet) landed on the back patio. The second bullet shot straight through the flower box, hit the left side of Lita's temple, and exited through her right ear, leaving investigators to surmise that she held up the box to protect herself.

The flower box sits at the base of the stairway, six feet away from where Lita's body collapsed, likely shoved aside by someone—maybe Bob, Officer

Thrall, or the paramedics. The box is white with a pink ribbon and, other than the fact it has blood spatters and a bullet hole straight through it, is unremarkable in that it lacks any identifying clues as to where it came from. Patrolmen begin canvassing local flower shops looking for its source. The box is sent to the Georgia Bureau of Investigation's crime lab for processing. Later, experts in the lab will open the box and find that it contains a dozen now-wilting pink roses, only five of which have wired buds. They also find a thumbprint on the side of the box and a partial palm print. The thumbprint, they'll later conclude, is Lita's, but they never learn who the palm print belongs to; she gets cremated before they have a chance to compare the print to Lita's own palm.

Other evidence at the townhouse includes a postcard on the foyer floor from one Ed Wheeler. On it, Ed had written to Lita,

Dear Lita, I fear we are in or have passed your birthday zone without sharing a toast . . . I finally talked to JVS last week. He responded that my testimony would hurt him, that he has not asked former friends to testify because he doesn't want 'to put them in the middle' and that he's tremendously concerned about what's happening to him. I'm convinced that contact between us in the future will only be at my instigation. What do you suppose I must do in this instance?

Best regards, Ed Wheeler

The cops find this perplexing and bag it as evidence. Later, while explaining the postcard, Ed will tell cops he'd chickened out; he opted to send a postcard instead of telling Lita in person that he wouldn't testify against Jim. The police soon learn that Lita was due in court that day, that she'd been embroiled in a bitter divorce to one JVS—James Vincent Sullivan. Harris takes note to investigate the husband's whereabouts as soon as possible.

After the eyewitness interviews, a police sketch artist creates a composite drawing of the shooter based on the description given by Bob

Christenson—white male, late forties, rough-looking, wearing a light green jacket with dirty blond hair pushed back off his forehead, like it was greasy. No hat, no glasses.

Homer Deakins gives a similar description, but says the man wore wire-rimmed aviator-style eyeglasses and shabby clothes. He guesses the man is, like him, in his early fifties.

Margaret McIntyre sees the emergency vehicles as she's driving back from breakfast and stops to tell detectives that earlier that morning she almost hit a man running "like a bat out of hell" coming out of The Coaches. The only thing she remembers about him is that he wore a greenish-blue windbreaker over a plaid shirt and some sort of work pants. "He was running like crazy," she said. "He was definitely not a Buckhead jogger."

Harris issues a department-wide BOLO for law enforcement—be on the lookout for anyone fitting the shooter's description.

The next day, the cops, canvassing the area, trace the flowers to the Botany Bay Florist at the crossroads of Peachtree and Pharr Roads, just half a mile from Lita's townhouse. Detectives interview the clerk, Randall Benson, who tells his harrowing story of the creepy man who bought the flowers, how he didn't care about color or freshness, how he was in a hurry. He explained the man didn't have enough cash, so he went out and got more money from a scruffy guy waiting in a dirty white Toyota with North Carolina plates. He gives detailed descriptions to the sketch artist, but it's puzzling; neither man looks anything like the neighbors' descriptions of the shooter, which leads the cops to believe three men are involved: a driver—bearded with shaggy dark hair, a low forehead, and facial hair; the flower buyer—curly light brown hair, unshaven with a sharp nose and widespread eyes; and the shooter—clean-shaven with a long face, big lips, and slicked-back dirty blond hair. The cops update the BOLO—now they're looking for three guys, white Toyota, North Carolina plates.

❖

When Jim's divorce lawyer calls him around 9:45 A.M. on January 16 to report the news of Lita's death, Jim is still in bed. He doesn't react like a man whose wife of ten years has been murdered; he doesn't crumple, he doesn't cry. Instead, he calls his mistress.

"Hey, guess what?" he tells Suki when she picks up the other end. "Lita's been killed."

Suki gasps. He waits. When she doesn't say anything, he fills the silence. "Listen, it's better for us." He says he must go make other calls, and they make plans to meet later. He showers, gets dressed, and looks out the window at the swarm of reporters gathering below. He muses at their scurrying, like mice fighting for cheese.

Later, when he heads out to play tennis, he offers no comment to the reporter shoving a microphone in his face or to the burly cameramen trying to block his way. He has no concern for these people, and he's certainly not going to give them anything to nibble. After all, he's got a solid alibi—he's here in Florida, hundreds of miles from any of the mess in Atlanta.

The moment the fatal bullet hit Lita's skull, Jim became a free man, as good as divorced, as good as never married in the first place. There will be no more court dates, no more mounting lawyer fees, no more worries that any of his fortune will go to Lita. Her death means Jim is free to pursue his million-dollar loan to pay off the mortgage, so he won't lose his mansion; he no longer needs Lita's signature because, dead, she is no longer his wife.

That afternoon, Jim's divorce attorneys agree to meet Lita's lawyer, Richard Schiffman, to tell the judge together that Lita has been killed. When they all convene afterward to discuss next steps, Jim's lawyers sheepishly convey to Schiffman Jim's request that Lita's parents not take any personal belongings or furniture from Lita's townhouse.

"I said I would not call the parents on the day their daughter was murdered and tell them not to steal the furniture," Schiffman said. "And then I told them in more colorful language what they could do with their request."

❖

Lita is murdered on a Friday and the McClintons arrange for the funeral the following Monday, a federal holiday for Martin Luther King Jr. Day. The service happens so quickly because the McClintons are doers; maybe they believe if they can get it over with faster, it'll hurt less.

Although Lita's death means Jim is instantly single, it doesn't, it seems, go both ways. The funeral director tells the McClintons that because Jim is technically still Lita's husband, they'll need his permission to have their daughter cremated.

"He was considered next of kin," says Jo Ann. "You're so upset, you're blind. Then you have to get his permission to cremate her." They need his response in writing. He complies by sending a telegram that simply says, *My permission given to cremate Lita Sullivan, James Sullivan.*

Condolences flood in from the McClinton family's many friends and acquaintances in Atlanta and across the country. At the funeral, mourners overflow into the street at Patterson & Sons Funeral Home in Decatur. Lita's friends from Spelman, friends of the family, relatives, neighbors, acquaintances from her many charitable causes—all devastated at the violent death of such a lively and beautiful member of their community—crowd in to give their respects. Finely pressed handkerchiefs get drenched with tears. Words stick like dough in the throats of many mourners while others wail in anguish. Throughout are astonished whispers about the one person who is noticeably absent. After more than a decade of being married to Lita, Jim doesn't attend the funeral, doesn't pay for it, never offers condolences, never sends a sympathy card.

He doesn't even send flowers.

CHAPTER 13
EARLY INVESTIGATION (1987)

I knew instantly Jim had done it. The second I heard she'd been shot I knew he had done it. Who else would want to kill her?" Valencia, Lita's sister, told writer Marion Collins, adding that to Jim, Lita was just a trophy. "The McClinton name had power in Atlanta and even in Macon, and he felt he could be part of that power when he lived here. In Palm Beach, the power base was totally changed. He didn't need her anymore to have any status or power at all."

While the McClintons know in their bones that their son-in-law is somehow responsible for their daughter's murder, they can't prove anything, nor can the police. Jim, after all, is down in Florida and vehemently denies any involvement in the murder. Instead, he unleashes a slew of unsubstantiated allegations he learned through the illegal Marvin Marable tapes. This information sends investigators scuttling off in many directions, which infuriates the grieving family. For the past year and half, Lita, living as a single woman, had dipped her toe back into the dating scene and rekindled old friendships with college pals and childhood friends. Jim inflames this information to reinforce accusations that Lita slept with other men while they were living as a married couple, none of which he can prove. He'd said in his divorce papers that he believed Lita was having extramarital affairs because "Mrs. Sullivan had a complete lack of interest in me."

In the week following her death, he releases a statement suggesting that Lita struggled with a cocaine addiction and had been involved with drug dealers. When the autopsy report comes back saying Lita had "traces" of cocaine in her system, though nothing remotely suggesting heavy use, Jim doubles down on his theory that Lita had been involved in some kind of drug deal gone wrong. He also accuses her of stealing diamonds from the safe; in her divorce affidavit she'd admitted to taking diamonds from one of her necklaces because she knew she'd need money. He paints himself as a hardworking husband, a man who single-handedly climbed out of a working-class existence on the power of his smarts and ingenuity only to be duped by Lita, a materialistic drug abuser, adulterer, and thief out for his money. The police investigators at first seem swayed by Jim's narrative. The McClintons, barely able to get out of bed in the morning because it means they'll have to face another day without their daughter, are sickened by Jim and the way he's manipulating the police. They allege that the detectives can't believe a Black woman could live in such luxury without being involved in something nefarious. Jim even points the cops in *their* direction, suggesting the McClintons offed their daughter so they could collect on her life insurance policy, of which they were the beneficiaries.

The McClintons are disgusted. "Just plain cruel," says Jo Ann. "This is what racism will do for you."

Nine days after the murder, on January 25, Detective Welcome Harris and his boss travel down to Palm Beach to interview Jim at his lawyer's office. Harris keeps the specifics of this conversation away from reporters but says they found Jim friendly and cooperative. On the advice of his lawyers, Jim takes a polygraph and passes—the results indicate he has nothing to do with the murder. He trumpets this news to investigators and the press.

❖

Police question anyone and everyone, especially the men in Lita's life. They look at three in particular: Bob Daniels, the friend Lita had dinner with the night before her death, was in his mid-fifties when he became interested in Lita. They sparked a friendship, but he wanted more. One night, just a couple of months before her murder, he rammed his blue Cadillac into her garage in a jealous drunken rage because he didn't like her talking to other men. Lita, terrified, called the police. When the cops came to arrest him, they threw him into the back of a squad car and he reportedly yelled out, "I'm going to kill the bitch!" You don't need to be a detective to see this as a giant red flag, but since then, Lita's friends and family say Daniels and Lita had talked it out. He'd apologized profusely and they'd reconciled as friends. The night before she died, he'd taken her out for dinner and given her two roses. The car ramming and roses make him a suspect except for one fact: a couple of weeks prior to Lita's murder, he'd undergone quadruple bypass heart surgery at a hospital in Alabama. His doctor tells detectives that he could barely walk, let alone run anywhere. He was at home in his pajamas at the time of the murder. Still, Harris interrogates Daniels, pulls his phone records, and looks at his bank accounts, but finds nothing that links him to Lita's murder or the hiring of a hitman.

Another suspect, Stephen Brumley, played soccer for the Fort Lauderdale Strikers, a soccer team based in Miami. Lita met him when she lived in Palm Beach and occasionally spent time with him in Atlanta. But, police soon discover, on the day Lita died, Brumley was serving time in jail on drug possession charges.

Finally, there's Michael Hollis, the president of Air Atlanta, the first Black-owned airline in the country. Hollis and Lita knew each other as teenagers and had rekindled a friendship and dated a few times. He'd sent her flowers—roses—on her birthday nine days before the murder. But, like Daniels and Brumley, Hollis has no motive, and nothing links him to the murder. He too is quickly eliminated as a suspect.

To the McClintons, it seems like the police are looking everywhere but at the man they believe to be responsible, polygraph be damned. The McClintons allege publicly that Jim is being treated with kid gloves because he is a rich, slick-talking white man. They ask: would authorities treat him differently if he were Black? Would they think about Lita differently if she were white?

❖

After the murder, Jim accuses the McClintons of taking some of Lita's property in the chaotic hours after the murder and quickly arranges a court order to block anyone—including Lita's family—from removing any belongings from the Slaton Drive townhouse. Then, on Valentine's Day, less than a month after Lita's murder, he arranges to have Emory and Jo Ann deposed at his lawyer's office. Not only have they been unable to sit with Lita's things, but they also now have to tell Jim's lawyer that they have not, in fact, stolen property from their dead daughter's home. Knowing the McClintons will be occupied for several hours, Jim arrives at the townhouse with a moving truck and orders the movers to pack everything, quickly. They are directed to box up and haul out everything.

A neighbor witnessing the movers calls the McClintons, but by the time they get the message, it's too late. When they arrive at the townhouse, everything is gone. Jo Ann can't retrieve the linens and chafing dishes she lent Lita for the party that will never happen. She'll never get a chance to save family photos, smell her daughter's clothing, hug the throw pillows, preserve Lita's journals or scrawled grocery lists or anything that could show the way she curled her S's or crossed her T's. Instead, Jim has taken it all away—the furniture, her jewelry, clothes, the silverware, even Lita's makeup.

"We had told the police on numerous occasions that there was something in the house Lita had concerning taxes, but Jim was given permission to go in the house and clear it out," said Jo Ann. "He just cleared it out while we were giving the deposition."

"That's an example of his deviousness," said Emory later, still angered by the thought.

"By then I was so numb," said Jo Ann. "The worst thing in the world had happened to me so it just sort of rolled off my back. Whatever he did, I would expect him to do."

❖

The police detectives who worked on this case—Welcome Harris, George Jackson, and Horace Walker—all passed away long before I began researching this book. What I know about them is they were all passionate about this case, they longed to get justice for Lita's family, and they were hopelessly overworked. I wish I could talk to them to find out what exactly they were doing to follow leads after the murder. These were the nascent days of the internet, so you couldn't just google anything. The AFIS (Automated Fingerprint Identification System) was new and not yet linked to a national database. No one had cell phones, so you couldn't track calls or texts—or do anything fancy like monitor cell tower pings. They did a lot of legwork, talking to neighbors, acquaintances, friends, and family. But they were missing key evidence, including viable fingerprints, the murder weapon, or anything that specifically linked someone to the murder. They had no shooter. They knew Jim had means and motive, but they had nothing that proved he had anything to do with it.

Three weeks after the murder, Bill Montgomery, a longtime reporter for the *Atlanta Journal* (which later merged with the *Atlanta Constitution* to become the *Atlanta Journal-Constitution* or *AJC*), who would go on to cover this story for decades, wrote, "Authorities are left with a chilling mystery, some speculative theories, but no prime suspects." He quoted Lieutenant Horace Walker, head of Atlanta's Homicide Task Force, as saying, "Everybody who was involved with her is a suspect at this point . . . We haven't ruled out anybody, and I mean anybody."

In mid-May, four months after the murder, the cops get their first big break. With help from the State Attorney's Office in Palm Beach, police subpoena Jim's phone records for the previous year and make a thrilling discovery. Among the calls Jim regularly makes to his lawyers, investment account brokers, and Suki, Jim's records show an incoming collect call from an unknown Georgia number at 9 A.M. on the morning of January 16, the day of Lita's murder.

Detective Harris decides to call it. It rings and rings. There's no answering machine—these are the days before voicemail. He tries again. And again. Finally, someone picks up.

"Hello?" says the voice on the other line.

"Good morning," says Detective Harris, noting the humming sounds of traffic in the background. "I'm wondering if you could tell me who this number belongs to?"

"I have no idea," the person says, chuckling. "I just picked up. This is a payphone."

"Can you tell me where exactly, please sir?" asks Harris. Turns out the number belongs to a rest area payphone off the highway near Suwanee, Georgia. Harris roughly knows the area—you pass by it en route to the Atlanta Falcons' football training camp. He waits until the next day and drives over to The Coaches, Lita's townhouse complex. At exactly 8:20 A.M., right after the time he believes Lita was shot, he begins driving. He follows the most logical route available to I-85, exit #44. He clocks the route: it takes him thirty-eight minutes to travel the thirty-seven miles. His heart's pumping when he realizes someone called Jim collect from here at 9 A.M., exactly forty minutes after Lita's murder.

A week later, Detective Harris and Lieutenant Walker again fly to Florida to question Jim at Casa Eleda. Of the collect call, he says he has no recollection, that it must've been a wrong number. There are many phones in many rooms in the house, Jim says, and housekeepers come and go all the time. The investigators speak with him for an hour and tell reporters he was "cooperative" but they have many leads still to follow. Harris tells reporters, "I ain't ruled out nothing and no one. The only person I know for sure didn't kill her is me."

In September, a reward for any information in the murder reaches $20,000, thanks to a $15,000 donation from an anonymous donor, $3,000 from private citizens, and $2,000 from Joe Frank Harris, the democratic governor and a friend of the McClinton family.

"I'm sure that whoever hit Lita, if it was a contract hit, killed her for a lot less than $20,000," Detective Harris tells the *Atlanta Journal-Constitution*. "We know only one person did the shooting, but we've got three actors. There are two other people involved who did not pull the trigger, but they can be prosecuted for murder."

Jim, undeterred by the heat swirling around him, sells the Atlanta town-house for $575,000, making a profit of $135,000 (around $367K in today's dollars). He's rid of his last tie to Atlanta, finally removing the shackles of Lita and her family.

❖

Johnny Austin Turner is broke, having just been released from prison, when he walks into the Jolly Fox Lounge, a strip bar on the southside of Atlanta. It's before noon and Turner takes in the deliciously sour scent of old beer and last night's depravity. The smell of freedom. He plants himself on a barstool and orders a draft, well worth the change in his pockets. He makes small talk with the bartender, and they both turn as the door opens and two men—one white, one Black—enter the bar. Turner realizes the white guy is his old friend Thomas Bruce Henley. They'd done time together, even escaped prison together back in 1979. He knows Henley to be an unabashed racist, so seeing him with a Black guy seems strange. Henley greets Turner enthusiastically, happy to see his old buddy, and suggests they go get high outside. Henley is around five foot nine, well-built, bearded with short brown hair, in his thirties. Turner's roughly the same age, but tall and lanky at six-foot-three. Turner follows Henley and they climb into a late-model Oldsmobile parked outside. Turner, in the passenger seat, asks his old pal about the well-dressed Black guy.

"I'm making all kinds of money with this n—," he says, sparking a joint. To prove it, he pulls a wad of hundreds out of his jeans pocket. He peels off a couple and hands them to Turner, who can hardly believe his good luck. Henley tells Turner that he and another guy, an outlaw named Clinton Botts, made some sweet cash "doing a hit in Buckhead." He said the Black guy set it all up.

CHAPTER 14

TRUCK STOP (FEBRUARY, OR MAYBE AUGUST, 1987)

It's the middle of the night, or maybe early morning, when Tony says it's time to go collect the second half of the $25,000. Belinda grabs her pillow and a blanket and climbs into the car. They'd been doing a lot of blow and pot at the time—balancing the ups and downs—and details are murky. She doesn't know which car they're in, but definitely not the truck. While he drives, she sleeps. She's not sure which of the fifty states they are in when she wakes up, whether they've driven north or south. She doesn't know if they've been driving for five hours or ten hours. It may be February, but it could be August. All she knows is that it's daylight when they pull into a Denny's or Stuckey's or a 76 gas station parking lot and she's hungry. The aroma of bacon grease and coffee makes her stomach growl.

"We're not eating," says Tony firmly.

"But I'm starving," says Belinda. He ignores her.

They walk into the busy diner and grab a booth by a plate-glass window that overlooks the parking lot. She slides in first, then him. She's looking out the window, not at him, sulking. She's tired, wants to eat. The restaurant is crowded. Most people, like them, look ordinary, wearing T-shirts and jeans.

She looks up and notices a tidy man with a newspaper tucked under his arm walking straight toward them. She later describes the man as, "Tall, slender, light hair, light complexion." He's forty-something, wearing linen clothing and deck shoes, yachty. She says she notices the shoes because she used to be an assistant manager at a Florsheim's, so she has an eye for these things. He walks over to them and sits down on the opposite side of the booth.

At this point Belinda gets scared, finally realizing Tony's telling the truth about the business in Atlanta. Up to this point, she says, she still thought he was full of shit. But now this guy. Tony is country through and through; he doesn't know anyone like this.

"Why did you bring her?" the man asks Tony in a funny accent, nodding at Belinda. "What's she doing here?"

"It's OK, she's my wife," Tony lies. "She'll keep her mouth shut."

The men mumble a brief conversation while Belinda looks out the window. She sneaks a peek at the man's manicured hands and wedding ring as he slides the newspaper across the table to Tony.

Shortly after, the man leaves, and they do too. Back in the car, Tony opens the newspaper—or was it an envelope?—and shows her a wad of cash. She doesn't remember how much. From there, they went . . . somewhere. Maybe back to Albemarle, maybe to Texas. No one can say for sure.

CHAPTER 15

FOR LOVE OR MONEY
(1987–1989)

On September 15, 1987, just eight months after Lita's brutal murder, Jim and Suki tie the knot in Palm Beach, marking Jim's third marriage and Suki's fourth. Their wedding is a small ceremony held at the Royal Poinciana Chapel, witnessed by a few friends. Standing in as Jim's best man is George Bissell, a financial investor and frequent tennis partner. Bissell was the one who'd broken the news to Jim that being married to a Black woman would obliterate his chances of gaining membership to the Everglades or any of the other private clubs. Their camaraderie, more of a schmoozy, what-can-you-do-for-me affair, is the closest thing Jim has to an actual friendship.

If the marriage raises eyebrows in Palm Beach, Jim doesn't care. Suki, it seems, is a trophy people understand. She knows how to navigate men and money and has found a lane: look gorgeous, have few opinions and ideas, and sit back to enjoy the spoils.

Two headlines in the Atlanta newspaper stand out on the anniversary of Lita's death: YEAR-OLD BUCKHEAD SLAYING STILL MYSTERY; WIDOWER IS INVESTIGATED, and ATLANTA OFFICERS FAIL TO GET REQUESTED RAISES. That Lita's death goes unsolved amid protests of overworked and disgruntled police officers is infuriating for the McClintons, who can only watch as Jim goes on with life, enjoying his wealth and freedom more than ever. Palm Beachers appear to have moved on too. The *Palm Beach Post* that day makes no mention of the fact that, a year after the murder, Jim is still the prime suspect, even though he's living free and easy with his new bride.

❖

Jim and Suki become fixtures on the "Shiny Sheet," the pages of the *Palm Beach Daily News* that inspire the town's gossip before lining the cages of exotic birds. They're pictured wearing haute couture, attending galas and parties around town. They travel around the world, splurge on extravagant shopping sprees. Suki's closets fill with expensive gowns and jewelry. She spends hours at the spa, plays tennis, and drives around town in Lita's old silver Mercedes. They enjoy slow easy days and spend evenings hobnobbing with anyone who can elevate their social status.

But authorities are keeping tabs on Jim, trying to find a paper trail that will lead somewhere. The Florida State Attorney's Office, at the behest of the Atlanta police, is investigating the almost $1 million loan application made on his house a few weeks prior to Lita's death. Jim needed the jumbo loan to refinance two existing loans, and the only way he could get refinancing would have been to have Lita sign the mortgage. When Lita refused to sign it, Jim instead listed himself as "single" on the application. But on his 1985 tax return, he listed himself as "married" with four dependents, even though Lita had left him and his children hadn't lived with him for years. Upon discovering that he'd lied on his application, the bank had reneged on the loan. But a month after Lita's death, Jim reapplied—death certificate in hand—and the bank gave him the loan.

Jim's financial gymnastics show authorities what they already know—he had irrefutable motive to have Lita killed. But none of this gets them closer to apprehending the killer—or determining how and if Jim was involved.

"This tragedy has left an open wound that will be with us the rest of our lives," Jo Ann tells reporter Bill Montgomery on the year anniversary. "The apprehension of the person responsible is a daily concern."

Jim rarely speaks to reporters and is usually testy and brief when he does. Montgomery catches him on the phone on the anniversary and manages to ask his thoughts about the search for Lita's killer. Jim says, "Any ideas I have would be shared only with the appropriate authorities. I've attempted to cooperate with them and if I share them, I'd be damaging their work." Asked if he thinks the killer will ever be caught, he replies, "I certainly hope so," and hangs up the phone.

❖

Around the first anniversary of Lita's murder, a letter arrives at the Fulton County District Attorney's office from police informant and convicted forger Johnny Austin Turner, who is currently incarcerated in a Georgia prison. His letter tells the story about how he met up with an old buddy at an Atlanta bar when he was out on parole in April 1987. His buddy, a guy named Thomas Bruce Henley, had been with a sharp-dressed Black man, had a wad of cash, and bragged about doing a hit on a Black woman in Buckhead just few months prior.

Alarm bells ringing, Detectives Harris and Jackson from the Atlanta Police and Special Agent Robert Ingram from the Georgia Bureau of Investigation rush to interview Turner. Seeming very eager to turn in his jailhood friend, Turner says Henley looks just like the composite of the driver. He didn't know the Black guy, but when the cops show him a photo lineup of six Black men, he looks carefully before pointing to #5 which, it turns out, is Poppy's husband, Marvin Marable.

On paper, this information looks astonishing. Maybe this is the hit team, the men they've been looking for. But also, maybe not. It could be that Turner is making the whole thing up, that he'd seen the papers and watched the news and fabricated a story in an attempt to reduce his own sentence. It's common for convicts to make up stories and rat each other out in hopes that a judge will shave off time in exchange for information. Of course, Marvin vehemently denies ever knowing Botts and Henley, and they deny having anything to do with it. The detectives dig but find nothing that connects them all other than Turner's story.

GBI special agent Robert Ingram, an expert in interrogation and behavioral sciences, has Turner take a polygraph. Before 1998, when results of polygraph tests became inadmissible in federal court, law enforcement leaned heavily on them. When Turner's responses to Ingram's questions show he's being repeatedly deceitful, it leads the agent to believe Turner's entire story is bullshit. The file gets shoved back in the cabinet.

❖

Meanwhile, Jim cements his status among the Palm Beach movers and shakers. In May 1988, the Palm Beach Town Council unanimously appoints Jim to a second three-year term on the Landmarks Preservation Commission *and* elevates him to chair. Now anyone wishing to renovate a portico or add a row of hedges must go through him. With social clout, the mortgage on Casa Eleda secure, and lovely Suki on his arm, Jim is riding high.

But, as reporter Frank Cerabino tells me, Jim's aspirations were always delusional.

"In Palm Beach, it doesn't matter how much money you have. If you come from the wrong start, if you have the wrong beginning, there's no amount of money that will cure that," he said. "Sullivan was never going to make it into the *Social Register.*"

The town's unofficial black book, the *Social Register*, published annually, lists the people that matter. It logs their contact information, the schools they attended, the clubs they belong to, names of their yachts, and locations of their summer homes. Cerabino says the value of your party is calculated by how many of your guests are listed on the *Social Register*.

"Sullivan went in and he kind of made a splash by buying that house and everything," says Cerabino. "But he wasn't really on the A-List either, he wasn't on the *Social Register*. Nobody was begging to have Jim Sullivan come to their house."

Eighteen months after Lita's death, in July 1988, at the height of Jim and Suki's spending, Jim gets in touch with his twenty-two-year-old daughter Deirdre and asks her to sign away her claim to a trust fund she has no idea exists, for a lump sum of around $15,000. Surprised by this sudden communication from her estranged father, she hires a lawyer. "I've had little or no contact with my father for the past eight years," she says in a court affidavit. The lawyer learns that Jim had started a trust for his four children in 1980, funded by the mortgage payments he collected on the Macon house, and now he wants the money back. Lita was trustee of the fund, and Deirdre was entitled to the money when she turned twenty-one. But she never knew anything about it. The attorney tells the court, "In the light of the lack of contact between the Sullivan family and James Sullivan, Catherine [Jim's first wife] and Deirdre were, at best, shocked and, at worst, suspicious about the letter and legal papers they had received from Mr. Sullivan."

Jim is confrontational and litigious by nature—in addition to trying to swindle his eldest daughter, he is in and out of court for everything from suing contractors who'd worked on his renovations to fighting unpaid parking tickets. In April 1989, an exasperated traffic court judge suspends Jim's driver's license for five years after Jim appears in court for his eighteenth violation; in six years he had amassed eleven speeding tickets and seven other traffic citations. Not one to be told what to do, Jim continues to drive around town in his 1973 Rolls-Royce.

CHAPTER 16

THE FEDS
(1988–1989)

R etired FBI agents aren't necessarily easy to find; they're not hanging out on Facebook or LinkedIn. They know how to hide because they've forged careers searching for hidden things, like criminals, clues, or money. I know of Special Agent John Kingston because of his early involvement in the Sullivan case, but also from the accolades of others. I hear it repeatedly: he was a stand-up agent who specialized in white-collar crimes, one of the bureau's best, brilliant, a true pro.

I finally get in touch with him, and our first Zoom call lasts two hours. Now, we're meeting in person for the first time at his house in Palm Desert, California. It's 106 degrees and I drive my rental car into a gated community where I punch in a code and drive to his house, a comfortable rancher overlooking a golf course. He greets me waving and smiling as I pull into the baking asphalt driveway. He's wearing shorts, loafers with white socks, and a green Hawaiian shirt—he looks nothing like my clichéd assumptions of an FBI agent. No suit, no frown, no firm handshake. Instead, he hugs me like we're old friends. He's tall, with a full head of hair with traces of its original dark brown peeking through the gray. He's sixty-eight, retired in 2005 at fifty, after nearly twenty-two years in the FBI.

Kingston was partially pulled into Lita's case in the spring of 1988, a little more than a year after her death. At the time, he'd been busy working on a murder-for-hire case where a man had answered an ad in *Soldier of Fortune* magazine to engage a hired gun to brutally murder his business partner. As such, Kingston had familiarity with a new and mostly unknown statute that had passed in 1984—18 USC § 1952A—"the use of interstate commerce facilities in the commission of murder-for-hire." Kingston told me this statute basically meant that if someone uses the phone (or internet) across state lines to orchestrate a murder, it becomes a federal crime. The cops believed the call from the Suwanee rest stop to Jim's house in Florida proved a connection between Jim and whoever shot Lita. Because the call had crossed state lines, it fell under the jurisdiction of the FBI.

After the hug, he invites me into his home and I meet his welcoming wife, Barbara, who's on her way to run errands. Their neurotically friendly cat can't wait to settle on my lap as we sit down at a table strewn with papers. Like me, John Kingston has a box of old Sullivan files. One by one, he takes out his treasures, including a transcript from an interview of the first time he met Jim.

"It's always stupid to talk to the FBI, so I was thrilled that he was dumb enough to talk to us," says Kingston. Of the sixty-five people Kingston has put in jail over the years, a good fifty of them were convicted because of a confession. "Almost every time they open their mouths, they get caught in some detail that hurts them," he says. So, when he and agent John Coffey flew down to meet Jim at Casa Eleda in April 1988, he was eager to hear what Jim had to say and, even more importantly, how he said it. He says an FBI agent's job is to take in as many details as they can from beginning to end, pick up on a suspect's nuance, inconsistencies, note any strange mannerisms, and ask the same questions over and over again.

Kingston said Jim was cordial when the agents arrived at Casa Eleda. Compared to Kingston, who towers at six foot one, Jim, skinny at five foot ten, seemed like a little guy. At the time, Jim was forty-seven, more than a decade older than Kingston. The agent watched Jim closely. He could see the wheels turning in the littler man's head as he tried to convince the agents that he'd been a hardworking husband duped by a troubled woman. He told them the same story he'd been telling the Atlanta cops—that Lita had been unfaithful and that she had an affinity for cocaine, that it was one of the causes of their divorce and a possible reason for her death.

"After all," Jim said. "Lita was killed with a 9mm. The Atlanta police tell me that's the preferred weapon of drug dealers."

This made Kingston raise his eyebrows. What a weird thing to say. Jim then volunteered his theory about the McClintons wanting the insurance money. He told Coffey and Kingston that, after the murder, Lita's parents had stolen twenty-seven items totaling $275,000 from the townhouse. The suggestion that the contents of the townhouse were his differed from his assertions throughout the divorce, when he'd tried to show that Lita was living in luxury and that he wasn't in fact trying to leave her with nothing.

The agents interviewed him for about forty-five minutes, and Jim got shiftier as it went on. When they finally asked him the question they were really after, about the collect phone call from the Suwanee rest stop pay-phone forty minutes after the murder, Jim shrugged.

"I don't have the faintest idea what you're talking about," he said. "I received no such call." At that point, he stood to signal the interview was over.

"Every time Sullivan lied, he got more furtive, and his eyes got more askance, looking down and not holding eye contact," says Kingston. "I wanted to slap him and say, 'You're lying your ass off, you idiot. It's so obvious.'" Kingston says when they first got there, he had no opinion of Jim's guilt. But when they walked back out into the Florida sun, the world looked a little different.

"I knew when I left that interview, I was a hundred percent sure he was guilty," says Kingston. Now, he just needed to prove it.

Kingston's involvement as a criminal investigator in the Sullivan case only lasted a handful of months before he was transferred out of the Atlanta office, but the evidence he uncovered in his short tenure would prove instrumental for decades to come. In fact, his work would likely have solved the case if it weren't for a series of bureaucratic blunders and blind spots that infuriate Kingston to this day.

❖

Busy finishing up another case, Special Agent John Kingston doesn't get his hands on the Sullivan investigation full-time until April of 1989, two years and three months after Lita's murder. One of Kingston's first acts is to subpoena Jim's phone records for the months before and after January 16, 1987. The Atlanta cops had looked at his phone bill, but Kingston wants to go deeper—who exactly Jim spoke with in the days before and after the murder. Why this didn't happen before is a mystery to me—wouldn't that be something the detectives should've done earlier? I had asked Kingston about this. Not necessarily, he'd said. The APD was busy with a record number of homicides and only had finite resources to dedicate to the Sullivan case.

Kingston already knows from eyewitness interviews that there'd been a knock on Lita's door in the early hours of January 13, and he knows Jim had called Bob Christenson out of the blue that day, asking him if he'd seen anything strange happening at The Coaches—so his internal alarm bells start ringing when the phone records show that a few minutes before talking to Christenson, Jim called a Howard Johnson motel about 5.5 miles north of Lita's townhouse. If there's one thing Kingston's learned about Jim already, it's that he's more of a Ritz-Carlton, Four Seasons kind of guy who seemed hellbent on hanging around people in the same stratum. Who would he call at a HoJo's three days before his wife was murdered?

Kingston drives to the hotel and asks to see past records. In a box labeled "1987," he finds a paper registration card and folio for room 518. The room had been registered to a "Johnny Furr" and showed three adults had checked in at 7:24 A.M. on January 13, three days before Lita's murder. They'd listed their car as a 1985 "Toy" and had given a Raleigh, North Carolina, address. This was consistent with the car described by florist Randall Benson—a Toyota with North Carolina plates. It also backs up the police's assertion that three men were involved (the flower buyer, the driver, and the shooter). The hotel phone records show a call was made from the room to Jim's house at 7:44 A.M. Jim's records show that he, or someone at his house, called the hotel back at 10:33 A.M., just before Jim talked to Bob Christenson.

The clerk who was working on that day had been eighteen at the time and now, more than two years later, remembers nothing of these specific guests. But she still works at the motel and tells Kingston the unofficial hierarchy of how they assigned guest rooms at her HoJo's. The motel was a small, five-story building serving mostly business travelers passing through on sales calls. The lobby was on the second floor, which is where they'd put women traveling alone (for safety); single men and families would get rooms on the third and fourth floors; and anyone who was "unusual or uncomfortable" would get the fifth, which staff referred to as the "sketchy floor." That she had given this Furr guy a room on the fifth spoke volumes.

Kingston gets to work and quickly ascertains that the address on the registration card is bogus. The street (Rural Route #40) didn't exist in Raleigh and the zip code (28112) isn't a Raleigh zip code—but, he discovers, it's similar to zip codes in another North Carolina town called Mooresville. He runs driver's licenses for the names Johnny, John, and Jonathan Furr and is surprised when more than 150 come up in a very small and specific area of North Carolina, near Mooresville. Kingston knows it could be a fake name, but he also knows that when someone picks an alias, it's often a name they're familiar with, a friend or acquaintance. He gets out his paper map and draws a circle around what he calls the Albemarle-Concord-Kannapolis circle.

"I am convinced that the people involved came from within that circle," Kingston says. "There's no doubt in my mind." He is armed with composite drawings of three men, drawn from the competing memories of eyewitnesses.

Kingston's plan is to drive up to this part of North Carolina with another young and energetic FBI agent named Todd Letcher. They'll hit every grocery store and business in the entire circle, talk to people, and show them the composite drawings, telling them the FBI needs info on the three men.

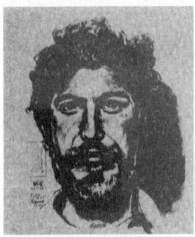

FLOWER BUYER   DRIVER

SHOOTER

"I also planned on knocking on the door of every single Johnny Furr and showing them the artist sketches," explains Kingston. If Kingston can't find the men, he's confident he'll find someone who knows them.

But he never gets the chance.

Per FBI protocol, before Kingston and Letcher can investigate in another state, they need permission from the special agent in charge (SAC) of the local field office—North Carolina's field office is in Charlotte. It's a way to prevent a jurisdictional pissing match between state agents and to alert local bureaus that agents from another state are poking around. Almost always, permission is granted in under eight hours. But they don't get a response. After waiting a week, the eager agents decide to go anyway. As they drive up I-85 N, their boss calls and tells them permission to investigate in North Carolina has been denied.

"It was the strangest thing," says Kingston. "Nobody ever says no. Of the fifty-six field offices in the entire bureau, we get the only one who won't let us come to his division." Instead, North Carolina agents meet Kingston and Letcher at a Cracker Barrel restaurant near the state border and say, essentially, *Sorry boys, we'll take it from here.* But Kingston knows there's no way they'll be able to take over with the level of detail he and Letcher were after—they'd planned to spend a week doggedly banging on doors. He was right. The search for the three men in North Carolina dissolves into nothing.

Which is too bad. Tony Harwood lives right in the middle of Kingston's circle.

CHAPTER 17

TICKING TIMEBOMB (1990)

In March 1990, Jim gets into a three-car fender bender just a few miles from his house. Jim's not at fault, but the cop notices Jim is driving on a suspended license, with an expired registration and expired Georgia tag, and writes him a ticket. Instead of just paying the fine, Jim shows up to Palm Beach County traffic court with Suki on his arm—she's part of his strategy for getting out of this trouble. The Sullivans look exceedingly Palm Beachy. Suki wears a gold dress and Jim a blue blazer, gray slacks, and a yellow tie. They're a cut above the regular West Palm Beach folks here to fight parking tickets.

Reporter Frank Cerabino goes to court that day with a photographer to try to capture a photo of Jim for an article he's writing about Lita's now-cold case and Jim's potential role in it, more than three years after the murder. Cerabino, a tenacious reporter, had tried to interview Jim at home, had offered to have a photographer come to him, but Jim repeatedly hung up on him.

Cerabino watches with interest when Jim, instead of paying the fines and being done with it, tells the judge Suki had been the one driving the car. Suki stands up, gets sworn in, and testifies, under oath, that she was indeed driving that day. Considering this confusion, the prosecutor drops the charges, and the judge dismisses the case.

Driving home later that day, Cerabino thinks about what went down in court. If the ticket was for an expired registration and tag, he thinks, what does it matter who was driving? Puzzled, he tracks down the ticketing officer who, after ranting about the fact he wasn't notified of the hearing, says, "Do you think I can't tell the difference between Suki and Jim Sullivan?!?" After all, it's not every day he tickets a Rolls-Royce. He confirms Jim was indeed driving that day; he was the only one in the car. And, as it turns out, Suki doesn't even have a Florida driver's license.

It seems like Jim is always in the newspapers. Aside from his legal troubles in Palm Beach, the Atlanta authorities are still trying to connect the dots in their ongoing search for Lita's killer. In April 1990, a federal grand jury convenes in Atlanta to begin hearing witness testimony—to determine whether prosecutors have enough evidence to bring charges against Jim, whom investigators call a "serious suspect."

A note about grand juries: much like a trial jury, a grand jury is composed of individuals that represent a cross section of the population—they are pulled from the same pool. Unlike a trial jury, which sits for the duration of a trial, a federal grand jury can sit for months, even years, meeting more sporadically as the prosecution builds a case. The grand jury isn't meant to decide someone's guilt or innocence, but whether there's enough evidence to bring the case to trial. In Lita's case, the grand jury learns about the evidence thus far: that someone bought flowers, delivered them to Lita, and shot her dead before fleeing the scene. They learn of the florist's description of the flower buyer and the shady driver in the car, the eyewitness accounts of the shooter, and the details of the phone calls between Jim's house in Florida and the Howard Johnson in Atlanta. They hear about the collect call to Jim's home from the Suwanee truck stop, forty minutes after Lita had been shot. They learn about Jim's money problems, how he stood to lose half his fortune in the divorce. It seems irrefutable, overwhelming flashing red arrows pointing to Jim, but all the evidence is circumstantial. The cops have never found the gun, so they don't have a murder weapon; they have no hitman, and still aren't sure if two or three men were involved. The calls to Jim are certainly suspicious, but they don't actually *prove* anything.

District attorneys generally won't try a case they can't win so, much to the anguish of the McClinton family, the Fulton County District Attorney drops the indictment until there's more direct evidence that links Jim to the murder. The grand jury doesn't dissolve, but it is running out of time. The statute of limitations on federal murder-for-hire cases is five years, and already more than three years have passed since Lita's murder.

While Jim is off the hook for now, he can feel the squeeze, a vise being slowly hand-cranked on his neck. The constant scrutiny wears on the newlyweds, not to mention the fact that money has become a serious issue again, especially after Jim loses roughly $1.5 million in a get-rich-quick scheme led by his one-time best man George Bissell. Over a decade, Bissell and his business partner had roped more than two hundred investors, including Jim, into financing an exotic plant business. The deal—put down money now and reap rewards when the expensive palms and orchids mature—turned out to be an elaborate Ponzi scheme, where old investors are paid with the money of new ones. Jim even becomes the spokesman for the duped investors when Bissell and his partner are later charged in federal court, but he is never able to recoup the losses. With the $1.5 million loss, extravagant living expenses, and the cost of keeping his new bride happy, Jim's fortune is dwindling fast.

As with Lita, Jim tries to rein in Suki's spending, track her whereabouts, and evaluate her every move. The tree of resentment begins to grow; branches of anxiety, stress, and pressure now blossom with buds of judgment and suspicion. In his day planner, he logs who she meets, where she goes, how much gas she burns. He calculates every penny she spends, follows her around the house waving the American Express bill. He chastises her for running the air conditioning and accuses her of excessively flushing the toilets. Where Suki once thought nothing of dropping thousands on extravagant couture, she must now beg to buy a bikini. Their lust for each other vanishes in the dark house, where heavy curtains shut out the sun to save on electricity but turn the place into a dank sauna. Their fights grow ferocious—neighbors report hearing them screaming at each other from a block away—and Suki realizes she has two choices: stay with this increasingly cheap and irritable control freak or begin planning her exit strategy. Jim, getting desperate, puts Casa Eleda on the market for $3.9 million, advertising in *Town & Country* and the *Wall Street Journal*, later upping the price to $4.9 million.

❖

When the State Attorney's Office catches wind of how Jim and Suki lied in traffic court, they wait till Jim is out playing tennis and send cops to arrest Suki and charge her with perjury. It is May, two months after the accident. The newspaper reports, "Palm Beach socialite Suki Sullivan, wife of the town's Landmarks Preservation Commission chairman, was arrested and charged with lying to a judge." A tearful and scared Suki tells the cops everything: Jim had asked her to lie for him, she was not anywhere near the car that day, Jim had taken her to the scene of the accident and coached her so she could reliably recount the details. She gets released that night when Jim pays a $10,000 bond, but she's a wreck. She is so stressed, she breaks out in shingles across her back, so painful she can barely function.

That night, though her tears and discomfort, she beseeches Jim to tell her why he was so adamant to have the police believe he was not driving that he let her lie in court. He holds his finger to his lips, gets up and closes the door, then cranks the volume on the TV. He sits Suki down next to him on the couch. "Anyone could be listening at any time," he whispers into her ear. "You need to understand; if I go to jail, I might never get out." He clutches her hands and looks her in the eyes. "Let's sell the house as soon as possible," he begs. "We can go anywhere you want, any place in the world."

A week later, on June 13, 1990, two stories on the front page of the *Palm Beach Post* inspire tongue wagging among the town's many gossips: first, there's an eye-rolling story about the governor's intent to prevent women from wearing thong bikini bottoms in state parks, and halfway down the page there's the scintillating news that, after thirty-three months of marriage, Suki Sullivan, Jim Sullivan's third wife, has filed for divorce.

CHAPTER 18

UNCIVIL WAR
(1990-1991)

The divorce drama that ensues between Jim and Suki is even more contentious and vicious than Jim's legal battles with Lita. Suki and Jim's messy and public demise electrifies the Palm Beach gossip columns and adds a shake of spice to ladies' luncheons and golf games at the Everglades. The chatter is incessant—it's a small world, after all. Suki is impossible to miss and Jim, well, it seems when he's not rattling around in his crumbling mansion, he lives in the newspapers. It's the talk of the town—first the Black wife, then her murder, the grand jury in Atlanta, and now *this*! Their chair of the Landmarks Preservation Commission, the man who can single-handedly greenlight their renos or stall their stucco is, it seems, falling apart.

In her divorce affidavit, which immediately goes public, Suki says that she's now terrified of Jim, a man she married less than three years prior. "My husband follows me about, watches my every move, and makes me account to him for every moment of my time . . . A year ago, he told me that I was dealing with a dangerous person in a dangerous game and that I had better watch out . . . He has left me in a highly nervous state and very scared." For anyone watching (and everyone is), it illuminates a pattern of Jim's controlling behavior, paints a picture of a man desperate to cling to his possessions—his wife among them.

Before the divorce case goes to trial, the judge quickly shuts down any talk of Lita's murder, saying that while the details of the case "might be terribly interesting," they have nothing to do with the matter of Suki and Jim's divorce. The judge must also address the issue of temporary alimony. Through her lawyer, Suki asks for $8,000 a month to retain the lifestyle she's grown accustomed to—shopping at boutiques on Worth Avenue and enjoying luxury vacations in Europe and Asia. She drives a Mercedes, he a Rolls-Royce. She says she needs $32,000 in attorney's fees and $20,000 in costs to cover things like the personal security guard she needs to protect herself from Jim.

Jim, now forty-nine, argues their life is not lavish, she actually shops at Marshalls and other department stores—and they subsist on a meager $2,000 a month.

"You're telling the judge that you and Mrs. Sullivan were rattling around in a $4.9 million mansion on $2,000 a month?" asks Suki's lawyer incredulously.

"Well, two to three thousand," Jim says.

Jim's lawyer, Joel Weissman, argues Suki has her own money from her three previous marriages. "Only in America," says Weissman, "could a woman with $360,000 have the chutzpah to walk into court and say she can't live without taking money from her husband."

The judge rules Jim must pay Suki just $2,500 a month in temporary alimony plus her attorney's fees. He'll continue to pay her subscriptions to *Vogue* and a Korean newspaper, and he'll keep Coco, their Maltese dog, while they await trial. He'd given Suki Coco for Christmas, even though she'd asked for a fur coat. When she'd questioned the gift, he'd joked, "You can make it into an ear muff."

Jim withdraws his request for court-ordered marriage counseling, saying, through Weissman, "a man can only beat his head against the wall so often."

❖

When the salacious divorce trial begins in September, it's the stuff of *Judge Judy*, *Nancy Grace*, and *Jerry Springer* combined. Jim enacts his legal team's strategy: he's an innocent, poverty-stricken patsy to Suki's conniving gold digger. Suki's lawyer, Ronald Sales, plays up the idea that Suki is a meek and frivolous woman who can barely understand English. He makes it seem like she has no idea what's happening around her, calling her "functionally illiterate"—even though, by this point, she's been in the United States for more than seventeen years.

Jim tells the court that Suki is a reckless spender, a pampered kitten who never does any work. Instead, she spends her days shopping, spending his money on hoards of clothes, luggage, cosmetics, and kitchenware, all of which she squirrels away under beds. He reports he found an obscene amount of pantyhose and crates of makeup hidden beneath the bed skirts. To prove it, to the delight of reporters everywhere, Jim comes to court and dumps hundreds of packages of pantyhose, a trove of Clinique cosmetics still sealed in green-and-yellow boxes, a dozen pairs of unworn shoes, and a massive pile of knitting yarn onto the courtroom floor. He floats the idea that she'd been planning her getaway, planning to sell this stuff to fund her next chapter.

While the trial traipses on with many embarrassing and scandalous moments—he calls her a scheming hoarder who stole the very sapphire earrings she's wearing in court; she calls him a controlling menace who hid her jewelry under lock and key—it's hard for anyone to look away. Then, on day three, a bombshell. Jim is on the stand when Sales, Suki's lawyer, attempts to get Jim to admit Suki's English is too limited to keep up with his brilliance in financial matters. He's trying to appeal to Jim's ego, lure him into admitting that Suki's not smart enough—or her English isn't good enough—to dupe him. Jim doesn't bite, but instead attempts to profess his love for her, his devastation that she wants to divorce him.

"I think everything Lita does, she does beautifully. She was my whole life," he says.

There are audible gasps throughout the courtroom.

"You mean Suki," says Sales.

"Yes, yes. Suki. I meant Suki," says Jim, swatting away his mistake. That he confuses the women could be chalked up to an honest blunder, but for the detailed and fastidious Jim Sullivan, who knows to the penny the cost of gas or the amount of the electric bill, it seems a telling error. Jim has said the quiet part out loud: this may be a trial about Suki, but Lita is still very much alive in the recesses of his brain.

❖

To this war of epic proportions, thirty-eight-year-old Suki brings her own bombs: when she's called to testify, tiny Suki walks quietly to the witness stand wearing all black—black jacket, black skirt, black stockings, and black heels—as if at a funeral. She's gorgeous but playing small, diminutive, a victim. The gallery of onlookers leans in as she tells the court in her soft Korean accent that on the night she was charged with perjury, when Jim cranked the volume on the TV and begged her to run away, he'd tearfully confessed to having Lita killed.

"He hired someone to murder her," she whispered in the hushed courtroom. "I thought I'd be next." To the McClintons, investigators, and everyone watching from Atlanta, this explosive testimony is a grenade—and Suki's just pulled the pin. Suki says she didn't ask questions because she was frozen in fear. Six days after the confession, she moved out, leaving her stuff—including the lipstick and pantyhose—behind.

Jim's divorce lawyers play it off as just another ploy by a thrice-divorced, money-hungry opportunist. Weissman, Jim's attorney, argues the confession is merely another in a long list of Suki's lies. He says Suki can read just fine, that she's astute and shrewd. He calls her "The Black Widow of Divorce" and says, "She married not for love but for dollars, and when the dollars ran out, so did she." He paints Suki as nothing more than a career wooer of wealthy men; he even floats the idea that Suki herself paid to have Lita killed.

At this, she gasps, "No!" before Weissman is reprimanded by the judge.

The battle rages on. Suki's lawyer claims that she should get half the house—Suki remembers when Jim took her to the courthouse to sign the legal documents making her co-owner. But, Jim reveals, he also had her sign a quit-claim deed that says she must give up her claim if they ever divorced. She doesn't remember that part.

He begs to keep Coco, saying the dog is all he has left in the world.

While they await the judge's decision, Jim loses his role on the Landmarks Preservation Commission. He's been on leave for five months and this volatile divorce isn't a good look, so the council unanimously votes to replace him. Suki gets a year's probation for lying about the car accident in exchange for her testimony in Jim's perjury trial slated for next spring.

Finally, on December 10, 1990, almost four years after Lita's murder and three years after Jim and Suki married, the latest rendition of the Sullivans is officially divorced. The *Palm Beach Post* headline reads, HE GETS COCO; SHE KEEPS HOSE. The judge rules overwhelmingly in Jim's favor. Suki gets to keep her $42,000 engagement ring, her platinum wedding band, a Cartier bracelet, and her suitcase full of pantyhose, but not much else. Jim retains Lita's old 1977 Mercedes, the deed to Casa Eleda, and Coco the dog.

❖

The day after his big divorce win, Jim appears in traffic court and pleads no contest to driving on expired tags and without a license. The judge sentences him to ninety days of house arrest, plus six months' probation. The house arrest is pretty cushy—he's allowed to go to "work" on weekdays even though he doesn't have an office outside the house and hasn't really worked in years. He plays tennis almost daily and shows up at parties, blatantly ignoring his curfew.

In March 1991, Jim pleads no contest to the two counts of perjury for telling the judge Suki had been driving. The judge orders an additional year of probation and a year in jail. But Jim's lawyers successfully argue against jail time and, instead, Jim gets another year of house arrest, this time with slightly tighter restrictions. He must wear an electronic ankle bracelet with a transmitter that alerts the sheriff's office if it is removed. He is allowed to swim in his pool, but he can't drink alcohol or go out at night. He, somehow, is allowed to go to "business meetings" between 9 A.M. and 7 P.M., even though he doesn't have a job. Many people, including the prosecutor, think the sentence too light. Regardless, Jim celebrates his fiftieth birthday confined to his dark, decaying house alone with Coco, the only one left he hasn't betrayed. Yet.

CHAPTER 19

I SPY WITH MY LITTLE EYE (SUMMER 1991)

I'm the last one left for the McClintons," private investigator Patrick McKenna tells me on the first of many phone calls. McKenna, along with his longtime pal, the McClintons' lawyer Brad Moores, and Atlanta lawyer David Boone, fought for the McClinton family for nearly three decades. When Boone and Moores died in 2018 and 2020, respectively, McKenna felt like the last of the old guard. When I began talking to him in the very early stages of this book research, I felt I'd found a kindred spirit, a delightful partner in crime, an essential connection to Lita and the McClintons. While his paper filing and organizational skills could be described as disastrous, his memory of people and details remains incredible.

When I fly into Palm Beach for the first time, I'm excited to meet McKenna in person. I arrive at night and I'm craving a beer. I pick up a rental Camry and drive to a gas station where there's a cage around the cash register and I need to ask for the fridge door to be unlocked so I can buy a six pack. I drive to my hotel, nothing fancy, sip the beer, and have a fitful sleep; the room is too hot, and I can smell cigarette smoke embedded in the carpet. In the morning, I wake up to a cockroach on my pillow, freak out, and quickly check out of the hotel. Already I'm wasting time, and I chastise myself for making poor choices. I troll Airbnb and find an affordable apartment across the water in the swanky part of Palm Beach. I drive over the bridge, past the Everglades Club, past the gates to Mar-a-Lago. My Camry's like an Amish wagon among the Bentleys and Aston Martins and Lamborghinis. Unlike in West Palm Beach, almost everyone here is white, with pastel clothing and leathery tanned skin. The only people of color are driving landscaping trucks or weeding carefully manicured gardens. The beach is gorgeous, right there, but hard to get to; the only public access points seem intentionally hidden behind hedges or overgrown trees. Lots of signs tell me to stay out—this section and that section and this other section are private. On the intercoastal side, the marinas are filled with sailboats and yachts four times the size of my house. For some reason, my clothes don't feel right; I wish I had nicer shoes. I am self-conscious. I can only imagine how out of place, how unsafe I'd feel, if my skin was black or brown.

I can't help but think about how Lita would've felt coming here nearly three decades earlier. I drive past Casa Eleda several times, stop and take photos, try to imagine Lita and Jim making a home here. The house is massive, but amid all the other palatial homes, it seems almost . . . reasonable. I can imagine Jim seeing this house on a corner lot, overlooking the glimmering ocean, and thinking, yes, this will work. From everything I've heard, Lita never wanted to move here—she knew she'd be far from her family and friends. She was used to being the only Black woman in the room and could hold her own in any circle, but she wasn't immune to the barbs of blatant bigotry. And Jim did nothing to help. He announced that he'd bought the mansion before she could have a chance to weigh in, and without any discussion about what their lives would be like as an interracial couple in Palm Beach.

The day after my arrival, I finally meet McKenna in person at O'Sheas Irish Pub downtown. He's every bit as welcoming and friendly as he sounds on the phone. He's wearing a suit because, even at seventy-six, he's still working and has just come from court. McKenna is somewhat famous around here. To know him is to respect him. A former marine in Vietnam, he's a guy who's seen it all. He's both a hard-ass who swears like a sailor and an old softie who believes in the good in people and will fight to the end for people he loves. Growing up in Chicago with nine siblings, he learned how to navigate the streets and fend for himself. He knows the law, having studied the criminal justice system at Southern Illinois University, where he sold pizza slices in exchange for whiskey and pot. He worked as an investigator in Virginia then moved to Florida to work for the public defender's office in West Palm Beach. He specialized in finding the human story behind a defendant, something that could change their narrative—turn lemons into lemonade sort of thing. He'd track down a defendant's high school teacher, a former employer, friends, anyone who could speak to the accused's character before they committed whatever crime. He was so good at it, he started his own private investigation business and would go on to figure prominently in the high-profile defenses of O. J. Simpson, Yoko Ono, F. Lee Bailey, Casey Anthony, and even members of the Irish Republican Army.

He's sipping a soda water with lime because he gave up drinking a few years ago. He gives me a big hug, invites me to sit down, and launches into his side of the story.

❖

In the summer of 1991, McKenna is sitting in his office on the west side—the working side—of Palm Beach when a call comes in from a reporter named John Connolly, a former New York City detective turned journalist who's in town researching an article for *Spy* magazine. Connolly has heard that McKenna's the guy to go to when you need an investigator.

"I got something you gotta hear," Connolly says.

McKenna's a sucker for a good story and agrees to meet Connolly at F. J. O'Donnell's, his favorite Irish saloon. The two men are straight out of central casting—Connolly with his heavy New York accent, McKenna with his Chicago twang. They volley f-bombs and check each other out; they are more comfortable in dive bars than courtrooms, but they've spent a lot of time in both.

Over beers and whiskey, Connolly tells him about his wild weeklong visit with a guy under suspicion of orchestrating the brutal slaying of his wife. McKenna listens but already knows Connolly's talking about Jim Sullivan, whose name has been a newspaper headline ever since his wife Lita was gunned down in Atlanta four years ago. McKenna occasionally sees Sullivan peacocking around town like he owns the place in his Rolls-Royce and preppy clothes.

Connolly tells McKenna that Sullivan has a trove of secrets, and Lita's parents are desperate to find evidence that connects him to their daughter's brutal murder. The cops aren't doing enough; it's taking too long. They need the help of someone like McKenna, someone unafraid to dig and push in the right places.

But McKenna, at forty-three, is busy. He's got his hands full helping attorneys build the defense for thirty-year-old medical student William Kennedy Smith, nephew of Senator Ted Kennedy, who is accused of raping a single mother at the family's Palm Beach estate—President John F. Kennedy's "Winter White House." Unrelated, but interesting nonetheless, in 1990, Jim led the Preservation Committee's attempt to designate the Kennedy estate a historical landmark; the family successfully fought the designation believing it would hinder the future sale of the property. Regardless, it's a high-profile Kennedy case dominating the national airwaves and all but halting life for the millions of people watching. When the trial ends in December (Kennedy is acquitted), it will become the most watched trial in history (until O. J. Simpson takes the honor a few years later—McKenna will work on that one too). For now, it's grown into an obsession for McKenna, so much so that his marriage has fallen apart; the kids are now living with their mom.

McKenna thinks for a bit. He's truly up to his eyeballs in work. But he orders another drink and sighs. "Alright, motherfucker," he says. "Tell me what you know."

❖

John Connolly and Jim Sullivan can credit their connection to—of all people—Donald Trump. In 1990, Connolly was researching a *Forbes* story he cowrote titled, "Manhattan's Favorite Guessing Game: How Rich Is Donald?" alleging that Trump, claiming untold wealth, was in fact broke. Connolly had needed someone to help dig up financial records and a friend recommended he ask Jim, who was an accountant and seemingly savvy businessman. While Jim did some digging around, the two men bonded over the phone, sharing their working-class Irish-Catholic roots and a mirrored brashness that made them feel like old friends. Jim liked Connolly and seemed happy to have someone to talk to.

In June 1991, while Jim was between house arrests, Jim invited Connolly to spend a weekend in the Hamptons with some friends. There, they played tennis and went out for dinners. Connolly got a kick out of Jim, the way he didn't hide his orneriness or arrogance. He'd seen Jim dress down a waiter, explode with road rage, get irritable at little mundane things. He'd also seen Jim flip a switch and become charming and confident whenever women were around. When Connolly learned Jim was a suspect in Lita's murder, he found himself not terribly surprised. After he got home, he read up on the case and got even more curious.

Months after that Hamptons trip, Jim invites Connolly to visit Casa Eleda to hang out for a week. Jim's stuck in the mansion on house arrest, lonely and bored. Connolly thinks it's odd—why would a murder suspect on house arrest invite a former cop journalist for a visit?—but he's intrigued so he pitches a story to his editors and figures, *Why the hell not?*

When Connolly arrives at Jim's hulking Palm Beach home, he sees the 17,000-square-foot mansion has fallen into disrepair. The house is humid and desolate, an apt prison. Jim keeps the lights off, lets dishes pile up, and refuses to run the air conditioning in the Florida heat. The paint is peeling, the pool is empty, and the fountain doesn't work. By this point, Jim has been booted from his position on the Landmarks Preservation Commission and is now the recipient of orders to clean up the yard and maintain the house or face fines from the very council he used to lead.

The men get into a routine—without a driver's license and limited movement due to the house arrest, Jim asks Connolly to take him to appointments and on errands, and in the evenings, they drink wine and smoke cigars on the veranda overlooking the empty pool and overgrown courtyard. They both glisten with sweat in the Florida summer evenings, but it's better outside than inside the stuffy, insufferable house. Jim talks, telling Connolly story after story; to Connolly, it seems like some sort of nihilistic self-sabotage. Jim is well aware Connolly's a former detective, now a journalist who covers white-collar crime. But still, Jim talks and talks.

Jim tells him about his uncle, whose death made him rich. "After I was there only ten months," Jim told Connolly, "the fat old bastard keeled over from a heart attack right onto a pallet of vodka."

When Connolly relates it all back to McKenna in the Irish bar a week later, McKenna is shaking his head. "I bet this asshole offed his uncle too," he says, echoing Connolly's thoughts.

In November, John Connolly's *Spy* magazine article is published and flies off the shelves. It's a sweeping first-person account of his trip to Casa Eleda. Connolly describes the crumbling mansion, Jim's fastidious and precise notetaking, their strange conversations, and his suspicions that Jim had a key role in the deaths of both his uncle and Lita. He writes that the days rolled together as the men adopted a consistent if strange routine . . .

> Dinner was usually set for seven o'clock, and afterward we would sit out on the lanai, facing a fountain that stands in the courtyard in the center of the house. The fountain, of course, didn't work, leaving us little to do but watch lizards run in and out of the overgrown bougainvillea. We talked of this and that, but mostly about him. Sullivan would sit in the same seat every night. His patterns never varied. Once, at dinner, he went to retrieve something from the kitchen, and I filled our wine goblets. When he returned, he looked from glass to glass, his eyes darting, and he briefly seemed angry. "John," he said evenly, "I believe you have my wine glass." It hadn't occurred to me that

he had a special glass, and I was astonished that he could tell the difference between what appeared to me to be identical goblets. "How can you tell?" I asked him. He told me that his glass had a small chip on the stem. The chip was minuscule.

After several nights on the lanai, I finally broached the subject at hand. "Jim," I asked, "did you arrange to have Lita killed?"

He puffed on his cigar thoughtfully for a moment before answering. "What husband," he finally said, "would be foolish enough to have his wife killed on the very day there is to be an important court decision?"

Later, Connolly writes, he went to Macon to interview people who knew Jim and his uncle. He learns Uncle Frank, who had been a healthy sixty-five-year-old, had planned to fire Jim. Connolly learns there was no autopsy, and it was Jim who'd moved quickly to have his uncle's body sent back to Boston. He becomes convinced Jim had killed Uncle Frank using a drug called Coumadin, an anticoagulant or blood thinner also known as warfarin, which was originally developed as rat poison. Jim's first wife, Catherine, told Connolly she'd been on it after giving birth to one of their children. At the time, Jim had long discussions with doctors about the potential side effects. In large doses, Coumadin can cause internal bleeding and violent flu-like symptoms, bouts of nausea, vomiting, and black stools—just like Uncle Frank experienced. Connolly writes that the chief of forensics for the New York State Police had told him, "[Frank] Bienert's symptoms were consistent with many conditions, one of which, however, was poisoning." When Connolly asked him if Frank's symptoms were consistent with Coumadin poisoning specifically, the expert said yes, in fact, they were. But by this point, Uncle Frank's body had been in the ground for more than fifteen years.

Hours have passed and Connolly and McKenna order another round. "It's an incredible story," says McKenna.

"Hold on," says Connolly, clinking the ice in his whiskey. "I haven't even told you about the guns."

CHAPTER 20

JUSTICE LEAGUE (FALL 1991)

When Connolly's *Spy* article about Jim was published in 1991, it was so damning and salacious that whatever friends Jim had left in Palm Beach distanced themselves in a hurry. Where before Jim was a "friend," he became an "acquaintance." Where he was "charming and likable," he was now "shifty and a charlatan." The respected chair of the Landmarks Preservation Commission became just another unfortunate blip in the town's history.

I spoke with John Connolly by phone in late summer 2022, more than thirty years after his *Spy* article hit the shelves. By this point, he'd had a long and successful career as a writer, including as the coauthor with James Patterson of the 2017 book *Filthy Rich: The Shocking True Story of Jeffrey Epstein*. He had a strong New York accent and a surprisingly high singsongy voice, not the machismo TV-cop tone I'd expected. When I asked Connolly about his unlikely friendship with Jim, he cut me off.

"I was never friends with him. No," he said. He'd simply used Jim as a source for the *Forbes* Trump article and sent Jim a copy when it was published. Several months later, when Connolly found himself back in Palm Beach, he called Jim and invited him to lunch. They ate at Testa's, an iconic hundred-year-old restaurant that closed permanently in 2017. Connolly recalled how the waiter brought Jim's sandwich on the wrong kind of bread and Jim berated the guy as though he'd personally put a dead rat between the slices of sourdough. When the waiter slinked away, Jim leaned in, "You know, you have to keep *those people* in their place." The waiter, Jim had assumed, was gay.

"That's when I came to believe this guy is capable of anything," said Connolly. Another time, when they were together in the Hamptons, Jim was convinced the driver in the car behind him was purposefully high-beaming him and grew enraged. He let the car pass and then trailed behind it, flashing his headlights and driving so close to the other car's bumper that he almost crashed into it several times. It was a fit of road rage like nothing Connolly had ever experienced.

"He was nasty. He was a real sociopath," he says. "He could be charming, but he could turn on you like a cobra."

When Jim invited him to stay at Casa Eleda for a week, Connolly was far too curious to say no. What compelled Jim, already a convicted felon with an even greater crime to hide, to invite Connolly, a former detective, to his house? Was he trying to show off? Was he getting a rush flirting with danger? Was it the same kind of hand-over-flame behavior that prompted him to sleep with other women in his and Lita's marital bed? What on earth compelled Jim to casually show Connolly his pistol, a shotgun, and other weapons?

❖

When I was further along in my research and had a better handle on the whole story, I called John Connolly again. I tried him a few times and never got a call back, which was odd because he'd been so willing to talk the first time. He'd been so full of piss and vinegar that I was truly shocked when I learned of his sudden death in January 2023, just a few months after we first spoke. He was seventy-eight and seemed like one of those people who would live forever. A former *Spy* magazine colleague gave his eulogy, saying, "[Connolly] always had something going on. John was never one to upstage somebody or hog the spotlight; he didn't have to. John brought the show. There was no ironic distance about John. He lived in a world inhabited by good guys and bad guys, and he wanted to catch bad guys."

I was truly saddened by his death, and disappointed in myself for not conducting a better interview the first time we spoke. I had so many more questions to ask him, one of which was, after he left Jim's house, what made him decide to call the FBI?

❖

FBI Special Agent Todd Letcher is in his mid-thirties when the tip comes in from John Connolly that Jim Sullivan, convicted felon and still the prime suspect in Lita McClinton Sullivan's murder, has guns sitting out in the open at his home—a clear violation of his house arrest. Connolly also tells Letcher about Jim's almost compulsive need to document every detail of his life in his daily calendars, and he keeps piles of neatly stacked documents—including receipts, legal papers, years of correspondence, and a paper Rolodex—in his home office. The various cops and special investigators have been circling around Jim Sullivan for years, but this tip from Connolly feels like a ticket into his inner workings. Letcher believes if he can get access to Jim's paper trove, he'll get answers to who killed Lita. He writes a sweeping affidavit to request a warrant to search Casa Eleda. While the report of guns certainly piques his interest, he's more interested in the paper trail, but the guns are a way in.

Letcher, who took over the murder investigation from John Kingston, is a soft-spoken, straightlaced kind of guy with an MBA from the Wharton School of Business. He loves being in the FBI. It suits him: follow procedures, protect people, capture bad guys. Something different every day.

The judge grants his warrant, so on the morning of Friday, September 6, 1991, Letcher and a dozen other agents, plus GBI special agent Bob Ingram and Detective Welcome Harris from Atlanta, meet at the Palm Beach police station to study blueprints of the house. It's a huge space with many rooms, so they need to be both thorough and efficient.

When they arrive at Jim's, local cops secure the perimeter to keep nosy neighbors and press from getting too close. Even though it's early, it's a hot, humid day that will become the second-hottest day of the year in Palm Beach. Wearing their navy windbreakers emblazoned with FBI in thick yellow letters, they're all sweating already.

Letcher rings the doorbell and tries the intercom system. Jim is under house arrest, but it appears no one is home. They call Jim's lawyers to try to locate him, but no one can find him. They walk to the back of the house. Letcher pushes open the pantry window, looks at the other agents, and shrugs—the warrant says they can enter with or without the owner's permission, so why not? Letcher climbs through the window and looks around the pantry for a key to unlock the back door. When he can't find one, he takes out his screwdriver and removes the door from its hinges. The team files in, fanning out to their preassigned rooms. An FBI photographer and videographer go around capturing footage and numbering the rooms with little yellow sticky notes to keep track of where they find what in the house.

The cavernous mansion is hot and stuffy. Letcher, Ingram, and Harris have the most familiarity with the case, so they take Jim's wing of the house, which holds his large master bedroom, a sitting room, and another bedroom used as an office. In the sitting room, Letcher finds little white Coco in a crate, seemingly unfazed by the strangers in the house.

The agents seize Jim's 1991 in-progress day planner—it's a leather-bound book where you swap out the pages year to year. The agents find previous years' pages and take those too, along with financial records and the Rolodex. Sitting right out in the open of Jim's makeshift office, leaning against a wall, is a fifteen-inch double-barreled shotgun. Throughout the house, agents find three more weapons, including a rifle, another shotgun, and a .38-caliber pistol. All are unloaded.

Once they finish bagging and tagging evidence, they all meet in the dining room and list the items they've confiscated. They leave a copy of the warrant and the list of seized belongings on the dining room table. The agents file out the way they came in; Letcher puts the back door back on its hinges, locks it, and climbs out the window.

Just as the agents are pulling away, Jim rolls up driving Lita's old Mercedes. He'd been at a shareholder meeting at a downtown hotel for one of his investments, an excuse to get out of house-prison ("conducting business" is allowed on his house arrest). A front desk clerk had handed him a handwritten message from his lawyer saying, *FBI raid. Go home.*

When he pulls up to his house, he rolls down the window and before the agents can say anything, Jim says, "Yes. I know." The agents ask to speak with Jim inside and he nods. Harris, Ingram, and Letcher follow Jim back into the house, and they all sit down at the big mahogany dining room table. In the event they'd have a chance to talk to Jim, they'd planned a set of questions and determined Ingram would be the one to ask them.

Once seated, Ingram, a serious, slow-talking Southerner who doesn't bother with pleasantries, launches in. "Do you know why we've asked to talk to you today?"

"Lita's death is the reason why," says Jim.

"Were you in any way responsible for her death?"

"No, I am not."

The air feels mildewy and thick as heat from the Florida sun permeates the dark curtains. The men glisten. Ingram sighs, wanting to ask how Jim survives without the freaking air conditioning. Instead, he wipes beads of sweat from his upper lip and asks Jim how he feels about being interviewed today. Jim looks down, takes a deep breath, then gazes up at the ceiling. He exhales. "Uncomfortable and pessimistic." He crosses his legs, removes an invisible piece of lint from his pants, and levels a look of impatience at Ingram. His voice is quiet, pleasant even with the Bostonian lilt. But the knobs of his jawbone pop as he clenches and releases, hinting that annoyance or fear or rage simmer just beneath his stony demeanor.

"Tell me," says Ingram. "Do you think that Lita's death was intentionally caused?" It's a strange question, worded just so to elicit a telling reply. If Jim says the killing was intentional, it implies he knows something about it. If he says he doesn't think it was intentional, it implies that he's hiding something because murder by gunshot is clearly an intentional act.

But Jim just says, "I have no idea." When Ingram asks Jim why someone would kill Lita, Jim unloads his satchel of stories: Lita was involved with drugs, maybe it was a drug hit; maybe it had something to do with Marvin Marable and his carton of illegally gotten tapes; maybe her parents wanted to cash in on their eldest daughter's life insurance.

"Tell me why *you* would do something like this," says Ingram.

Jim again takes a long gaze at the ceiling. "Unthinkable and inconceivable," he says at last. Jim is composed, not sweating like the other men, as though he's acclimated to the weather inside his jungle.

"What do you think should happen to the person who did this?" asks Ingram.

"Well," says Jim. "They should be put away."

Sweat beads slither into the folds of Ingram's belly as he asks Jim about the telephone calls he made in the week leading up to Lita's murder. It's been four and a half years, but Jim's been over this many times. Yes, he'd called Marvin Marable to discuss Lita's running around. Yes, he'd called Bob Christenson to ask about any strange activity in the days before Lita's death—because a process server had been trying to subpoena some of Lita's acquaintances. No, he does not recall receiving or answering a call from the Howard Johnson's, but suggests maybe he'd called to make a reservation. The agents exchange looks. They've spent the last few hours searching through this man's 17,000-square-foot mansion; he's not a HoJo's kind of guy. When asked about the collect call he got the morning of Lita's murder, he thrums his fingers on the table, clenches, sighs as though he's bored by this question, and once again denies having received such a call.

In the days that follow, agents comb through Jim's old day planners, including the years 1986 and 1987. While they never find a HoJo's receipt or anything showing a large-sum payment to a third party (like a hitman), there are plenty of interesting notations. On November 21, 1986, about six weeks before Lita's murder, a note said *Furn P.U. in Macon* followed two days later with *Furn delivery here.*

In both years, Jim fastidiously noted Suki's every move, especially in the lusty days before they married, including when she'd go on dates with another man. It's also clear he had her followed because he knows her every move, down to the minute. Letcher zeros in on the days around the murder. Among the many notations, there is little about Lita. It's all about Suki, Suki, Suki.

> January 15, 1987 (day before the murder): *Suki says she has a headache and wants to stay in. He picked her up at 7:40 P.M. She didn't return home until 1:15 A.M.*

> January 16, 1987 (day of murder), included with notes to call his investment broker, play tennis, and write a letter: *Suki with me tonight till noon Saturday.*
>
> That night, even after the news of Lita's murder, the couple dined out at Jo's, an upscale French restaurant.

> January 17, 1987 (day after murder): *Suki supposed to be with me tonight . . . said she'd call me. Didn't.*

> January 18, 1987: *She went to dinner party with him, said she would try to get away early and stay with me. Didn't. Went to his house instead.*

> January 19, 1987 (day of Lita's funeral): Nothing

> January 22, 1987: *Suki and I had caviar and champagne at home tonight.*

But while the FBI came for his papers, they got him for his guns. Four days after the FBI raid, Jim is arrested and charged with possession of firearms by a felon and possession of an illegal sawed-off shotgun, which is three inches shorter than the legal limit. Jim's lawyers try to say the guns belong to someone else, friends who had stored stuff in his basement, but the judge doesn't buy it. Because Jim has violated the conditions of his house arrest, he is ordered to serve out the remaining nine months of his year-long house arrest sentence in the Palm Beach County jail.

Finally, Jim Sullivan is behind bars.

CHAPTER 21

GOOSE CHASE
(WINTER 1991)

As part of Special Agent Todd Letcher's affidavit requesting permission to search Jim's house, he unearths the police informant Johnny Austin Turner's assertion that his buddy Thomas Bruce Henley and another guy were hired by Poppy's husband, Marvin Marable, to put the hit on Lita. He's convinced that Turner's story has merit. He builds such a convincing case that, a week after the raid on Jim's house, police arrest Henley, who's living at a drug treatment facility in Rome, Georgia. Henley's rap sheet is riddled with charges of car theft, forgery, assault, firearms possession, and impersonating a police officer. Letcher believes Henley, along with a violent felon named Clinton Botts, orchestrated the hit, while Marvin acted as the go-between who'd brokered the deal between the trio and Jim.

It all seems so tidy—it all fits. Until, once again, it doesn't.

Henley is arrested, sits in jail for a month, but is never indicted. Over the next weeks, a thorough investigation ensues but nothing sticks: Henley's lawyer discredits Turner as a media-seeking informant rat with a litany of prior convictions including perjury. Henley's boss gives him an alibi, saying he was at work at the time of the murder. Botts is an unsavory individual with a long list of prior convictions, but police find no evidence that ties him to the crime, and he's never arrested. Marvin vehemently denies any involvement and, other than the reckless wiretapping of his wife and Lita's phone calls, no hard evidence ties him to Henley, Botts, or the murder. Investigations into the three men are eventually dropped.

While both agents Kingston and Letcher believe there could be some validity to Turner's story—maybe Marvin did at some point try to find a hit squad for Jim, maybe Henley and Botts were considering taking the gig—nothing ever transpired that backs up those hunches.

"Johnny Austin Turner was a piece of work. He was always angling to get what was best for himself," says Letcher. "We wasted a lot of time chasing all that down."

❖

By this point, private investigator Patrick McKenna has jumped into the Jim Sullivan situation with both feet. He's pulled in his lawyer pal Brad Moores—the two met decades ago in college, then worked together at the West Palm Beach DA's office. They knew a lot about the case due to media coverage, but also because Palm Beach can be a small, gossipy place. Together, they fly to Atlanta to meet Emory and Jo Ann McClinton. With boyish good looks and youthful enthusiasm, Moores believes he can get justice for the McClinton family. But the McClintons, at first, aren't so sure.

"When he came up and knocked on my door . . . there was this teenage-looking person standing in my doorway," Jo Ann says after meeting Moores for the first time. "I was expecting an attorney, like an elderly gentleman. And here was this . . . teenager."

But as Moores and McKenna sit with Jo Ann and Emory for a couple of hours, the group bonds—little do they know at this point that the bond will last the rest of their lives. They share stories of Lita, what she went through with Jim, frustration at the slow progress of the case. They've all been anxiously watching as the grand jury in Atlanta creeps toward an indictment against Jim, but it's running out of time—the five-year statute of limitations on federal murder-for-hire cases is just months away. Worried the grand jury is taking too long, Moores suggests they file a wrongful death civil suit in Florida. Unlike a criminal case, a wrongful death case is tried in civil court, where judgments levy fines instead of jail time. In a civil case, the burden of proof is also less stringent; a jury must decide there is a "preponderance of evidence" to convict, whereas in a criminal case, the jury must decide guilt beyond a reasonable doubt.

The McClintons agree and Moores files the suit. But justice costs money, of which McKenna and Moores have little. While the lawyers get paid once a judgment is settled, they have little to kick off the case, so they partner with Atlanta attorney David Boone, a more experienced lawyer with at least something of a war chest they can draw from.

After meeting the family, Moores and McKenna are more motivated than ever. "Emory and Jo Ann are truly extraordinary people," Moores told me later. "I think in twenty-four years of practicing law, I've never represented any one I like more."

McKenna agrees. "There's no more lovely people on the planet," he says. "We truly believed we could help them."

❖

From jail, with the help of his lawyers, Jim sells the crumbling Casa Eleda for $3.2 million in cash and buys a smaller but still upscale house in nearby Boynton Beach. Brad Moores, now officially representing the McClintons, tries to legally freeze Jim's funds pending the outcome of their civil suit, but his motion is denied. It is at this point, Moores believes, that Jim begins to squirrel away his fortune in offshore accounts. But he can't prove it . . . yet.

Regardless of where his money is stashed, things are looking pretty bleak for Jim. By the end of 1991, almost five years after Lita's murder, he's divorced from his third wife, sitting in prison on firearms charges, the defendant in a wrongful death suit, and facing the prospect of a federal murder trial.

CHAPTER 22

FEDERAL FIASCO
(1992)

F inally, on January 10, 1992, while Jim sits in the Palm Beach County jail, the federal grand jury indicts him on five counts of "conspiracy to commit contract killing by the use of interstate phone calls." It's in the nick of time—there are only six days to spare before the five-year statute of limitation expires. If convicted, Jim could face life in prison and up to $1.2 million in fines. The criminal trial will start in November.

Reporters flock to the McClintons' home, where the couple is headed out of town to get away from the chaos. They hurry past, giving a brief statement that, while they feel relief at the indictment, they regret it took five years. "James Sullivan was the primary suspect as far as my family was concerned from the beginning," Jo Ann tells *Atlanta Journal-Constitution* reporter Bill Montgomery. "Our contention was always that he initiated and orchestrated the murder."

The federal case hinges on the series of "interstate" phone calls, including calls to and from the Howard Johnson's three days before the murder, and the collect call to Jim's house from the Suwanee rest area forty minutes after Lita was shot. Jim is being charged with four counts of using the phone to arrange Lita's murder, plus one count of causing others to carry a firearm.

I wanted to understand the nature of the charges against Jim, so I reached out to former U.S. Attorney Bill McKinnon, who was one of the prosecutors in the case.

"Generally, murder or homicide is not a federal crime," McKinnon said. "So there has to be a particular jurisdictional element that the feds have to prove in addition to the homicide itself." That element was the federal statute that makes using the phone across state lines to commission a murder a federal crime. In other words, the onus is on the prosecution to present enough compelling evidence for a jury to decide beyond a reasonable doubt that Jim played a role in the homicide, and that he used interstate telecommunications to do so.

In addition to Richard Lubin, Jim's Florida attorney, Jim hires two hotshot Atlanta defense attorneys, Ed Garland and his partner Don Samuel. It's an intimidating force. The famous legal duo will go on to successfully defend some of Atlanta's most notorious cases, including Baltimore Ravens linebacker Ray Lewis, who was acquitted on double murder charges; Larry Gleit, CFO of the now-defunct Gold Club, who walked away with a misdemeanor charge in his federal racketeering case; Jim Williams, protagonist in the nonfiction tale of *Midnight in the Garden of Good and Evil*, acquitted of murder in his fourth trial; and Pittsburgh Steelers quarterback Ben Roethlisberger, who was accused of sexually assaulting a Georgia college student.

Ed Garland tells the press that the government's case "is obviously based on testimony by people unworthy of belief" and he firmly believes the charges are false and Jim will be acquitted.

In February, while awaiting trial, Jim gets into a scuffle with his cellmate in the Palm Beach County jail. Paul O'Brien, who is facing charges for a series of armed robberies, had told authorities that Jim confessed to orchestrating Lita's murder. As a result, he'd been subpoenaed to testify in Jim's upcoming firearms case and, catching wind of this, Jim rages at O'Brien, calling him a "snitch." A fight ensues and Jim lands in the infirmary with a broken nose and a gash behind his ear. Jim accuses O'Brien of making up the confession to ease his own sentence and presses charges for aggravated assault.

In April, the U.S. Marshals accompany Jim from the Florida jail to the courthouse in Atlanta so he can be arraigned. Jim is hustled into court in handcuffs, looking like a shrunken and sour version of his former self. It's the first time the McClintons have seen their son-in-law in seven years. He looks rough and surly.

"I plead not guilty, your honor," he tells the judge. He is ushered out by his attorneys, who confidently tell reporters: "Jim denies his guilt as vehemently as he can . . . The prosecution has nothing to go on but innuendo, suspicion, and desire to end an unsolved crime."

Jim is just two weeks away from the end of his perjury sentence, and while he still faces firearms charges in Florida, he's gunning to spend the summer a free man. Federal prosecutors oppose bond, saying if Jim is let out on bail there is a "serious risk he will flee." But at the bond hearing, he is granted bail, with some caveats: the court will freeze his $2.9 million in assets, but it will dole out a $1,500 a month allowance, plus the $8,000 monthly mortgage for the new Boynton Beach house. Once again, he will be electronically monitored and limited to visiting his doctor and lawyers, going to "business meetings," and exercising pretty much whenever he wants.

❖

Finally, on Monday, November 2, 1992, the trial begins. Looking refreshed and slick after a summer of relative freedom, Jim comes to court wearing an expensive gray suit, blue shirt, and red tie. His curls, unruly and unkept at the arraignment six months ago, are now trimmed and tamed into submission, his gray pallor now golden from his months in the sun. He tells reporters he's looking forward to his "six-year ordeal" coming to an end. "Obviously, I am innocent," he says, adding that he fully expects vindication. "The truth will come out."

The jury—composed of ten white and two Black jurors—is set, and Judge Marvin Shoob begins hearing opening statements. All the lawyers—two prosecutors and three defense attorneys—are white men.

"James Vincent Sullivan is a cheap and miserable man, who is so preoc-cupied with his wealth, it was the be-all and end-all of his existence. He arranged to have his wife murdered," begins prosecutor Assistant U.S. Attorney Robert Schroeder. "He arranged to have other people commit the brutal execution of his wife. He is cheap and miserly; he didn't want to lose anything." He explains how Lita was gunned down just hours before a divorce hearing that could've given her a substantial chunk of Jim's fortune. "He wasn't about to take that risk," says Schroeder.

Schroeder tells the jury about Jim's fervent desire to hold the divorce in Florida instead of Georgia because, there, he would've felt supported by a cul-ture and court system rooted in protecting wealthy white men. Jim believed a Palm Beach judge—who would also likely be a wealthy white man—would side with him and allow him to hold on to the money he loved so dearly. Lita was an outsider in Palm Beach, he explains, because of the color of her skin. A jury in Georgia might side with Lita because, presumably, a good portion of the jury would be Black, reflecting the Atlanta population. Schroeder is not explicitly calling out racism or talking about racist institutions—it'll be many decades before this is openly discussed—but he's painting a picture of Jim's entitlement, his belief that ultimately he's the only one who matters.

Finally, Schroeder says the prosecution will show that Jim used a series of telephone calls to orchestrate Lita's brutal murder, and the jury will have no choice but to find him guilty.

But Jim's attorneys paint a starkly different picture.

"This is a case of how an innocent man can be charged with a crime he did not commit," begins defense attorney Ed Garland. "The prosecution's case lacks solid evidence or believable witnesses. The investigators have blinders on—they look at the facts and see only speculation and guesswork and what they want to see." He pauses, walks along, making eye contact with each jury member. "You will not be told any details about the telephone calls made between the mansion and the motel," he continues. "You will not know what was said or who said it, because all they have is speculation. There's no proof about who made the calls and what was said. What you have here is a theory."

While the prosecution hammers the fact that Jim had irrefutable motive to kill Lita, the defense says the Sullivans' divorce was just a regular dissolution of a marriage that had run its course, that Jim had showered Lita with gifts and money, even bought her a townhouse in Atlanta to make her happy.

"Lita didn't work, and she didn't contribute financially, and she lived in a mansion and drove a Mercedes and had the finest clothes," says Garland. "He had no motive to murder her, having spent lavishly on her." He then suggests Lita had been the one responsible for her own death because, he alleges, she'd been unfaithful with a variety of men, and had abused drugs—though he offers nothing to prove these allegations. He softens the attack with, "The death of Lita Sullivan was a great tragedy. She didn't deserve to die under any circumstances. That is not the issue here; I am not trying to slander her."

Through the first days of the trial, the judge and jury hear from the eyewitnesses, including neighbor Bob Christenson, who describes how his neck hair stood on end at the sight of the man delivering flowers at Lita's door on that cold January morning.

"This was the same kind of instinct you have when you're going on a patrol or something like that, and you are afraid you're going to get hit," he says, likening his experience in Vietnam to the instinctual alarm going off in his body when he locked eyes with the delivery man. "You can't lay your hands on why you are concerned. You just are. That's the instinct I had with this guy, like just stay away from him." A couple minutes later, he heard two shots and saw the man running. He says he waited a few seconds, stunned, before running to Lita.

"What did you do upon entering the town home and seeing Lita Sullivan lying there?" asks Schroeder.

"Well, the first thing I did was go to Lita to see if there was anything I could do for her. I have some military training. I'm no medic or anything like that but . . . you do know some things to do for trauma victims, so I went over to see her to see if she was still breathing. She was, not well, but she was still breathing."

"Was she conscious or unconscious?"

"She was unconscious," says Christenson, looking down at his hands.

"Did you notice whether or not she had sustained any injuries of any kind?"

Christenson swallows hard and looks at Schroeder. "It looked to me like she had been shot in the face," he says, clearing his throat. "I knelt beside her to see, to ascertain if she was unconscious or what the situation was. I opened her mouth to see if she had swallowed her tongue and put my hands underneath her head to see if I could find any wounds or anything like that. I could see there wasn't a whole lot I could do for Lita. So, I ran to the kitchen and called 911." He goes on to describe the chaos as the ambulance arrived, followed by the cops and detectives.

Neighbor Homer Deakins describes how he too saw the flower deliveryman and heard the shots. Mary McIntyre details how she almost drove into a man running out of The Coaches "like a bat out of hell" just after the murder, how she had to swerve not to hit him.

The florist, Randall Benson, testifies that the cops came to interview him on January 17, asking about a specific box of roses. "I thought I was in trouble because I didn't wire all the roses," he says. He describes how the suspicious man who purchased them had been in a hurry and didn't seem to care about the color or quality of the flowers.

"I picked pink roses because they were the freshest," he says. He says the man didn't want a card and needed to go out to his friend waiting in a white Toyota to get more money to pay for the flowers.

Marvin Marable, who has an immunity agreement saying that the wiretapping charges against him will be dropped in exchange for his testimony against Jim, tells the court that yes, he taped calls between Poppy and Lita without their consent—and then shared those tapes with Jim for a sum of $30,000, which Jim said he would give Marvin if things went his way in divorce court.

"Could you please explain to the members of the jury the conversations you had with James Sullivan about these taped phone calls and what he told you?" asks Schroeder.

"Well, I can't remember them all verbatim, but he was aware that the device was on the telephone," says Marable. "I made him aware of the conversations that were on the tapes, and he asked me if I could testify in his divorce trial." He says Jim wanted him to keep the recording device on the phone longer, so he could get more damning information to use in the divorce. Over the next months, they spoke a couple dozen times, sharing information and discussing how they could use their wives' private conversations to gain advantage in their respective divorces.

"He was very pessimistic about the outcome of his divorce," Marable says, adding that Jim complained incessantly about money and mounting legal fees. He admits he has no proof as to whom Lita was dating, and no proof she was doing drugs.

Schroeder asks, "Regarding the arrangement you had with the defendant—I believe it was $30,000. Did you ever receive any money from the defendant?"

Marable looks down and says, "No." When asked the whereabouts of the tapes, he replies that he thew the tapes in a dumpster in a mall parking lot.

"And as a result of that recording device being placed on the telephone, did you ultimately plead guilty to a criminal charge?" asks Schroeder.

"Yes, I did," says Marable.

"What was the charge you pled guilty to?"

"Invasion of privacy."

"Could you please explain to the jury what was the result of pleading guilty, what was the result of the sentence you received?"

"It was a two-year probation at the end of which the records were sealed and there would be no record of it." In other words, his record was expunged in exchange for today's testimony.

Finally, he tells the court that Jim called him on the morning of January 13, three days before the murder, sounding desperate. "He said, I need some information. He said 'It's very important. It's critical I get this information.'" He asked if Lita was still living in the condo, or any information on her whereabouts or activities.

"What did you say?" asks Schroeder.

"I said I didn't know," says Marable. He told Jim that he and Poppy were now divorced, and he hadn't been to Lita's in ages.

That Jim was desperately trying to get information on Lita in the early morning three days before her murder seems damning enough, but even more startling information comes to light on day four of the trial when prosecutors play a taped conversation between Jim and his friend Clyde Marlow, Jan's now ex-husband. The call took place a month after Lita's death, and on it the men discuss the murder. The recording isn't stellar, so everyone—the judge, jury, and reporters and onlookers sitting in the courtroom—leans in to hear.

> "This is what is called a nine-millimeter automatic pistol," says Jim in his unmistakable Bostonian accent. "The police tell me that the weapon that was used, Clyde, is a weapon never seen in Atlanta."
>
> "Really?" says Clyde who, knowing Jim is a suspect, is taping the conversation.
>
> "It apparently has nine shells or cartridges, whatever you call the bullets, instead of the normal five or six. It's automatic, and it is the weapon of choice of Colombian and Cuban drug-hit people," says Jim.

This bombshell moment lingers when Detective Harris testifies that the police had never revealed to anyone outside of law enforcement what type of weapon was used to kill Lita.

"It is the Atlanta Police Department's policy never to give out the type and caliber of a weapon used to commit a crime," said Harris. A ballistics expert from the Georgia State Crime Lab goes even further and tells the court the bullet that killed Lita came from a 9mm Smith & Wesson. He says that unless Jim had familiarity with the gun, there is no way he could know how many cartridges were in its clip.

Detective Harris also suggests that whoever did the hit were likely a bunch of amateurs.

"The shooter had taken the gun with him. A professional hit man would have used a stolen gun that could not be traced back to him, and dropped it at the scene," he says. He said a 9mm gun was generally not used in these kinds of crimes. "It is a semiautomatic weapon and once it's fired, it ejects shell casings, and therefore you leave these things lying at the scene."

He also drops the chilling thought that an experienced hit team would have waited until Lita was alone in the house. Clearly the shooter didn't know Poppy and her daughter were hiding upstairs. Otherwise, he could've gone for them too.

❖

In the second week of the trial, the judge dismisses the jury as he hears testimony from two friends of Jim's former lover Tanya Tanksley. The women's history of methamphetamine and cocaine use, among other drugs, has rendered their credibility dubious. The judge wants to hear what they have to say before letting them testify in front of the jury. Both women tell the court that Tanya was afraid she'd be called to testify in Lita and Jim's divorce. They say when Tanya told Jim her fears, he told her not to worry, saying he'd "take care of it where you never have to testify," and added, "Watch the newspapers.'"

The friends both testify Tanya told them about this conversation, but Tanya now denies the conversation ever took place and her lawyers assert that if asked about it, Tanya will take the Fifth. The judge decides the friends lack credibility and throws out their testimony altogether, which is a blow to the prosecution.

When thirty-three-year-old Tanya briefly takes the stand, she looks young and scared as she sneaks glances at fifty-one-year-old Jim. She reluctantly tells the court that she'd had an ongoing affair with Jim since they met outside of a Macon convenience store in 1976—the year Jim and Lita were married. They'd had sex "dozens" of times in the Macon home when Lita was away. They'd hook up in a hotel in Atlanta sometimes, and he'd give her prepaid airline tickets to Palm Beach so they could have sex in the big luxurious bedroom in Casa Eleda. Sometimes, she says, he had sex with her friends.

❖

Roughly two weeks into the trial, the prosecution's star witness, Jim's third wife Suki Sullivan, takes the stand. She's now been divorced from Jim for almost two years. U.S. Attorney Bill McKinnon asks her to point out Jim and describe what he's wearing.

"He's over there," Suki says softly, quickly glancing at Jim then looking away. "Beige suit with maroon-colored tie." She tells the court how she met Jim at a cocktail party while he was married to Lita and she was married to Leonard Rogers. Soon after, she began dating Jim.

McKinnon asks Suki to speak up several times and there are moments when she struggles to understand his questions, but they find a groove. She tells the court how Jim was frustrated at having to pay temporary alimony to Lita, and he wanted to bring her back to Florida so he could divorce her there.

"Because he say Georgia law is lot better for woman's side," says Suki.

"What else did he tell you about what was happening in his divorce from Lita?" asks McKinnon.

"He said she from Georgia and he mentioned about her parents' influence, and he say he been married long time, like ten years."

"Did he say what type of influence her parents would have?"

"They Black. They live in Georgia. It would be in her favor. Because lot of percentage Black people live in Georgia and he say her parents have big influence, power." She says Jim knew he was losing in the divorce.

"Do you remember how long before Lita got killed that he said that?" asks McKinnon.

"I don't know exactly," says Suki. "Maybe a month."

"Did he ever talk to you about what he might get people to do for him?"

"Sometime he mentioned . . . he said that in Georgia countryside, you can hire people to do anything you want to have done or want to do."

She tells the court that on the morning Lita was killed Jim called and told her, "After all, it's better for us."

When McKinnon asks her if Jim kept cash around the house, she says Jim kept stacks of hundred-dollar bills locked in a barrel inside a vault in the wine cellar in the basement of Casa Eleda. Suki had access to the cellar, would run down to retrieve wine, but she'd hurry back because it was dark and scary in the basement. Where the cash came from, she didn't know. This line of questioning attempts to settle a problem the prosecution has—so far, they have no record of Jim paying anyone a large chunk of money. Suki's testimony offers a possible method—maybe he paid a hit team by digging into his barrel of cash.

At one point during a break in the trial, Suki complains Jim is boring his eyes into her, prompting the judge to instruct Jim: "You can look, but don't stare." Jim shakes his head and sighs.

Suki tells the court about how Jim compelled her to lie in traffic court, how even after her arrest, he urged her to claim ignorance and say she didn't know what she was talking about because she didn't understand English. She says the night she was arrested for perjury, she was sitting on their bed, crying after spending six hours in jail. She'd broken out in shingles from the stress. That's when he led her from their bedroom to the TV room and cranked the volume on the TV.

"He say people can hear through telephone your conversation, he say 'They definitely listen to my telephone.' So he turned the volume higher."

"What did he say to you?" asks McKinnon.

"He say he hire somebody to kill Lita." Though everyone knows this is coming—she's the prosecution's star witness—hearing her whisper it sends a shiver through the packed courtroom. "He doesn't want to go to jail."

"What did he think would happen if he went to jail?"

"Never get out."

"What else did he tell you?"

"He say, 'Let's sell this house as quick as possible. Let's go anywhere in the world you want to go.'"

When it's the defense's turn for cross-examination, Ed Garland is quick to point out that Suki knew Jim was a suspect in Lita's murder but married him just eight months after her death anyway. Even after he'd allegedly given this loud-TV confession, Suki stuck around for another two weeks.

He reminds the court that Suki is a convicted perjurer for lying in Palm Beach traffic court. Then Garland points out everything Suki asked for in her divorce from Jim.

"So, you listed that you needed $2,000 per month for rent; is that correct?" asks Garland.

"Yes," says Suki.

"And you also asked for $850 a month, didn't you, for a housekeeper?"

"Yes."

"You were going to have a housekeeper at your apartment and wanted Mr. Sullivan to provide you with a full-time housekeeper. Is that correct?"

"Um, yes."

"And you said you wanted for yourself, alone, $400 a month for food, correct?"

"Yes."

"And another $500 a month for dinners out, correct?"

"Yes."

"All right. And you wanted $2,000 a month for clothing. Is that correct?"

"Yes," says Suki, now barely a whisper.

He continues . . . and you wanted $200 a month for dog care, $1,000 a month for vacations, plus $10,000 a month in lawyer's fees, plus half of the mansion . . .

Suki simply replies yes, yes, yes. Soon after, now seeming smaller than ever, Suki leaves the stand. Jim's divorce attorney slips into the hotseat and testifies Suki "has great difficulty telling the truth." He tells the court Suki "is the most manipulative woman I have ever met, a sheer fabricator of the first resort."

❖

When the wife of Jim's old pal and now bitter enemy George Bissell takes the stand, she tells the court she was at a small dinner party at Jim's on January 14, 1987, two days before the murder. She says Jim received a series of phone calls that left him agitated and nervous. During the final call, around 10:30 P.M., she overheard Jim say, "Well then, get flowers."

Once again, defense attorneys bat this damning testimony away, noting George Bissell was convicted two years ago of fifty-seven counts of securities fraud; Jim had been a key witness at the trial and his wife's convenient story is a simple case of retribution. When FBI agent Todd Letcher testifies that a notation in Jim's day planner on that day also said, *Get Flowers*, the defense points out it also said *Get Firewood* and *Get Pool Chemicals*—a simple list of items needed for the house.

After the prosecution presents its witnesses, the court will take a weekend break before the defense brings its side of the story. Before it does, defense attorney Don Samuel makes a plea to the judge to dismiss the case. It's a common occurrence in these kinds of trials for defense attorneys to discredit the prosecution and throw up a Hail Mary to get the case dismissed. Samuel argues that in the two-and-a-half weeks the prosecution's been presenting its case, the government has failed to prove Jim used the calls between his mansion and the HoJo's to arrange Lita's murder, or that the call from the rest area to his home had anything to do with the commission of a crime. "The government cannot show who was on the line, or what was said," he says.

After nearly three weeks of long days in court, everyone goes home to wait out the rainy weekend.

CHAPTER 23

UNREASONABLE DOUBT (1992)

Over the weekend, tornadoes rip through Georgia, killing several people and leaving hundreds more injured, without power, or homeless. The forecast calls for more rain and severe winds. When everyone returns to court on Monday morning, they are breathless and windblown and not quite settled when the bailiff says, "All rise," as Judge Marvin Shoob enters the courtroom.

He sits down and the room fills with the quiet rustling of people settling as though they're in a theater and the play's about to start. Shoob looks around, not saying anything. Finally, he takes a deep breath and announces he spent the weekend reviewing attorneys' briefs.

What he says next sends a different kind of storm through the city.

"It is my opinion that the government has failed to establish a case that a reasonable jury could conclude, beyond a reasonable doubt, that the defendant was guilty of contract murder."

The courtroom is overcome with stunned silence.

"Your daughter was a bright, attractive woman in the early stages of her life," says Judge Shoob, looking apologetically at Emory and Jo Ann McClinton, sitting with Emory Jr. in the front row. The family has been in the courtroom every day, listening to endless testimony in hopes that justice will be served. But their hopes plummet as the judge tells them, "Hopefully, the murderers will be apprehended and convicted. But this court is obligated under case law to dismiss."

Just like that, the trial is over.

While baffled onlookers, who'd been ready for a long day in court, begin to whisper and then talk more loudly as they try to sort out what happened, Detective Welcome Harris collects his coat and mutters, "I feel sick, I feel sick, I feel sick," as he leaves the courtroom.

Outside on the windy courthouse steps, Jo Ann, newly elected to the Georgia House of Representatives, is shaking and unable to speak. She grips her husband's hand as he gives a restrained statement to reporters.

"Judge Shoob should have allowed the people, that is, the jury, to decide, and instead he usurped the people's responsibility by making this decision," Emory McClinton says, keeping his manners in check as always. "In not allowing the jury to complete its responsibility, he sided against the victim, and we feel he erred."

Assistant U.S. Attorney Bill McKinnon, who would go on to prosecute hundreds of cases in his thirty-five years as a federal prosecutor, is shocked. He says he felt confident they'd presented sufficient evidence to let a jury determine beyond a reasonable doubt that those calls, particularly the one from the rest stop just forty minutes after the shooting, proved Jim arranged the murder. "We just ended up having a judge who didn't see it that way," he says.

Jurors, later interviewed in the *Atlanta Journal-Constitution*, say they agreed with the judge's decision. "The telephone calls were disturbing, but they weren't conclusive," said one juror, a schoolteacher from Stone Mountain. Another says, "You want to know what happened, but . . . you just don't."

On the afternoon of November 23, 1992, just three days before Thanksgiving, Jim walks out of court a free man.

"I had nothing to do with Lita's death," he says into a TV camera on his way out of the courthouse. His emotionless delivery is slow and deliberate, like he's rehearsed this script, maybe practiced it in front of a mirror. He seems honest and almost gentle, and his quiet voice and the lilt of his New England accent makes him seem smart, even likable. "Her death was a great tragedy and I thank God—and my attorneys—that this ordeal is over." He turns to his lawyer, Richard Lubin, and they share a smile. It's both disturbing and somehow convincing. Watching it out of context you might feel relieved for him, believe that justice has, in fact, been served.

CHAPTER 24

WRONGFUL DEATH
(1993–1998)

After the federal dismissal, Jim enjoys freedom before facing his next legal hurdle. Despite herculean efforts by his lawyer Richard Lubin to get the gun charges resulting from the FBI raid thrown out, in June 1993 Jim pleads guilty to possession of firearms and is once again sentenced to eighteen months house arrest, followed by forty-two weeks probation. No jail time. It's another relatively cushy sentence—between 10 A.M. and 10 P.M. he's permitted to go to "work," run errands, hit the gym, or smash a few balls on the tennis court. He wears an ankle monitor and rides around town on a bicycle because he no longer has a driver's license. He spends most of his time meeting bankers and lawyers.

To say the McClintons were crushed by the federal dismissal is a massive understatement. "We had very high hopes and they were dashed by the judge's ruling," says Jo Ann. "We were hurt and disappointed. We were not angry. It takes energy to be angry and we just didn't have the energy to be angry."

Now, all hope rests on the civil wrongful death suit brought by the McClinton attorneys, Brad Moores and David Boone. The case has been on hold pending the outcome of the federal trial. Now, there's a palpable sense of urgency and the lawyers, the McClintons, and investigator Patrick McKenna are chomping at the bit to get going.

"If we can't get him one way," says Jo Ann, "we will try to get him another."

The McClintons and their lawyers believe Jim's wealth and ability to pay for crafty high-priced lawyers got him out of the federal case, so their suit goes after the thing he cares about most: his money. Unlike in a criminal case, where a guilty verdict means a prison sentence, a guilty verdict in a civil case results in a monetary award.

The lesser burden of proof in a civil case is also in their favor. In civil court, a jury can convict if there is a "preponderance of evidence," unlike in a criminal case, where a jury must decide guilt "beyond a reasonable doubt." In other words, if a whole bunch of circumstantial evidence points to the very likely scenario that someone hired a hitman to kill his wife, say, a jury in a civil case can find that person guilty. In a criminal case, like the federal trial in Atlanta, a jury—or in this case a judge—could say all that damming circumstantial evidence means nothing if you can't prove, beyond a reasonable doubt, that this guy hired someone to kill his wife.

Ironically, investigator Pat McKenna's office is down the hallway from the office of Jim's lawyer Richard Lubin. McKenna sees Jim a lot, watches as he steals postage stamps and office supplies from his lawyer while using his photocopier. They're civil, barely, but McKenna can't stand Jim and thinks it's astonishing that he is once again a free man.

One night, Jim, who has no license and is technically under house arrest, has the audacity to ask McKenna for a ride home—even though he knows McKenna is working for Lita's family. McKenna's surprised that Jim would ask, but even more surprised when he hears himself say sure. The whole ride Jim yammers on, arguing about the merits of a certain brand of scotch. "He's talking like I don't know shit and he's some sort of aficionado," says McKenna. "The arrogance of this guy is just incredible."

Lubin lobbies to get the wrongful death charges dismissed, claiming the charges fell outside of Florida's two-year statute of limitations. Under the criminal justice system, there is no statute of limitations on murder, but in the civil justice system, the family has a finite amount of time to bring charges. In Florida, it's two years. Given that Lita was killed in 1987, Lubin argues, the ability to file a wrongful death suit should've expired in 1989. Moores, with the help of appellate attorney Richard Kupfer, argues the statute shouldn't apply because Jim had deliberately covered up his role in the crime.

Lubin tries another approach, saying Emory McClinton isn't authorized to bring a wrongful death suit because he isn't the administrator of Lita's estate. Earlier, Jim had argued *he* should be the administrator of Lita's estate because he'd been her husband at the time of her death. Emory McClinton had argued *he*, as Lita's father, should be named permanent administrator. A probate court had denied both requests and appointed Fulton County as the permanent administrator of Lita's estate. Moores tells the court that the administrator would happily ratify the suit.

All of Lubin's attempts at dismissal fail. For McKenna, running into Jim at the office becomes markedly less cordial. One day, Jim wags a finger in McKenna's face, raging about the civil suit and attacking McKenna for working against him.

"I remember saying to him, 'if you ever stick your fucking finger in my chest again, I'll throw you off this balcony,'" says McKenna. This is the last time they pretend to tolerate each other.

❖

The civil trial begins on Valentine's Day, 1994, seven years after Lita's murder. Just days before the trial begins, Jim suddenly fires his lawyer, Richard Lubin. He claims indigence, saying he lacks the funds to get proper representation. Instead, he says, he'll represent himself.

"I think it was a strategic decision," says Moores. "I think the strategy was that in a trial against two lawyers, a jury might feel sorry for him, might give him the benefit of the doubt."

In his opening address to the jury, Jim, two months shy of his fifty-third birthday, leans into the lectern and looks the jurors in the eyes. ". . . it is terrible to be wrongly accused of murder, to have to live through that and with that is another form of death, another form of murder of the spirit." Waving over in the McClintons' direction, he says losing a child "is the worst thing that can ever happen to a parent." He adds that though he was only a "mere husband," losing a wife violently "is the worse thing that can happen to a husband."

He plays up the fact that on his side, there's just him and his yellow notepad. On the other side are three lawyers in suits, plus Emory and Jo Ann, McKenna—all these people gunning for him. He fumbles along, apologizing that he can't afford to have someone there taking notes.

"Simply because I was going through a divorce from Suki—I mean from Lita—in no way cancels out the feelings that I had," he says, seemingly unfazed by his gaff. Amazingly, he's done it again. It was just a few years ago when he invoked Lita's name instead of Suki's in his divorce trial. "A woman I married because, and solely because, I loved her."

The McClintons feel sick. In the years since Lita's death, Jim has never once shown remorse, let alone spoken of his love for their daughter. He's completely relinquished his own children and seems woefully uninterested in anyone other than himself. They are witnessing a performance, watching Jim embody his arrogance like an actor under a crown of thorns.

"We all know the resources the government has put into this thing—the FBI, the Atlanta Police Department, the GBI, and the Palm Beach County State Attorney's Office," continues Jim. "If there was any way I was truly responsible for Lita's death, I would not be standing here today."

Like the doomed federal murder-for-hire trial, the civil trial is full of impassioned testimony. Emory describes his daughter as a take-charge kind of person, outgoing, the kind of individual everyone enjoyed being around. Jo Ann says Lita was trusting and empathetic. "When a friend fell off her bicycle and scraped her knees, Lita cried," Jo Ann says, tearing up at the memory. "Basically, that was Lita."

The McClintons tell the jury they never got so much as a note from Jim after Lita's murder. "We heard from his former wife. She called and his children called. They sent flowers but I have yet to hear from Mr. Sullivan," Jo Ann says.

The jury hears of the phone calls between Jim's home and the HoJo's, the collect call to Jim's house from the Georgia rest area, the roses and the man who delivered them. They hear testimony from FBI special agent Todd Letcher about how Jim's obsessive notes detailing Suki's whereabouts bordered on stalker behavior, about how he'd confessed the murder to Suki and to Paul O'Brien, the convicted robber who had broken Sullivan's nose in jail.

Jim has taken the Fifth Amendment, asserting his right to protect himself against incrimination, so he will not testify, nor can he be questioned by the McClintons' attorneys. But because Jim is representing himself, he gets to question Emory and Jo Ann McClinton on the witness stand.

"I know this must be difficult for you," Jim says to Emory.

"No, you don't know," Emory replies.

Jim, hinting at his worn suggestion that the McClintons arranged their eldest daughter's murder in order to reap a $250,000 life insurance payout, asks Lita's father, "Why would a perfectly healthy woman take out such a large policy shortly before her death?"

Emory looks Jim in the eye. "I don't know," he says, shaking his head. "I have no idea."

Later, Emory will tell reporters, "It was horrible to be questioned by the killer of your daughter. I don't think anybody can imagine what that's like."

❖

The closing arguments are brief. Jim proclaims his innocence. He's just as much a victim, he says, and the wrongful death suit "pitting victim against victim is to disfigure Lita's memory." He pleads with the three-man, three-woman jury: "Do not allow this victimization to continue. Please stop this slow death. Please vote my innocence."

Does the jury buy Jim's bluster and play-acting? Do they view him as a lonely widower wrongly accused by a broken system? Do they feel sorry for him, a simple man overpowered by lawyers? After all of Jim's begging and pleading, the jury takes just three hours to deliberate. Jo Ann and Emory hold hands and weep as the verdict is read. The years of sorrow and long days of having to watch their former son-in-law feign love for their beloved daughter are just too much to bear.

On February 23, 1994, the jury, applying the lesser burden of proof required in civil matters, finds Jim guilty of murder and concealment of murder. Guilty. Finally, guilty. Jim is ordered to pay the McClintons $3.5 million in compensatory damages, and another $500,000 in punitive damages, a total of $4 million. It's a huge victory for Lita's family, for McKenna, Moores, Boone, and Kupfer, and for precedent in future cases.

"For us, it was never about the money," says Jo Ann. "We wanted Jim to be held accountable for what he did to our daughter." Emory vows to continue his efforts to have criminal charges brought against Jim in Georgia. His lawyer, Brad Moores, agrees.

"We hope this will move the needle for Georgia authorities to reopen the criminal case," Moores tells reporters. "We think there's a good chance of it with this jury's verdict."

In the *Palm Beach Daily News*, the "Shiny Sheet" where Jim and Suki used to flash their bleached white teeth while wearing tuxes and shimmery gowns, is a photo of Jim looking grim-faced as the verdict is read. What must be going through his head as he hears the words "guilty" and "four million dollars"?

❖

What's going through his head is how soon he'll be able to appeal. Now quick to hire top Miami attorneys, Jim immediately appeals the civil court decision, tying the case up in a legal morass for years to come.

His dedication to staying in the legal ring pays off. In 1997, three years after the initial civil court win, the Florida Supreme Court overturns the verdict, ruling the two-year Florida statute of limitations had indeed expired. Once again Jim is off the hook. It's a crushing blow and the McClintons and their supporters are incredulous. Brad Moores and Rick Kupfer are quick to counter appeal. "You shouldn't be able to beat the system because you're clever and fraudulent," reasoned Moores.

Again, they wait.

In early 1998, Jim sells his place in Boynton Beach and buys a condo in Costa Rica. Before he leaves the country, acquaintances see him loading up on canned goods and other supplies at Costco, as though he's planning to disappear.

CHAPTER 25

BELINDA
(JANUARY TO APRIL, 1998)

Belinda Trahan, now thirty-nine, lives on a farm with a controlling ex-con husband and spends her days working as a receptionist at a small law office in Beaumont, Texas. She mainly answers phones and photocopies documents for attorney Ed Lieck, who defends clients throughout rural Texas. Her son Jimmy, now an adult, lives with his own family in Oklahoma. It has been eleven years since Lita's murder, and a long time since Belinda left Tony Harwood and Albemarle behind.

A few months after Lita's murder, Belinda moved out of Tony's trailer and rented a small house across from the Albemarle fire station while Jimmy finished school. As soon as she made enough cash, she hightailed it back to Texas.

At first, she heard from Tony frequently. Sometimes he'd show up unannounced, swinging through Texas in his eighteen-wheeler. They'd hook up briefly, then he'd go away again. This went on for about three years, but when they both got married to other people, Tony faded out.

She's relieved to have him out of her life, but she's always nervous he'll resurface again. After all, she knows too much.

One day, in January 1998, Belinda leaves the law office to pick up lunch at Schlotzsky's Deli. When she returns, she doles out sandwiches and tells Ed, "I need to talk to you . . . about something personal."

Ed, who is cranking through a legal brief on a desk strewn with case files, sighs. He shoves some papers aside to make way for his sandwich and tucks a napkin into his collar to ensure no mustard hits his tie. He takes a big bite and motions for Belinda to sit down. "What's up?" he asks through a mouthful of meat.

She looks down at her hands, winds a paper napkin through her fingers, and doesn't say anything.

"Look Belinda," says Ed, wiping his mouth, "I gotta finish this brief. If it can wait . . ."

She launches in. A long time ago, she says, she dated a guy named Tony. They lived in a trailer in North Carolina on his family's land. And Tony, well, he was involved in a murder in Atlanta. Once she starts, it all floods out, the whole story, about how Tony moved furniture for a man in Florida, how the man wanted Tony to kill his estranged wife in Atlanta. The man was white; the woman was Black. She tells him everything, how she'd suggested Tony deliver flowers, how she knew it was real when the man slid an envelope full of cash across the table at a diner somewhere. She's relieved to unload her decade of anxiety, but Ed, with a mountain of stress and a mouthful of salami, is incredulous. He doesn't know what to think.

She goes on, telling him she's been hearing from Tony again. He wants her to meet him this week at a nearby Petro truck stop; after all this time, he wants to talk.

Ed swallows hard and wipes his mouth. "Well, don't do that," he says, still struggling to catch up with this sudden tale. He shoves his sandwich aside and jots notes on a legal pad. Finally, he rubs his eyes and scratches his head. "Look, I need to finish this brief and think about how to handle this. Don't do anything, and definitely don't go meet this guy."

At home that night, he sits down for dinner with his wife, Cheryl, who is also an attorney.

"You're not going to believe what Belinda told me," says Ed, relaying the story, but midway through, Cheryl interrupts him.

"Stop," she says. "I bet I can tell you the rest."

A few days before, while waiting for reruns of *Seinfeld*, Cheryl caught a primetime episode of *Extra!*, a tabloid show covering the cold case of

the 1987 murder of Lita McClinton Sullivan. In it, a lawyer named Brad
Moores and a couple named Jo Ann and Emory McClinton made heartfelt pleas for any information in the killing of their daughter. Ed and Cheryl
start putting pieces together—the flowers, the timing, an interracial
couple, the orchestrated hit. It all jibes with Belinda's story.

The following day Ed makes some calls. First, he reaches the *Extra!*
producers in Los Angeles, who direct him to call authorities. He tries the
Atlanta Police Department, but they don't know anything about the show,
and all this time later no one's around who can recall the case. He makes
repeated calls to the Fulton County DA's office before hunting down FBI
agent John Kingston, who has long since moved on from Lita's murder. Ed
tells him the story and Kingston's intrigued enough to make a call.

"Bill," he says to his old pal, Assistant U.S. Attorney Bill McKinnon.
"It's John Kingston. Don't toss your Sullivan files just yet."

❖

Georgia Bureau of Investigation inspector Robert Ingram is dubious at
first—after all, they've been chasing unproductive tips for over a decade. The
case has been tried in federal court and in civil court. There's no new evidence, still no gun, still no clues on the hit crew. But when he finally calls Ed
Lieck in Texas, his ears perk up and his pulse quickens. Belinda has intricate
details no one has heard before. He feels it in his bones; this is the real deal.

A month later, on February 27, 1998, Ingram is sitting across from
Belinda and Ed in a room at the Chambers County courthouse in Ana-
huac, Texas. Flanking Ingram is an assistant district attorney from Fulton
County, and an investigator from the Atlanta police. All three know this
woman has information about a potential hitman and can't hide their
eagerness to learn more. Across the table Belinda looks tiny and terrified,
eyes darting, arms folded across her chest, like she doesn't know what side
she's on. She feels her lack of education as these intimidating city men in
suits throw words around she can barely catch, let alone understand. Beside
her Ed, in protective papa-bear mode, taps her knee to reassure her.

Pens poised, recorder rolling, the men lean in, and Belinda starts talking. From 1984 to 1987, she says, she lived in a mobile home on the outskirts of Albemarle, North Carolina, with her boyfriend, a long-haul trucker named Phillip Anthony "Tony" Harwood. In the winter of 1986, Tony returned from a trip to Florida sort of nervous and out of sorts. It was around Thanksgiving. He'd moved some furniture from Macon to Palm Beach, and while she usually went with him, she'd refused to take this particular trip. She couldn't face another long, cold ride.

"After he got back from that trip, he didn't seem the same anymore," she tells the men. She says she assumed he had found another girl somewhere along the way. He'd begun hanging out and going to bars with a guy he referred to only as "The Bartender," which was unusual. Tony was a party-at-home kind of guy and not a big drinker.

"This bartender's name?" Inspector Ingram interjects.

"I have no idea," says Belinda.

"Go on," says Ingram, nodding.

"He said the less I knew about it the better off I'd be," Belinda continues. "I kept at him, asking him what was going on. He finally told me that a rich white man he'd delivered furniture to wanted him to 'take care' of a woman, a Black woman, in Georgia," she says. The men sit frozen, listening intently. "I didn't believe him. 'Take care of her'—what do you mean? I just figured it was his excuse to go out with this bartender guy and go to titty bars or whatever."

The men shift in their seats, look down at their notepads.

"Did he say why he hired Tony to take care of the Black woman?" asks Ingram.

She says Tony had said the people in Palm Beach didn't approve of the interracial marriage. "They were getting a divorce," says Belinda. "She was going to take him for everything he had."

Belinda explains Tony went down to Atlanta twice to do the job. The first time was a bust; they'd been unsuccessful climbing a retaining wall at the back of the property, and when they went to the front and tried ringing the bell, no one came to the door. She says she told Tony that any idiot knows if you want a woman to open a door, all you have to do is bring flowers. She says this was a flippant suggestion, a joke. But the second time he went to Atlanta, he came back and told her, *it's done*. She says she still never believed him, thought it was all just a bunch of tough guy bullshit to cover up a bender.

"And this man in Florida, this 'rich white man,'" says Ingram. "What man are you referring to?"

While it feels scary and surreal to get these words out, she can already feel the pressure of this story, this guilty secret she's been carrying around, finally being released.

"Mr. James Sullivan," Belinda replies, confirming this is the man Tony delivered furniture to in Florida, the same man she'd met in person more than a decade ago.

❖

Ed Lieck quickly sets to work drafting a transactional immunity agreement, which will protect Belinda from being convicted of anything related to Lita's murder. He's concerned her suggestion to "get flowers" might prompt an overzealous prosecutor to think she's part of a bigger conspiracy. After all, it doesn't look great. If she knew about the murder, why'd she wait till now to say anything? Her confession is timed perfectly with the *Extra!* show, even though she swears she hasn't seen it. She says it took her so long to come forward because she feared for her and Jimmy's lives; if she talked, she thought, Tony would hunt her down and kill her.

Fulton County district attorney Paul Howard signs the immunity agreement that day, releasing Belinda to tell the entire story without fear of prosecution.

When Agent Ingram, who is on the doorstep of retirement, returns to Atlanta, he hands Belinda's file to Special Agent John Lang. After a decade of one limp lead after another, they finally have a firm lead, and he needs someone with energy to go chase it down.

He tells Lang, "She's the real deal. Go get her."

❖

Special Agent John Lang was a former marine and Georgia state trooper before he joined the Georgia Bureau of Investigation and became a top criminal profiler. At six foot four, he's imposing, with thick hair, chiseled features, and a swagger like a winning football coach. He's a commanding good ol' boy, a Georgia native who cracks f-bombs like peanut shells and makes no apologies for taking up space in the world. He prides himself on eagle-eyeing every aspect of a crime scene, seeing things and asking questions others don't. Lang's father was also a marine, then a sheriff's deputy and private investigator. Young John would tag along with his dad on surveillance details, work the video camera as they spied on adulterous spouses or committers of insurance fraud. Once, John was riding around on his bicycle and spotted a guy who was supposed to be bedridden with back pain muscularly mowing his lawn. John sped home to tell his father; he knew right then his calling was to investigate crimes and bust bad guys.

Death fascinated Lang. He'd go to the morgue for fun.

"I wanted to learn every aspect of death," he told me. He found it enthralling to learn what motivated people to do horrendous things. By the end of his career, he'd witnessed hundreds of autopsies, reconstructed untold crime scenes.

So, in March of 1998, he's more than happy to go stir some shit up in Texas.

❖

After the first meeting with Belinda and Ed Lieck, things move quickly. Agent Lang partners with Atlanta homicide detective Steve Balkcom and they head to Texas to show Belinda a photo lineup in the hopes she'll identify Jim Sullivan.

Belinda plans to meet the investigators with Ed at the courthouse, but Ed's running late. She doesn't want to go alone, so she stops at a Mexican restaurant to kill time. She orders a margarita to calm her nerves and pops a valium, thinking it will help. She slurps down a second margarita before driving over to the courthouse. When she meets Lang in person for the first time, he towers over her.

Lang smiles and assures her everything will be OK. Detective Balkcom doesn't smile or say much; a good five inches shorter than Lang, he's clearly not the alpha here. They are all a little anxious with the weight of the moment. If Belinda positively identifies Jim as the man she met in the diner, then the whole house of cards could finally fall.

They sit down and Lang pulls out the photo lineup, a single sheet of paper containing six black-and-white mugshots. He slides it over to Belinda but immediately pulls it away when he catches a whiff of booze on Belinda's breath. He looks at Balkcom, tips his hand near his mouth, the international symbol for drinking. Balkcom nods; they can't do this now.

"Miss Trahan, have you been drinking?" asks Lang sternly. Her eyes widen as she looks over at Ed and nods. She was nervous, she says, so she had a couple margaritas. She's never done anything like this before. Lang, swearing under his breath, pulls a smile, not wanting to scare her more.

"It's OK, Sweetheart. Just let Ed here take you home and sleep it off," says Lang, adding that they'll reconvene in the morning. He nods at Ed and frowns, a silent command: *don't let her fuck this up.*

The next day, before showing her the photo lineup again, Lang confirms she's consumed no cocktails, popped no pills. Shaking and nervous, a sober Belinda studies the photo lineup carefully. At first, she says the person in position #3 looks familiar. In the upper right-hand corner of this checkerboard of men, photo #3 shows a man with a slight smirk and curly hair. Several minutes go by until Belinda taps her fingernail right on Jim Sullivan's face. She nods at the investigators. "I'm sure that's him."

Now, they need to get Tony.

❖

A month before Belinda sat down with Agent Lang, Tony Harwood sent her a letter. Of course, Tony knew nothing of her conversations with

Ed or the cops or the FBI, but he likely knew about the *Extra!* show and could feel the heat coming on. In the letter, he doesn't mention anything about Lita or James Sullivan, "The Bartender," the money, or the murder. Instead, he complains his wife doesn't love him the way he wants, like Belinda used to.

"I cherish our moments and at times still long to hold you and taste your lips," he writes. "Your smile lingers in my memory even after all this time." He reminds her of their passionate sex life and asks her to send a recent photo of herself, preferably naked. He wants, it seems, to get back with her—maybe as a way to ensure she keeps her mouth shut. "You were my friend, someone I came to trust and giving you my trust was everything," he continues. After all these years, he says, he still loves her.

As part of her immunity agreement, Belinda must set up an oral intercept device—a bug—on her home phone and Ed's office phone. She begins calling Tony, talking to him like a conspirator, under the guise of helping him get more information about the *Extra!* show and how the investigation has been reignited.

Unbeknownst to Tony, Special Agent John Lang is listening too.

Saturday, April 11, 1998 (transcript excerpts):
TH: Hello.
BT: Hey. You told me to call you back if I found out anything else.
TH: Hold on. Let me get on another phone. OK.
BT: Where's your wife?
TH: Sitting in the living room.
BT: What are you going to tell her?
TH: Nothing.

Belinda tells him the news program said three guys rented a room at a Howard Johnson's in Atlanta. He hasn't seen the *Extra!* show. These are the days before on-demand, so you'd have to wait to see a rebroadcast.

TH: Three?

BT: Three.

TH: Huh.

BT: They're calling this the 'Flower Box Murder.'

TH: Yeah.

BT: And they've got a composite on there. Three of 'em. I've never seen the dark-haired ones but one of them looks just like—it's you. Someone's ID'd you, OK? You need to know that. It looks just like you, Tony.

TH: Well, that's impossible.

He says his wife, Donice, also saw the composite on TV and commented that it favors him, but still he's never told her anything about the case or his role in it, despite the fact they've been married eight years. Tony asks Belinda to mail a copy of the drawing and other materials she has to his mother's house, marked PRIVATE so no one else will read it. She tells him to look it up on a computer, but he says he doesn't have one. She tells him she can't be photocopying and sending stuff at work. She needs to get him talking, so she says:

BT: They say police found fingerprints on the flower box.

TH: Well, there can't be no fingerprints.

BT: There can't be? All right. Well, were you at the hotel? That sounds familiar, right?

TH: Well no, that ain't even right. And the number of people is wrong.

BT: Oh. Well maybe I got the wrong thing. But the picture looks like you. I haven't seen you in a while, but it damn sure looks like you at the time.

TH: Yeah. What's the other guy look like?

BT: He's got dark hair and a beard and . . . He looks like Charles Manson or something.

TH: So, it's long hair?

BT: Spooky looking guy.

TH: Wearing glasses or anything?

BT: No.

TH: Look, the main thing is that you don't know nothing. You can't testify to nothing. You seen nothing. You heard nothing.

BT: All right.

TH: You know nothing.

BT: Well, I don't.

Tony tells her not to worry. He wonders why the cops are digging in again, and she tells him she guesses they want Sullivan. She asks him about the bartender, and he tells her, "That was just a bunch of smoke," a cover so she wouldn't find out he was going to strip bars, the very thing she'd accused him of at the time.

BT: Now you're telling me you *were* going to titty bars that whole time?

TH: Well, there wasn't too many other places to go at that time of night.

BT: Well, I'll be damned Tony.

TH: Well, don't get out of shape about it.

There's a long pause while both figure out what to say next.

BT: I just never figured it was really real.

TH: Oh yeah. It was real. I live it every day.

BT: Geez.

TH: Sometimes I cry myself to sleep at night thinking about it.

Monday, April 13, 1998 (transcript excerpts):

Tony asks Belinda if she's put anything in the mail yet. She tells him no. Tony has no experience with computers and, at the time, the idea of googling something is beyond him.

TH: Well, I just been thinking and—like I said, what's gonna happen is gonna happen and you ain't got nothing to worry about cause your name will never come up.

BT: What about the time we went to that restaurant and picked up the money?

TH: Don't make no difference. He still don't know your last name. He thinks your last name is my last name.

BT: All right. OK.

TH: I've thought about it and thought about it and thought about it since we first spoke.

BT: God, I've been thinking about it too.

TH: Well. There's nothing you have to worry about whatsoever.

BT: Uh-huh. Well—

TH: I would never do anything to hurt you in any way.

She tells him she's at work, can't talk right now. He ignores her.

TH: You got more stuff I want to hear? Lay it on me real quick.

BT: That *Extra!* show said the woman's name was Lita.

TH: I don't know.

BT: Sullivan's wife's name was Lita. OK?

TH: Right.

BT: They said the murder took place in Atlanta.

TH: All right.

BT: And it showed a composite of you and that other guy that I told you looked like Charles Manson.

TH: Right.

She tells him to speak up, but he can't. He's on the phone in the yard and doesn't want Donice to hear the conversation, says she's already suspicious and keeps asking who he's talking to. Belinda can feel him getting antsy. Fear flutters in her chest—does he know he's being recorded?

She tells him Sullivan was tried in civil court and ordered to pay Lita's family $4 million. He knows about it, but not the details. Belinda suggests that's why there's renewed interest in the case.

TH: He's stupid as shit. If he pays it off it would be the best thing he could do and let it die away. If he'd done paid them, we'd been done with it.

Again, they discuss how the police found fingerprints on the flower box.

TH: You said they found fingerprints?
BT: Fingerprints on the flowers. You told me that you bought . . .
I don't know what kind of flowers you bought . . . Did you buy a flower box or just flowers?
TH: A flower box.
BT: That's why they're calling it the 'Flower Box Murder' then.
TH: All right.
BT: There must be a fingerprint on the damn box.
TH: Ain't mine.
BT: Well, they showed a lot of shit on there. Remember when you told me that y'all went there and there was a big wall? You know, around the condo?
TH: Yeah. Right.

This is a huge moment for the investigators. They now have Tony admitting he bought the flowers, admitting he was at the scene, and that he'd told Belinda about the retaining wall at the back of the condo. She tells him again that an eyewitness had described the shooter, that the composite looks just like him.

TH: They couldn't've seen me cause I wasn't there.
BT: Well, that's what I hear on TV or read on this damn computer . . .
TH: The main thing is just keep yourself quiet. Cause you know more than what you did. You're still involved.
BT: How am I involved?
TH: You took part of the money and you knew what it was for. So just keep yourself out of it. Just keep quiet.

At this point, Belinda feels afraid. What if Tony comes after her, what if he finds out the cops are listening in? What if the cops change their minds and cancel her immunity agreement? But Tony seems unfazed and tells her about the Wachovia bank account they'd set up in her name, where he deposited $7,500. She says she doesn't remember any of this, and he suggests she was out of her mind on drugs at the time and not paying attention. He says the money may still be in the account. She's surprised by this and talks about how she had to scrimp to get by after she left him, had to work two jobs just to get enough money to feed her son and get back to Texas. Why didn't he tell her about the money then? He suggests she come up to North Carolina to see if it's still in the bank. She says she can't. She's married now and can't just take a road trip. Belinda sighs.

TH: Drop me a line, send me a picture of you. I want a new picture. Send me some good naked pictures.
BT: Yeah, right.

They talk a couple more times, but Agent Lang is already licking his lips. After listening to Belinda's recording, he calls Detective Balkcom at the Atlanta Police.

"Steve," he says. "Pack your bags. Let's go get this motherfucker."

CHAPTER 26

TONY'S ARREST
(APRIL 1998)

While Agent Lang has Tony on tape admitting he bought the flowers and divulging he was at the scene of the crime, he still has nothing concrete tying Tony to Jim—no evidence of money exchanging hands, or that the men ever met other than Belinda's recollection about meeting Jim at the diner in Florida. She'd been using drugs heavily at the time, and her credibility is shaky. Any good defense attorney could say she'd watched the *Extra!* show and made the rest up to reap the substantial reward for information leading to the arrest of Lita's killer. Lang has already contacted all the banks in Albemarle to find a paper trail, but none of them have records of Tony or Belinda having accounts—and if they ever did exist, the records have long since been purged. He found a receipt for a down payment on a used '78 Buick Riviera Tony'd bought for Belinda shortly after the murder, but nothing shows where Tony got that money. Then Lang remembers how Belinda told them that Tony drove a truck for North American Van Lines at the time they were living together in Albemarle. He finds the number for the trucking company and calls the owner.

"Good afternoon," says Lang. "I'm wondering if a man named Phillip Anthony Harwood—goes by Tony—worked for you in the late 1980s?"

Lang doesn't want the owner to tip Tony off, so he makes up a story about how Tony may have been a witness to a fatality down in Macon back then.

"Oh sure, Tony worked for us," says the owner.

Lang asks him if he happens to keep any records.

"I've tossed a lot of them but still have some up in my attic," he says. "It's a mess up there but feel free to come take a look."

Lang and Balkcom, who've already made the trip up to North Carolina, drive over right away.

Up in the attic, dusty boxes sit stacked against the windowless walls, and the air is insufferably hot. Lang thinks his chances of finding anything are slim, but he rolls up his sleeves, squeegees his brow, and opens the first box. Nothing. The second, nothing. But when he opens the third, he strikes gold.

"Steve, look at this fucking thing!" His hands shake he's so excited, barely believing his good luck. He shows Detective Balkcom an invoice with Tony Harwood's name on it, dated November 21, 1986—less than three weeks before Lita's murder. The invoice, sitting in a box in this sweaty attic after all these years, is the paper trail they've been searching for. On the invoice, casually scrawled in black ink: James Sullivan's name, address, phone number, and signature. Paydirt.

❖

By the time Lang and Balkcom and a handful of local police knock on Tony Harwood's door, they know all about him. They've been casing the house he shares with Donice and her two kids, a humble single-story home, near the intersection of Austin and Efird Streets in Albemarle, with white siding, brown roofing shingles, and a detached garage. They know he spent seven years in prison for burglary and attempted escape (twice) in the 1970s. They know he has three brothers and a sister. He's forty-seven years old. He's still a long-haul trucker and has a reputation as a loner who likes to tinker with old cars, like the classic 1963 Ford Galaxie convertible sitting in the yard. They know he's had some brushes with the law, but he's kept fairly clean ever since he got married in 1990 and found Jesus.

It's 8:50 A.M. on Sunday, April 19, 1998. In a while, Tony will be heading to church with Donice and her kids, but he's not dressed yet, still in his pajamas. He hears the knock on the door and opens it wide. He takes in the cops and the guys in suits and leans against the doorframe. He knows exactly what this is.

He tells Agent Lang, "I've been waiting for you boys for a long time."

Lang asks Tony to come to the Albemarle police station, and he does so willingly. He folds into the back seat of Lang's black Crown Victoria, unrestrained, and they drive the short distance to the station.

They sit in a small interview room, not much bigger than a broom closet. Prior to Tony's arrest, Lang printed out signs that said "Harwood Homicide" and "Homicide Task Force" and taped them to empty cardboard boxes and filing cabinets, all to make Tony believe they have a whole lot more than they do, to rattle him before they even begin.

Tony sits—leg splayed, knees bouncing—on a metal chair on one side of a metal table bolted to the floor. His crossed arms are the size of tree trunks, hands baseball mitts, fingers thick sausage links. He's compliant, friendly. Lang sits across from him, his hand strategically placed on a thick folder. Balkcom stands behind Tony, leaning against the wall beside a chair he'll periodically sit in throughout the day. The only daylight comes through a window in the closed door. Tony can't see out.

They chat for a bit, about last night's fog, about how it'll be good to get all this squared away. But the air becomes thicker once the interview starts.

For the audio recording, Lang says, "I'm Special Agent John Lang with the Georgia Bureau of Investigation. This is detective Steve Balkcom with the Atlanta Police Department. Before we talk, we just want to go over some things . . . you have the right to remain silent. Anything you say can be used against you in a court of law. You have the right to talk to a lawyer and have him present with you while you are being questioned. If you cannot afford a lawyer, one will be appointed to represent you for any questioning, and you can decide at any time to exercise your right not to answer any questions or make any statements."

The shootin'-the-shit part of this conversation is clearly over.

Tony wipes his palms on his legs, his eyes blink faster as heat warms his cheeks. He needs a cigarette. "So, at any time I can stop and say I want an attorney?" says Tony. "Cause I don't want any bullshit because my brother just got locked up for something that he didn't really—well, he did, but . . ."

Lang confirms he can ask for a lawyer at any time.

"I'm between a rock and a hard place," says Tony, shifting in his seat. "Do either of you smoke?"

"Yeah," says Lang. "But you can't smoke here. Public building and all."

Tony grunts and thinks maybe it's OK. Maybe this won't take long. Maybe he'll be out in a couple of hours, explain everything to Donice, eat a big breakfast, and get some forgiveness at church.

"Mr. Harwood, the reason we're talking to you is that there's been a television program about a murder that happened down in Atlanta in 1987," says Lang. He tells Tony there are composite drawings created from eyewitness accounts, and one of them looks just like Tony. Tony asks to see the picture and Lang pats the folder, still closed beside him. He says he'll show it to him later. For now, he wants Tony's side of the story.

Tony takes a deep breath. "So, this Sullivan guy . . ." he begins. He tells Lang about how he moved furniture from Macon to Palm Beach in November 1986. How, while his hired laborers were working, he began chatting with Jim.

"For some reason everybody wants to dump on me about all their dadgum problems and crap," says Tony. "He told me he had a problem with an ex-wife, and she was going to take him through the hoop. He said he really needed somebody to take care of her. I said, 'what do you mean take care of her?' and he said, 'you know, get her out of the way.'" Tony looks Lang in the eye. "And, you know." He shrugs. "I've been in prison."

Lang nods, Balkcom doesn't move.

"I looked at this guy and saw a chump," continues Tony. "I thought, I can take this guy for a loop. So, I said I'll take care of her for $25,000. He

kind of looked at me and said, 'You have someone who could do it?' I just
winked at him."

A couple of weeks later, Tony says two certified checks totaling half
the money arrived in the mailbox at his doublewide on his parents'
property in Finger.

"What did you do with the checks?" asks Lang.

"Cashed 'em," says Tony, obviously. He says he cashed the checks at a
Wachovia bank in downtown Albemarle. He says he spent the money a little
at a time, paid some bills. He fails to mention the $1,200 down payment he
put down on the Riviera for Belinda. Doesn't mention Belinda at all.

Lang asks about the rest of the payment and Tony says he met with Jim
at a motel, or maybe a restaurant, in Florida, he can't remember.

"If someone would give me some money, I certainly would remember
where it was, a substantial amount of money," says Lang. "How did things
go down?"

"I was sitting at a restaurant," says Tony, again not mentioning Belinda.
"He came in. We went to the bathroom and made the exchange." He says
the money was in a white envelope, mostly hundreds, that Jim had tucked
in his sock. "We sat back down, had a cup of coffee, and he left then I
left." He says Jim looked "sloppy," wearing shorts, flip-flops, and a shirt.
"Looked like somebody from Florida," he says.

He tells the investigators that soon after the first money arrived three
guys wearing suits came to his house. At first, he thought they were cops,
or FBI or CIA, but then he thought maybe the mafia. From behind Tony,
Balkcom looks up. He and Lang exchange glances, curious.

Tony says the men instructed him to drive down to Atlanta and meet
them at a restaurant. He drove his brown Buick Skylark to Atlanta—about
a five-hour drive—early in the morning, before daybreak. He said two men
walked into the restaurant and instructed Tony to buy flowers at the florist
next door as soon as it opened at 8 A.M. Then they told him to get into a
small white car waiting outside. Tony, a lifelong car guy, can't recall the
make or model. He says the keys were in the ignition and a third man, who
was waiting in the back seat, gave him directions to a condo development,

told him to park against a big concrete wall outside of Lita's condo and wait. The man from the back seat, who Tony says was a chunky guy wearing glasses, pulled on a ski mask, took the flowers, and left the car. A couple of minutes later, he came back running at full speed and jumped into the passenger seat. "He had a blue ski mask on," says Tony, and it was spattered with blood. "Jumped in the car and said 'drive.'" The two of them drove forty miles up I-85N to the rest area in Suwanee. The man wore the ski mask the whole time. Tony says he used his calling card to call Sullivan's house in Florida. While he was on the phone, the guy in the bloody ski mask jumped in the driver's seat and took off.

It's an understatement to say Lang and Balkcom are dubious of this story.

Tony says he thumbed it back to North Carolina. A few days later, his friend drove him back to Atlanta to pick up the Buick Tony had driven there. But Lang and Balkcom can't confirm this story—the friend killed himself with a shotgun in 1995.

Lang peppers Tony with questions: the color of the car, the flowers, the cost of the flowers, the shop, about the guys. Tony doesn't remember a lot of details—after all, it was eleven years ago. Lang suggests Tony doesn't remember things because he was so jacked up on cocaine, that it's convenient he got a ride from a guy who's not around to verify anything.

"Got any coffee?" Tony asks. Balkcom says he'll see if he can rustle up some but doesn't move.

"Well, I think we got some problems," says Lang. "And you know you're not telling us the whole truth on this matter, Tony."

"I'm telling you everything I know."

"Well, I'll tell you this. I know you made another trip to Atlanta." Lang's trying to get Tony to admit to the first attempt three days prior to the murder.

"Not on this," says Tony. "No way Jose. I go to Atlanta a lot. I was going down there to titty bars, but—"

"Where in Atlanta? Let's do this now," says Lang, getting annoyed. "If you feel it's necessary to tell something that's not true, then just don't say anything at all, OK?" Balkcom leaves the room and returns with black coffee in a paper cup. Tony thanks him, rips open two packets of sugar, and gently stirs it with a brown plastic stir stick. Afterward, he slides the stick into his cheek, chews it like a stalk of wheat.

"We know quite a bit about Tony Harwood," says Lang. "Since we've been down here working on this task force, we've been digging up information on you." Lang looks Tony straight in the eye. "I want you to be honest about it, be man enough to accept responsibility for this."

Tony chomps the stir stick, knees bouncing.

Lang continues, "You got caught up in a situation where this man used you, he took advantage of you. He's a very wealthy man and he took advantage of someone who's not in the same ballpark as him, financially, educationally. He used you to have his wife murdered. He put you out front and you're the scapegoat on this thing."

"Where does that leave me?" asks Tony, his face flushing as surprise tears spring to his eyes. He clenches his jaw to will the emotions away.

Lang tells him, don't protect anyone. It's time to talk.

"I don't remember. I'm serious," says Tony. He says he doesn't remember staying at the Howard Johnson, or calling Sullivan, or even the day of the murder. "I have been . . . ever since I found out about the composite on the TV, I've been racking my brains trying to figure out dates and times, events. Because I knew you was coming."

"How did you find out about the composite on TV?" asks Lang, wondering if Tony will bring up Belinda.

"A friend of mine called me and told me about it."

"Well, what about the eyewitness that identified you as being the person that delivered the flowers?" asks Lang. "How can that be mistaken?" Lang opens his folder and pulls out a sheet of paper with the composite drawing of the shooter, based on Lita's neighbor Bob Christenson's description. The man in the drawing has a long, clean-shaven face, a prominent nose, and thick lips. His eyes are close-set and deep, hair receding.

"Wheew, rough looking. Yeah, it does look a lot like me," admits Tony. "I hope my mama don't see that." He says that, despite the resemblance, it isn't him. The witness, he says, must be a liar.

Lang tells him he'll have to participate in a photo lineup.

"Well, like you said, I'm up shit creek anyhow, so it don't really matter."

Lang asks him what he was wearing in Atlanta on the day of the murder.

"I have no idea," says Tony.

"How would you normally dress?" asks Lang.

"Hat, jacket, and boots. Dress like a cowboy. I always dress like a cowboy." He says he only started wearing glasses recently when he had a cataract removed.

Lang pivots. "Who had the gun?"

"I guess he did 'cause I sure didn't. I ain't never owned a gun."

"You haven't?"

"Nope. Don't want one. I guess it's against the law. Since I've been out of prison, I make it a habit not to break the law . . . I'm a truck driver. I cheat on log books, but other than that . . ."

Balkcom, who has been patiently sitting behind Tony, sometimes pacing, looking up, down, listening intently, and exchanging glances with Lang, interrupts. "How many shots did you hear before he came back to the car?"

"Two."

"Were they rapid shots?"

"Don't know what you call rapid," says Tony. "You know, it was like: Boom. Boom."

"How long after you heard those two shots did he get back to the car?"

"Wheew. Well, my heart was beating a thousand miles an hour. I don't know—a minute, thirty seconds."

"What did you say?"

"Nothing."

"So you knew what had happened?"

"Yeah," says Tony. "I knew what was gonna happen before I got there."

❖

As Tony's earlier visions of a breakfast at home begin to fade, Lang asks him if he'd give permission for the cops to search his house. Tony says yes and signs the waiver.

"Do me a favor," says Tony. "Call my wife and tell her you're coming." His wife, he says, will be pissed by all this. His mama will be so disappointed.

"You can't imagine the nights I wake up in the truck crying."

"Why?" asks Lang.

"Cuz I ain't got prayer one," says Tony. He begins to weep. He knows his story doesn't add up, but he longs for the burden of it to be taken off his shoulders. "Look, I'm trying to be just as straight up as I can remember. I don't give a rat's tail about this Sullivan guy. I don't care what happens to him, it's immaterial. I just . . . I've got a perfect life right now. I've got a wonderful wife and everything. I don't know why God blessed me this way. And why this is coming back to haunt me."

Lang doesn't have time for the waterworks and leaves the room with Balkcom while Tony pulls himself together. When they return, Lang says there's a hard way to go back to Georgia or an easy way, but regardless, Tony will have to face the music in Atlanta. Tony can either waive extradition and return to Georgia or fight the charges and drag it out while being locked up in the Stanly County jail.

"I ain't got a snowball's chance in hell of getting out of this, do I?"

Lang doesn't want him to lose hope and clam up, because he knows there's much more to the story they aren't yet getting. "Probably," he says. "But you gotta tell the truth. My patience is wearing just a little bit here, and I think Detective Balkcom's is too." Balkcom stands there, arms crossed, pissed off, tired, fed up with this nonsense.

They go back and forth again about the hotel, whether it's Tony's handwriting on the hotel registration, why he used the fake name "Johnny Furr," and why, if he was coming to Atlanta to go to strip clubs, would he stay in a motel in Buckhead, miles away from the downtown clubs. To most of the questions, Tony replies that he can't remember.

"Don't take this whole thing by yourself Tony. Don't go down by yourself pal," Lang says. "Let me tell you about a truism we use in police work, and you can live by this: the first one off the bus gets the best deal. And I'm not saying there's any deals, but certainly don't protect anybody else, OK? You have the opportunity to help yourself right now. You're the first one off the bus. If you need to tell on somebody else, tell on them now. But don't leave here taking the whole hit, OK?"

"If I could give you somebody else, don't you think I'd jump on it?"

"You need to think about it then," says Lang. "Because what this tells us is that you're the man."

"I ain't hurt nobody," says Tony.

"Tony, she died fifteen minutes after you bought the flowers," says Balkcom, getting heated. "What are we supposed to think?"

"I don't know," says Tony.

Lang opens his folder and pulls out the list of damning telephone calls between Tony and Jim. "Let me read this to you, it's from my affidavit." Lang tells him the telephone toll records reveal the following:

1. January 13, 1987, 7:44 A.M.: A call lasting between two and three minutes made from room 518 at the Howard Johnson motel on Roswell Rd. to James Sullivan's residence.

2. January 13, 1987, 10:33 A.M.: A call from James Sullivan's residence in Palm Beach to the Howard Johnson motel.

3. January 16, 1987, 9 A.M.: A collect call lasting one minute made from a payphone at the Suwanee rest stop on I-85N to James Sullivan's residence in Palm Beach.

Tony can't remember anything about the motel. He says he uses "Johnny Furr" whenever he needs a fake name. He doesn't know why he wrote that there were three people on the registration. He says he was probably out all night partying and crashed at the hotel. He says maybe he was with two women.

"Who would the women be?" asks Lang. "Dancers?"

"Titty dancers, yeah. I ain't never went to a titty bar I didn't come out with one," he says, winking.

"Did you do any cocaine with them?"

"Probably," says Tony.

Tony admits to meeting Jim and that Jim paid him $25,000. He says yes, he bought the flowers just after 8 A.M. on January 16, and he admits to calling Jim from the Suwanee rest stop. But still, he says, he wasn't the shooter.

"Tony, you need to get this right, get right with the Lord," says Lang.

"I've already got right with the Lord," says Tony. He's getting jumpy now, hungry, tired, confused.

"If you're not the shooter, and I seriously believe that you are, OK—then Tony why would you not . . . Did he ever say what race this lady was?"

"No," says Tony.

"He never told you she was a Black woman?"

"No."

"You never heard that before from anybody?" asks Lang.

"No. I knew he was white and that's all I knew. I thought maybe she was white woman. I don't know." Tony says he can barely remember last week, let alone eleven years ago.

"Let me tell you something about traumatic things that happen in your life," says Lang. "I'm a Vietnam veteran. I remember very well things that went on in Vietnam. I'm a veteran police officer. Detective Balkcom's a veteran police officer. We have both shot and killed people in the line of duty, all right? Let me tell you something: those details are as clear today as they were back then."

"And if I'd shot that woman then it would be very clear to me too," says Tony.

Lang ignores him and continues, "If you are involved in something like that and you know this woman died, she's going to be killed, she's gonna be executed, you damn sure would remember everything. You would remember from the get-go when this thing started." Lang's getting heated too. He wants justice for Lita's family. He wants a drink but knows he can't buy even a beer in this goddamn dry county. He wants to finally go and arrest Sullivan and then take a vacation, get a break, kiss his wife.

"I box like a heavyweight," says Tony. "I know a lot of martial arts. I could hurt anybody I want to without any type of gun or knife or anything. But I just can't hurt people. I might slap you; I might hit you, but as far as hurting you—uh uh. Because at the sight of blood, I'm through with it. I cannot hurt nobody. It's not in me."

"Look," says Lang, nodding at Balkcom. "We're on a multiagency task force and I'll tell you what, we know more about Tony Harwood than Tony Harwood knows about Tony Harwood. We know that you're a decent person, that you are a hardworking person now. That your wife loves you and you love your wife. You've straightened your life out. But now it's time to come clean about this case . . . The only hope you've got is to provide the names. Because let me tell you this, if you don't, then you're taking the hit. You're taking the murder charge."

"But I didn't do it," says Tony, and Detective Balkcom makes a long hissing sound, like he's blowing out through clenched teeth. Tony turns to him and says he'd swear on the Bible that he wasn't the shooter, "And I don't do that lightly."

Balkcom grabs the folder on the table and spreads out the crime scene photos. There's the blood-spattered flower box, photos of bullet casings and blood—so much blood. But the most devastating photo shows Lita dead on a hospital table with a bullet wound on the side of her head.

"You think this lady doesn't have a mama and daddy?" says Lang. "You don't think they grieve every day about their daughter dying?"

Tony looks away.

"Look at it," growls Balkcom, slapping the table.

"I ain't looking at it," says Tony. "I have no remorse except for her."

"You have no remorse?" says Balkcom.

"That she's dead, because I didn't do it."

"Come on," says Balkcom. "You want us to believe that you're not the shooter?"

"I am not the shooter," says Tony. "And God as my witness knows I'm not the shooter. Y'all can believe what you want to believe but when I go through them pearly gates, I know. I would give anything if I could tell you who it was."

"If we were sitting in front of a jury today," said Balkcom, "do you know who most likely would be the first one they'd believe killed Lita Sullivan?"

"Me," says Tony. "But I didn't do it."

"When did you find out the lady's name?"

"Just now."

Balkcom is sitting now with his elbows on his knees, leaning in. He rubs his eyes. It's been a long three hours trapped in this stuffy little room, now sour from so much sweating. "So, you killed someone," he says. "And you didn't even know her name."

CHAPTER 27

ON THE RUN
(1998–2002)

After Tony's interview and arrest at the Albemarle police station, he's allowed to meet briefly with his wife, Donice, who is so pissed off she tells authorities that she doesn't know or care what Tony got into in the past, and she doesn't want anything to do with it. In a few months, she'll file for divorce. Before facing the music in Atlanta, he also gets to see his mom, Mary. All she can do is weep.

Tony waives extradition and says he doesn't want a lawyer. Lang and Balkcom drive him to Atlanta, about a five-hour trip with various stops for snacks and bathroom breaks. Tony's friendly and cooperative, talks a lot about cars and long-haul trucking. When they get to Atlanta, they drive by Lita's townhouse so Tony can pinpoint where he parked the day of her murder, the route he drove out of there, where the gun was tossed out the window. But it's been eleven years and it's getting dark, everyone's exhausted—and Tony can't confirm anything in the coming darkness. He gets booked at the Fulton County Jail. Among his personal effects, Lang finds a folded piece of paper in Tony's wallet with Jim Sullivan's name and phone number. How odd: Tony's been carrying this scrap of paper around for more than a decade.

❖

With Tony under arrest and facing charges, newly elected Fulton County district attorney Paul Howard, the county's first Black DA and a man who won his seat with promises to crack down on crime, holds a press conference. He announces Tony Harwood's arrest and tells the media more arrests are imminent. The McClintons and their lawyers are dumbfounded and furious at Howard's announcement—the DA may as well have called Jim to say, "Hey! Heads up, you're about to be arrested."

By this point, Jim has found relative peace in his condo community of Faro Escondido, an exclusive beach resort near the town of Jaco, on the Pacific coast of Costa Rica. He's left alone to do whatever he wants. He frequently drives his brown Jeep Cherokee up the highway to the Pelicano Restaurant, where he's befriended the owner and his family. He occasionally sips wine with neighbors and flirts with women at the pool. Sometimes neighbors see him with an Asian woman but mostly he's alone, save for Coco, the small white dog he takes everywhere.

But it all falls to pieces when they arrest Tony Harwood. It's April 26, just a couple of weeks past Jim's fifty-seventh birthday, when he learns of the warrant out for his arrest. His pulse races as he looks around the luxury condo he's furnished with the few antiques he saved from Casa Eleda and thinks hard about his next move. He knows the walls are closing in.

But the crazy thing is, the authorities don't know where Jim is. His most recent address lists his mother's modest retirement home in Boston. His mother, in her eighties and shaken at the news that her son is a wanted man, says she recently spoke to Jim but refuses to give the cops his phone number. Jim's defense attorney, Don Samuel, says Jim's location is attorney-client privilege, but he assures the press Jim will turn himself in and he will once again be exonerated. But Jim doesn't turn himself in, which surprises even Samuel.

"Paul Howard called and told me they were arresting James Sullivan and I said, 'For what?'" Don Samuel tells Court TV. "And he said, 'We found the hitman.' So I called Jim and he said he wanted a bond, so I called Paul

Howard and he said great, but here's the deal: I'll be seeking the death penalty. I told Jim that they were seeking the death penalty and then: click. I didn't hear from him again for years."

After he hangs up on his lawyer, Jim packs a garment bag and a small suitcase and drives over to Pelicano's. He invites the owner's sister, a young woman named Tatiana, to go on a trip with him to Panama City, where he says he has to pick something up. He says they can go shopping, have a little adventure. She wants to go, but her brother, Fabricio, doesn't want his sister driving all that way alone with Jim, so he says he'll go too. It's a harrowing trip. Jim takes the twelve-hour drive at full speed, swerving around curves and prompting Fabricio to beg him to slow down. When they finally get to Panama City, Jim drives to the airport, takes his bags out of the car, and throws Fabricio the keys.

"I'm not coming back to Costa Rica," he says. He hands Fabricio some money for gas and walks away. Fabricio and Tatiana are so shocked they don't think to ask about his beloved Coco, who's waiting at Tatiana's mother's house. They, and Coco, never hear from Jim again.

When they finally track Jim down in Costa Rica, federal authorities must request an "unlawful flight to avoid prosecution" warrant from a magistrate judge, but by the time the paperwork is complete and the FBI and the U.S. Marshals go to get him, Jim is long gone.

Jim simply vanishes. No one—not his mother, not his lawyers—has any clue where he is. It's as though he vaporized in Panama City. The McClintons and their lawyers keep pressure on the GBI, FBI, and Fulton County District Attorney's office, and they keep the story in the media by offering and upping rewards for information leading to Jim's arrest. *America's Most Wanted*, the popular television show that features reenactments of heinous crimes, devotes an episode to Lita's murder and the hunt for Jim. John Lang and FBI special agent Mike Greene, whose job is to hunt down fugitives, chase the tips that roll in—erroneous sightings of Jim in Vegas,

Florida, Panama. They hear rumors that Jim's in Thailand, but there's no record of him entering the country. They learn that before his arrest, Jim had obtained an Irish passport, so they contact Interpol to look for him, but find no luck in Ireland.

About eighteen months after Jim's disappearance, the Florida Supreme Court reverses Jim's winning appeal in the 1994 civil case and reinstates the $4 million judgment (plus 12 percent interest) that he owes Lita's estate. The McClintons' lawyers successfully argued that, since the murder occurred in Georgia, the case should've abided by that state's statute of limitations, which was five years. Lita's family doesn't want the money, but nor do they want Jim, when he's finally captured, to use their daughter's estate to fund his defense.

"It's blood money," says Jo Ann, going so far as to call his attorneys complicit in his crimes, especially if they stoop to defending him once he's apprehended.

The McClintons' lawyers, who know Jim has money stashed away in offshore accounts, believe the reinstatement of the civil judgment is a big step in stripping Jim of the thing he loves most: money. After all, wherever he is, he's certainly getting money from somewhere.

"I'm optimistic," says appellate attorney Richard Kupfer, admitting he has no clue where in the world Jim Sullivan is. "At some point he'll be careless. At some point he'll make a mistake, and then we'll collect."

Another year passes. By 2000, Jim's landed on the FBI's "Most Wanted" list alongside Eric Rudolph, the felon responsible for Atlanta's Centennial Olympic Park bombing in 1996. The GBI monitors the phones of anyone Jim could potentially call. Prior to his disappearance, he'd make periodic calls to his mother in Boston. But from 1998 to 2002, he calls no one, not even his mom.

On January 14, 2002, as the world is still reeling from the 9/11 terrorist attacks on New York, DC, and Pennsylvania, a brief article in *USA Today* commemorates the fifteenth anniversary of Lita's death. Under Jim's mug shot the caption reads WANTED FOR MURDER. His photo is everywhere: on local and international news programs, plastered in post offices, airports, police stations, and on the FBI's web page. But still, Jim is nowhere to be found.

CHAPTER 28
THAILAND (2002–2004)

Just when it seems Jim is beyond the reach of the long arm of the law, authorities get a break. In May 2002, a man in Thailand watching a rerun of *America's Most Wanted* recognizes the man on TV as the fastidious and cranky American living in his resort community. He calls the police, who alert the FBI. At almost the same time, another tip comes in—someone saw Jim's mug shot on the FBI website and also recalled seeing him in Thailand. Special Agent Robert H. Cahill Jr., the FBI's legal attaché assigned to the embassy in Bangkok, finds no record of Jim having come through the border, but the tips lead authorities to the Springfield Resort in Cha-am, eighty miles south of Bangkok.

The Springfield is a luxury resort with a lagoon-shaped pool, a cabana stocked with fluffy white towels, beachside restaurants, and guards to keep out the riffraff. Jim lives in a lavish two-bedroom apartment overlooking the white sand beaches that rim the cobalt Gulf of Thailand.

The FBI does not have jurisdiction to arrest in another country, so Agent Cahill must work with local authorities to make sure the paperwork is airtight for such a high-stakes international arrest. For two months authorities from the Royal Thai Police and FBI watch Jim as he strolls along the beach, lazes by the pool, plays tennis with one of the hotel's chefs, and reads the finance section of his American newspapers on his big veranda. And he's not alone. Also living in the apartment is Thai-born Chongwattana "Nana" Sricharoenmuang, who once traveled in the same Palm Beach circles as Jim. Her immigration-inspired marriage to Dr. Howard Reynolds, Palm Beach Junior College athletic director and a popular basketball coach, had been amicably dissolved in 2000, although Nana and Jim had hooked up before then.

Through binoculars, the cops note that Jim, now sixty-one, looks tanned and fit, not dissimilar to all the other rich white Americans who've come halfway across the world so they can stretch their dollars and live like royalty under the Thai sun. Nana is often away, for weeks at a time, in the States or visiting family in Bangkok, but Jim doesn't venture far. He gets up late, exercises at the gym, plays the occasional tennis match if he can find a partner. When Nana's home, he drives her to the food market in his late-model BMW. The staff at the resort know him for his stinginess and simmering irritability—he frequently complains about loud neighbors—so they mostly leave him alone.

Every month $1,400 USD drops into Jim's Thai bank account—but how it gets there is uncertain. Regardless, in a country where the average monthly income is $340 USD, he's got plenty of disposable Thai Bahts to throw around, but the couple rarely socializes and mostly eats in. Jim keeps a low profile but has his name on the door of his apartment, as though he isn't the subject of an international manhunt.

Now that the FBI knows where he is, they're able to piece together where he's been. After driving like a maniac over the mountains from Costa Rica to Panama City, he flew to Caracas, Venezuela. A couple of days later he landed in Thailand, where he obtained a retirement visa that allowed him to live there. He'd likely slipped in with his Irish passport before it was flagged. He bought the apartment for an easy $128,000 USD around the time he was indicted for murder, four years ago.

As he smokes his cigar in the evening gauze of the setting sun, he is oblivious to the fact that he will soon be a caged man. If he knew, would he take Nana out for fine wine and fresh prawns? Would he walk into the sea and never look back? Would he flee again? Where would he go?

❖

On July 2, 2002, four Royal Thai Police officers finally knock on Jim's door. Jim and Nana just returned from a stroll on the beach, and Jim is utterly dismayed to see the cops on his doorstep. The police captain tells him he's under arrest for unlawful flight to avoid prosecution and the murder of his wife, Lita McClinton Sullivan. Mouth agape, Jim nods, befuddled and panicked, like he's been told the building's burning, and he must leave now.

He goes willingly, quietly, with Nana following close behind him.

❖

Back in Atlanta, the McClintons had been informed authorities were watching a man in Thailand who appeared to be Jim Sullivan, but they didn't get their hopes up—they'd experienced sightings in the past and knew enough not to climb onto that emotional rollercoaster. But when they get the call from the FBI telling them, finally, they have their former son-in-law in custody, they break down all over again.

"I knew this day would come," Emory McClinton tells *Atlanta Journal-Constitution* reporter Bill Montgomery. "The final chapter on bringing Jim Sullivan to justice has begun, but there will be no final chapter for her mother and myself. We can't bring our daughter back." He says that even all these years later, he'll see a woman on the street or on a television commercial and his heart leaps before his brain kicks in and reminds him, *it can't be Lita.*

❖

Fulton County district attorney Paul Howard tells reporters the day after Jim's arrest, "This is a great day for the family and friends of Lita Sullivan." He confirms his office will seek extradition immediately, and he intends to seek the death penalty.

In Thailand, Special Agent Cahill interviews Jim briefly while he's in police custody at the Crime Suppression Division station in Bangkok before he's transferred to prison, where he'll wait out the extradition process. He reads Jim his Miranda rights.

"Do you understand the charges against you?" asks Agent Cahill.

"I'm shocked at these charges," says Jim. "I was previously exonerated."

"Well, you understand you were indicted in Atlanta four years ago," says Cahill. "There's a warrant out for your arrest."

"I was unaware there were outstanding warrants," says Jim, then shuts it down. He won't say anything further without a lawyer.

Cahill also speaks briefly to Nana, who doesn't offer much. She says although she met Jim in 1995 or 1996, she had no idea his former wife had been murdered, knows nothing about any of it, and that's all she'll say.

Three days after his arrest, Jim makes his first appearance at the Bangkok criminal court. He's wearing khakis and a white striped shirt, still looking like a rich American. Nana, draped with gold jewelry, wearing a white dress and heels and carrying a Louis Vuitton duffle, scuttles alongside. Jim is not handcuffed, and he's escorted only by the Thai police captain. "He's an old man," the captain tells reporters. "If he runs, I can chase him. I run faster."

❖

A month prior to Jim's arrest, Amnesty International published a report about the abhorrent conditions in Thai prisons, including at Jim's new home in the Lard Yao section of the Klong Prem Central Prison on the outskirts of Bangkok. In addition to severe overcrowding, lack of adequate food, and medical care, the report says, "Prisons in Thailand have a high rate of deaths in custody from diseases such as AIDS and tuberculosis. Many prisoners with a wide variety of diseases, some of them life-threatening and contagious, receive no treatment."

It goes on to say that prison guards are allowed, even encouraged, to beat prisoners with impunity: "Detainees in police or military custody are sometimes subjected to torture and ill-treatment, usually in the form of kicks and punches or beatings with batons."

Prisoners wear shorts and T-shirts and share overcrowded cells with no air conditioning and poor sanitation. Convicted murderers live among accused rapists and drug dealers, or those awaiting trial for simple petty theft. Privacy is nonexistent and food consists of inadequate servings of mushy rice or weak soup. No special treatment is given to foreigners. Each prisoner is allowed one twenty-five-minute visit each weekday. Nana visits Jim almost every day, impeccably dressed and always carrying a basket of food. Prisoners and visitors are separated by three feet of bars and wire. Each visiting room has four telephones, but the audio is so terrible that many prisoners choose to yell through the wire. Nana and Jim whisper into the phones in the cacophony of the visiting area.

He quickly hires a lawyer in Thailand and at first says he won't fight extradition, will return to the United States to face the charges in Atlanta. But then, at a court hearing in October, three months after his arrest, he changes his mind. Jim reasserts his innocence and says he should not be extradited back to the United States. To Jim, staying in the rat- and cockroach-infested, overcrowded, humid Thai prison seems like a better option than returning to Atlanta, where Tony Harwood is ready to blab, the DA will show no mercy, and his former in-laws could take every last cent he has.

❖

The whole time Jim's been toking on stogies in Thailand, Tony Harwood's been sitting in a jail cell in Fulton County, still refusing to take the prosecution's plea deal, which would have him testify against Jim and get twenty years instead of the death penalty. Tony writes letter after letter—to judges, district attorneys, court clerks—complaining about his lousy court-appointed lawyers, the slow, painful churn of the judicial system, the terrible conditions in the jail, the food, the inability to contact his family. He's a people person, he says; he's lonely sitting in jail limbo while they search for Jim. He still denies firing the bullet that killed Lita and is hoping the DA will be forced to either let him go or give him a greatly reduced sentence. Yes, he moved the furniture and took Jim's $25,000, and yes, he drove to Atlanta, and yes, he bought the flowers. But he still insists he was an accomplice, not the triggerman. After all, he thinks, Sullivan is the one they want; once they find him, they'll surely see that Tony was just a middleman. Right?

Once Jim is arrested, things change. Fearing the plea deal could go away altogether, Tony, wearing orange scrubs and handcuffs, stands in front of a judge on February 12, 2003, some sixteen years after Lita's murder, and pleads guilty to a reduced charge of voluntary manslaughter in exchange for testifying against Jim. Taking advantage of a Georgia law that allows a victim's family to comment during sentencing, Emory McClinton calls Tony "scum of the earth" and tells him, "The only person worse than you is the person who paid you twenty-five pieces of silver." Jo Ann, now a busy state representative, isn't there but sends a statement recounting a recurring nightmare. It's read aloud in court: "Lita and I are talking and then she vanishes, and I'm left reaching for her, screaming her name," she writes. "I have panic attacks in the middle of the night, only to awaken my husband and we cry together."

Tony is transferred to the Georgia State Prison in Reidsville. Opened in 1937, the maximum-security prison is the state's oldest. Like many other prisons in Georgia, Reidsville is a dangerous place, where weapons and drugs flow freely while the showers back up and the toilets clog. The majority of prisoners are Black, and when it gets around that Tony shot a Black woman, he realizes he must watch his back. Maybe he was better off rotting alone in the Fulton County Jail.

❖

Two days after Tony's sentencing, a Thai judge denies Jim's attempt to avoid extradition and orders him back to Georgia. His Thai lawyer appeals, and Jim pulls in the big guns by rehiring Don Samuel and Ed Garland, the defense duo who brokered his acquittal in his earlier federal trial. Samuel flies to Thailand to represent Jim in court and argues that Jim's Irish citizenship should prevent extradition—Ireland opposes capital punishment and will not support extradition in cases where one of its citizens faces the death penalty. Samuel also argues Jim should not be extradited because of the US constitutional protection against double jeopardy. Given that Jim was already acquitted in federal court in 1992, he says, he should not be tried again for the same crime. He warns they will appeal on the same grounds, even if Jim is eventually sent back to the US.

While they await a decision on the appeal, Samuel announces that Jim married Nana in prison. The McClintons' lawyers believe it's a ploy, that maybe Jim believes that marrying a Thai national might help keep him in the country and avoid prosecution in the US. Regardless, Nana becomes the fourth Mrs. Sullivan, after Catherine, Lita, and Suki.

❖

"Sullivan stayed ahead of us because he had the money to stay ahead of us," says private investigator Pat McKenna, who is watching news of Jim closely with the McClintons' attorneys in the US. The McClintons are still owed the $4 million civil judgment, now calculated at about $8 million with interest.

In the summer of 2003, lawyer Brad Moores uncovers evidence that Jim has squirreled away between $5 and $10 million in offshore accounts. Moores sues a Palm Beach lawyer for knowingly funneling funds to Jim in Thailand. Moores also believes Jim had set aside money to fund his defense in the event he was ever caught, so when Jim again hires Samuel and Garland, Moores takes notice. The renowned lawyers will not work for free; they'll get paid somehow, and Moores and McKenna are determined to find out how.

❖

In January 2004, Jim, wearing an orange prison shirt and ankle shackles, shuffles into court to hear that the Thai Supreme Court is rejecting his final appeal to avoid extradition. It's a closed session, but through a window he signals a thumbs-down to Nana and blows her a kiss.

In March, Jim is officially transferred from Thai authorities to the U.S. Marshals to accompany him on the trip back to Atlanta, along with FBI special agent Mike Greene, who's been in Thailand interviewing anyone Jim had contact with. Jim is in rough shape, having had a couple of skirmishes with other inmates during his two years fighting extradition. He looks scrawny and scruffy, well beyond his sixty-two years. He is quiet on the airplane, reading *Newsweek* between frequent naps.

When he limps off the plane at Atlanta's Hartsfield International Airport, he's wearing handcuffs and shackles, a face mask, and a single shoe. He has serious dental problems, the mask is a precaution against SARS, and the bare foot is because his right foot is swollen from severe gout. He is transported to the Fulton County Jail, where he'll await trial. A few days after Jim's arrival, Fulton County district attorney Paul Howard serves Jim notice of the state's intent to seek the death penalty against him.

Samuel says Jim Sullivan's defense is simple: "He didn't do it. He is not guilty."

❖

The article I first wrote about this story was published in *Atlanta* magazine in October 2004, after Jim had been brought back to Atlanta and everyone was awaiting the trial. Before the article came out, I'd visited Jo Ann and Emory McClinton at their stately home on East Lake Drive, where they had lived for nearly thirty years. I was so nervous at the time. Though it had been seventeen years since Lita's murder, it was relatively new for me and it felt fresh, tender. I'd been researching the story for months, traveling to Palm Beach to look at court documents, trying to understand and unravel the story up till now. I felt close to them, even though we'd never met. When I knocked on their door, I carried assumptions about their anguish, as though I'd ever understand it.

We sat on comfortable overstuffed couches in the living room. Photographs of Lita were as prevalent as photos of Valencia, Emory Jr., and the McClintons' two grandsons. Portraits of ancestors lined the walls. The home was furnished with antiques and heavy brocade furniture. Generous magnolia buds sat submerged in water in a big glass bowl on the coffee table. Talk radio murmured in the background. I asked them if they felt a sense of closure now that Jim was back on US soil.

"Closure does not have meaning to me," Jo Ann said. "There's no such thing as closure because our daughter is dead and that can never be erased or changed." She said Jim's being in jail awaiting trial was just another piece of the puzzle, but the jigsaw was nowhere near complete.

After fifty-three years of marriage, the McClintons were the kind of couple who finished each other's sentences. At seventy, they were aging but still full of life, and they were determined to see Jim pay for what they say they know in their hearts he did to Lita.

"In this society we have allowed people with means to get away with violations of the law, of humanity," said Emory, wearing shorts and a green T-shirt, with sneakers and white athletic socks pulled halfway up his calves. He's a tall man with a gentle but determined voice. "And we were determined that that would not happen in this case." They wanted Jim to pay for his actions, wanted to make sure his wealth wouldn't let him slide away again. "He should have known," said Emory. "He should have known that we would not let him get away with this."

CHAPTER 29

UNCLE FRANK
(MARCH 2005)

For years, rumors flew in Macon, Atlanta, and Boston that Jim must've had something to do with his uncle's early and sudden demise. Uncle Frank was just sixty-five, in robust health, when he suddenly dropped dead in 1975. That this happened just before he had planned to fire Jim raised eyebrows that never again settled on the faces of family and friends. Frank's death was attributed to heart failure, and no autopsy was performed. Jim had swiftly sent his uncle's body to Boston to be buried in a cemetery in Braintree, Massachusetts.

While preparing to prosecute Jim, Fulton County DA Paul Howard arranged to have Uncle Frank's body exhumed and autopsied to rule out foul play. Fulton County investigator Chris Harvey accompanied GBI agents to Boston to witness the exhumation in March 2005.

"It was a rainy day," Harvey recalls, describing it as a scene from a movie. Several people, including the Georgia medical examiner and Massachusetts police, stood by in the gloom and watched as they dug Uncle Frank's coffin out of the ground before transporting it to the morgue where the body would be autopsied.

"They did the autopsy right there in the coffin," Harvey says, remembering that the body was still clothed. "They took some tissue samples and closed it back up." He said the whole thing was over in a matter of minutes. "Then we went for lobster and flew back to Atlanta."

When the results came back several months later, they were negative, showing no verifiable indication of foul play. This meant that if ever there was poison running through Frank's body, it was absent from the tissue samples now.

"Jim Sullivan had nothing to do with the unfortunate death of his uncle," defense attorney Don Samuel tells the press.

District Attorney Paul Howard says, "We realized the exhumation was a longshot. But it was the right thing to do under the circumstances."

CHAPTER 30

PREPARING FOR JUSTICE

E very year, defense attorney Don Samuel makes the list of Best Lawyers in America and has done so since 1993. He has literally written the book—several actually—on Georgia law. If you're talking about the biggest cases in Georgia history, his name comes up alongside his law partner Ed Garland. Garland, nearly twenty years older than Samuel, is a forbidding trial lawyer and the guy TV personality Nancy Grace said, out of anyone in the country, she'd call if she ever needed a defense attorney. The two have worked together for more than forty years.

The first time I speak with Samuel over Zoom, he's sitting in his backyard on a sunny Friday in 2023. Birdsong fills the air as though in a Disney movie, so many birds that I half expect them to drape him with a crown and cape or turn his T-shirt into gold. Samuel is a formidable guy—in addition to being a top defense attorney, he's married to the award-winning author Melissa Fay Greene and raised nine children, including one adoptee from Bulgaria and four from Ethiopia.

Samuel is jovial and smiley, with a big bushy beard and twinkly eyes; it's hard to reconcile that this cuddly teddy bear has spent his career defending some of the worst criminals in Georgia's history. He's helped get acquittals for accused Al-Qaeda defendants, motorcycle gang leaders, and Jim Williams, the Savannah antiques dealer and accused murderer featured in the movie and book *Midnight in the Garden of Good and Evil*. He's defended sheriffs, football players, mafia lords, rappers, and politicians. He believes deeply in the concept of innocent until proven guilty, that everyone is entitled to a fair trial and access to the best defense they can get.

Samuel was just thirty-two during Jim's 1992 federal trial. It was Samuel's first big case, and it was his job to argue a "directed verdict motion," which pointed out that no one could possibly know the contents of the phone calls that constituted the circumstantial evidence upon which the prosecution's case hung. His argument was so compelling that the judge threw out the case and Jim was acquitted. At the time, Samuel was giddy with the result, as though he'd just shot a Hail Mary from center court and somehow sunk a swoosh. Jim, realizing Samuel wasn't just some shmuck junior lawyer, put him on speed dial.

"He's always been an odd guy," Samuel says of Jim. "He'd get mad at us when we'd FedEx something. He'd say, 'Why spend the $7 when you could put a .55¢ stamp on it?' That was kind of emblematic of his behavior in general." Scrimping seems ludicrous when you're fighting for freedom or, in the case of the pending state trial, your life.

Samuel visited Jim in Thailand twice, even toured Bangkok with Nana, who he says was sweet and shy and spoke fluent English, having lived for many years in the United States. He spent months in trial preparation with Jim. He said they worked hard to delay Jim's extradition because "the more years you can prolong the proceeding, the longer your client stays alive." His attempt at claiming double jeopardy—the notion that you can't be tried for the same crime twice—didn't fly in Jim's case. In the federal trial, Jim was charged for violating a federal statute with the "use of interstate commerce facilities in the commission of murder-for-hire," which is a law that doesn't exist at the state level in Georgia; therefore it couldn't be considered the same crime. In other words, in the 1992 case Jim was tried for using interstate phone lines to commit murder; in the state's case, he was charged directly with murder.

Jim's upcoming state trial would be Samuel's first death penalty case, and he knew the resources it would take to save Jim's life. Samuel believes, above anything, that everyone, no matter who the defendant is or what they've been accused of, deserves a fair trial. When the McClintons' attorneys sued Samuel and Garland, arguing Jim shouldn't be able to pay their hefty fees while the civil judgment is open against him, Samuel told reporters, "A civil judgment is a debt. It doesn't bar him from his Sixth Amendment right to hire counsel."

Georgia death penalty trials are bifurcated, meaning they are conducted in two stages: the guilt-innocence phase (determining whether a defendant is guilty or not) and the penalty phase (determining the sentence—in a Georgia death penalty case, the sentence is determined by a jury, not a judge). Samuel said that in most death penalty cases a defendant gets convicted, so defense attorneys focus more on the penalty phase by selecting a jury least likely to impose the death penalty; their goal is to keep Jim alive. Whereas the prosecution focuses more on the guilt-innocence phase; while they seek the death penalty, their main goal is to get Jim convicted.

❖

Former Fulton County prosecutor Clint Rucker is at home making chicken pot pie when we finally connect over Zoom. We discuss the genius of his using flakey biscuits instead of pie crust, and he gets busy chopping vegetables while we talk. Rucker is a big, burly Black man and an impressive litigator, famous for his courtroom theatrics. He knows how to talk to people, how to connect. He is a master at captivating juries and creating dramatic tension around key moments. It's easy for juries to get lulled into the procedural humdrum of a long trial; Rucker can tell when they're getting bored, sleepy, or distracted. He knows how to wake them up. He is an eloquent storyteller and a mesmerizing character; no one can rock a closing argument quite like Clint Rucker.

"He's like a Baptist preacher," Charles Mittelstadt, Samuel and Garland's defense investigator, once told me. "He can turn chicken shit into chicken salad. On game day, no one brings it like Clint."

Rucker went to Emory University in Atlanta and became a prosecutor in 1995. He specialized in prosecuting murder cases—by the time Jim's case went to trial, he'd tried more than fifty homicides and a few death penalty cases.

But Rucker was only one member of Fulton County district attorney Paul Howard's prosecution team ready to go up against Garland and Samuel. In addition to Rucker, the team included three experienced assistant district attorneys: Kellie Hill, a young Black woman who was responsible for anything related to Jim's flight, and two white women, Sheila Ross and Anna Green, who were responsible for the divorce and for any legal questions that arose during trial, respectively. They knew full well that Jim had been acquitted in the past, and they weren't going to let it happen again. Every move they made was strategic.

They also knew the death penalty sentence would be an uphill battle. "The statute in Georgia for death penalty cases has three criteria," Rucker explained, outlining that to qualify, a defendant would have to have killed multiple people, killed a law enforcement officer, or hired someone else to commit murder. Clearly, Jim qualified on the third one, but his age and lack of prior criminal arrests meant it wasn't a sure thing. "Really all we had was he was just a person that people didn't like. He was an asshole. He was greedy. He was a misogynist. He cheated on his wife," said Rucker. "He was just generally a bad person." But that didn't mean a jury of his peers would send him to death.

The prosecution's case hinged on the testimonies of their star witnesses, Belinda Trahan and Tony Harwood, who'd be as comfortable in a courtroom as a vegetable in Rucker's steaming pot pie. And their stories kept changing. It wouldn't take much for the defense—two lawyers considered top experts in Georgia law—to paint Belinda and Tony as undereducated former drug users, disgruntled ex-lovers whose stories varied wildly. Tony acted alone, they could argue. Just because he moved furniture for Jim doesn't mean Jim paid him to kill his ex-wife. As it was in the 1992 case, the evidence was largely circumstantial. There was still no murder weapon; Tony still said he wasn't the shooter, and no accomplices had been identified; and still, no one could prove the contents of the phone calls. And no financial paper trail shows the money ever exchanged hands. All the defense needed to do is sow reasonable doubt—they'd done it before, they could do it again.

❖

After all the pretrial motions, requests for discovery of evidence, motions to suppress evidence, appeals, witness depositions, bureaucratic delays, etc., it takes two years after Jim is returned from Thailand for the trial to begin. All eyes are watching, waiting to see if the district attorney can succeed where the U.S. Attorney could not.

"I've talked to a lot of people in our county," District Attorney Paul Howard said. "I was surprised when Sullivan was returned that so many people I've never met would just walk up to me and say, 'we want you to make sure he understands that you just can't get away with something like that in Fulton County.'"

By the time the case comes to trial, it's been nineteen years since Lita's murder. The DA says, "I think we've waited long enough."

CHAPTER 31

THE STRIPPER
AND THE BARTENDER

A s both sides prepare for trial, they must contend with the chaos that is Tony Harwood. While prosecutors know Tony moved Jim's furniture and that Jim paid him $25,000, Tony still says he wasn't the shooter, and no accomplices have ever been identified. The details of how it all went down remain concerningly murky as the case heads to trial. Since his arrest in April of 1998, Tony's story has changed, reversed tracks, grown thorns, and sprouted new heads. This can present many challenges in court—for both sides—because no one knows exactly what will come out of Tony's mouth.

Six years after Tony's arrest, while Jim was in the Thai prison awaiting extradition, Tony offered a new story. GBI agent John Lang, who by then was fed up with Tony's changing narratives, made the three-hour drive to the prison in Reidsville to hear the latest one. Reidsville was the state's largest maximum security prison, famous for housing the most dangerous inmates in the state's history and as the backdrop for the movie *The Longest Yard*.

"It's just a bad bad place," Lang told me. Tony was isolated from the general prison population, considered a highly at-risk prisoner because he was an alleged murderer of a Black woman and had become a "snitch" when he pled guilty to manslaughter in exchange for testifying against

Jim. When Lang went to visit Tony, he was isolated in his own cell, but guards had to secure public areas every time he walked through. Tony was on constant alert, the lowest man on the prison totem pole.

Tony told Lang he was ready to tell the truth, the whole story that would straighten everything out. He wanted out, wanted parole, and thought this new information would be his ticket. In this new story, he said his old friend Tracy, a topless dancer at the Palace Lounge Strip Club in Matthews, North Carolina, helped him find someone to carry out the murder. He said Tracy had introduced him to a guy called "John the Bartender," who Tony hired to shoot Lita. Before the hit, Tony said he had second thoughts and wanted to call the whole thing off, but by then John had already spent the money and was committed to going through with it. He told Lang that he, John, and Tracy all went down together on January 13 and, after knocking on Lita's door—the first failed attempt—they checked into the HoJo's and exchanged calls with Jim, telling him Lita wouldn't come to the door. The trio then drove all the way back to North Carolina. Tony and John the Bartender returned three days later, on January 16. Tony admitted he bought the flowers but now said John did the shooting and it was John who chucked the gun out the window on the way to the Suwanee rest area, where Tony made the collect call to Jim.

Lang, though dubious, considered that maybe Tony was finally telling the truth. The specificity of the details prompted him to track down Tracy and John. But by the time investigators found them, it had been more than seventeen years since the murder, and both struggled to remember the years they worked at the Palace, let alone what they were doing on a specific January day in 1987; their alibis were impossible to verify. Nothing, except Tony's story, connected either one of them to Lita's murder. But that was the story Tony decided to stick with.

And so it remained heading into trial: no one knows the truth of what really happened that day—no one but Tony himself.

CHAPTER 32

THE TRIAL
(2006)

Jury selection in the death penalty trial of the State of Georgia v. James Vincent Sullivan takes a painstaking six weeks before the list of 450 potential candidates gets whittled down to sixteen—twelve jurors and four alternates. Of the thirteen women and three men on the jury, four are Black, eleven are white, and one is of Asian descent. Finally, on February 27, 2006, nineteen years, one month, and eleven days after the murder of Lita McClinton, the trial begins.

The courtroom in the Atlanta Justice Center Tower is spacious. Judge John Goger, a former defense attorney, civil trial lawyer, and highly respected judge known to be fair, smart, and a tolerator of no bullshit, presides over the court. He sits on a raised wooden podium at the front of the court- room; the court reporter sits at a table below him, a woman whose fingers never stop moving. From the judge's view, the jury box is on his far right. In front of him, the prosecution's table is on the right and the defense's table is on his left. An old overhead projector sits in the middle, along with a lec- tern, an easel, and stacks of carefully organized evidence. The large gallery is packed with reporters and Lita's aunts, uncles, cousins, and friends. Her parents, now seventy-two, have been there every day since jury selection began, sitting in the front row, letting their former son-in-law feel their presence like fibers in a noose around his neck. Emory and Jo Ann are often accompanied by their grandson Harrison Wiener, the baby who was in Valencia's belly the day her sister was shot. He's now nineteen—he's been alive for the same amount of time the aunt he never met has been dead.

At the prosecution's table, Executive District Attorney Clint Rucker is joined by Assistant District Attorneys Sheila Ross, Anna Green, and Kellie Hill. At the defense's table, lawyers Ed Garland, Don Samuel, and Josh Moore sit with a quiet and straight-faced Jim Sullivan. Jim, now sixty-four, wears a blue suit, white shirt, and red-and-blue striped tie. The overhead fluorescent light glints in his wire-rimmed glasses. His receding gray hair is combed back so he looks a little windswept. Throughout the trial, he'll fiddle with a small tube of Vaseline he occasionally applies to his chapped lips.

Assistant District Attorney Sheila Ross, an Atlanta native, begins the proceedings with the prosecution's opening statement.

"On January 16, 1987, Lita McClinton Sullivan opened her door to a hitman carrying flowers. She greeted her killer with 'good morning' as she opened the door—and 'good morning' was the last thing that Lita ever said," Ross begins nervously, knowing how important it is to get all the details right. She's in her thirties, athletic, with short black hair and wearing a black skirt and suit jacket. She is tasked with introducing the state's case, all the major players, the nuances of the legal system, and she must somehow untangle the yarn of this convoluted story without confusing the jurors. "The evidence will show that this defendant paid $25,000 for a guaranteed victory in what was a long, protracted, very expensive divorce," she continues. "And while Lita was lying on her floor gurgling in her own blood, struggling to live, before she had even taken her last breath on this earth, that man gets a collect phone call to his Palm Beach mansion." Ross points to Jim. It's clear he's been coached to not react or show any emotion. He fiddles with a pen and occasionally jots down notes on a yellow legal pad.

As she gets more comfortable, Ross picks up steam and recaps the failed federal trial, the civil case, and the series of incriminatory phone calls made to and from Jim around the time of the murder. She tells the jury they'll hear from the prosecution's star witnesses—the alleged hitman Tony Harwood and his former girlfriend, Belinda Trahan, a woman whose testimony will be so damning, the state gave her immunity from any further prosecution.

Ross talks about how the case went cold. "Everyone moved on but Lita's family," she says.

When it's the defense's turn, Don Samuel keeps it simple. "Jim Sullivan did not murder his wife. He did not hire anyone to murder his wife," he says. "The last thing Jim Sullivan wanted in 1987 was for Lita to be murdered." Samuel, forty-six, wearing a red tie and dark gray suit that matches his bushy gray beard, tells the jury how Jim has had to endure nineteen years of gossip and speculation, how the TV tabloid shows and magazine articles have dragged his name through the mud, and how he's glad to be here now, to finally clear his name, once and for all. He says the prosecution's case is no stronger than it was in the 1992 federal trial. He says the state's case relies on purely circumstantial evidence and the testimony of "con man" Tony Harwood.

"There is not one shred of physical evidence that links Jim Sullivan to this crime," Samuel says. "No DNA, no hair, no fingerprints, nothing like that at all." He says Tony Harwood is the only link to Jim, and Tony's a guy who has written threatening letters to judges and lawyers, who never tells the same story twice. He compares Tony and his stories to a "snowflake," saying, "No two versions are the same." He proceeds to discredit Belinda, pointing out she was blitzed on margaritas and Xanax when she first saw the photo lineup, and she recognized Jim only from his appearance on *Extra!* He claims everything she knows, she learned from television or from Tony.

"There's not one shred of evidence that shows that he paid anyone anything," says Samuel. "Despite the efforts of the U.S. Attorney's office, the Florida Department of Law Enforcement, the GBI, the North Carolina police, the FBI, choose your agency . . . There's not one shred of evidence that Mr. Sullivan ever paid anybody anything."

Samuel is so compelling, dazzling even, that there's a discernible tension in the room; maybe this isn't a slam dunk after all. Samuel argues that Jim made the calls to neighbors three days before the murder because his lawyers were looking to subpoena witnesses in the upcoming divorce trial. Jim didn't flee when he left for Costa Rica, he just happened to move at the time of his indictment. Samuel says Jim was simply unaware he was the target of an international manhunt.

Finally, Samuel contends that the jury will find Jim innocent, that someday soon he'll once again walk out a free man.

❖

A long list of witnesses spend the first days of the trial recounting the day of the murder or giving expert opinions, including the medical examiner, ballistics experts, phone company record keepers, Detective Welcome Harris, and FBI agents John Kingston and Todd Letcher. Jo Ann and Lita's friend Jan Marlow confirm Lita reported hearing a knock in the early morning of January 13, three days before her death. A clerk reads the 1992 testimony of the florist Randall Benson, who died in 2002. The jury hears how a creepy man came into the Botany Bay Florist to buy roses on the morning of January 16, how the customer seemed impatient and jumpy, how Benson feared he was going to be robbed. Bob Christenson, Lita's neighbor, now in his sixties, describes seeing the shooter delivering flowers, how he made eye contact with the man, how he heard the gunshots and found Lita gasping for her life on the foyer floor.

Poppy recounts hearing Lita say "good morning" before she heard shots, followed by the awful thud of her best friend falling to the floor. She tells the jury how she hid with her young daughter in the closet, fearing for her life. Lita's divorce attorney, Richard Schiffman, explains the finances of the divorce, how he was sure a jury would've decided in Lita's favor.

Suki Sullivan gets on the stand and misspells her own name, omitting the 'i' in Sullivan, before telling the jury that she left Palm Beach and now lives on a farm, growing grapes. She recounts the story about how Jim had complained about his divorce from Lita being tried in Georgia, fearing an Atlanta jury would side with her because she was Black and her parents had power.

The real drama comes on day five of the trial when Belinda Trahan takes the stand. At forty-seven, Belinda is slender and pretty, with prominent cheekbones, thin lips, and deep, suspicious eyes. It's hard to believe she's a grandmother to her son Jimmy's three kids. She's wearing a fashionable black blazer and black slacks, an outfit picked out by prosecutors that she'd probably never wear in Texas. Her newly straightened long blond hair shines with new highlights, and she's got fresh tips on her painted pale pink fingernails. She's been staged and prepped by the prosecution—all she must do now is tell the truth.

The prosecution selects Assistant District Attorney Kellie Hill to question Belinda.

"Start at the beginning," Hill prompts. Belinda's hands shake as she tells the court how she met Tony Harwood in Texas, how she moved to North Carolina with him and lived in his trailer on his family's property outside of Albemarle, where Tony's three brothers and sister also had stakes of land they planned to one day build upon. She describes the Harwoods as "real nice people" and a very close-knit family.

Belinda describes how she'd go along with Tony on his jobs for North American Van Lines, how they'd take his eighteen-wheeler on long road trips and she'd do the paperwork, wrap furniture, and help haul boxes. They'd lied and said they were married so she could go along on jobs.

"How did you get paid?" asks Hill.

"I guess I got fed and a roof over my head," says Belinda. She says while it was fun for a time, it grew to be long and cold and boring. Finally, when Tony got a delivery from Georgia to Florida around Thanksgiving in 1986, she refused to go. She told him she was done with the moving van, maybe even done with him.

Nothing was the same after he returned.

"He was kinda acting strange and I asked him what was the problem," Belinda tells the court in her slow Texas drawl. "He was nervous and antsy. At first, he told me the less I know the better off I'd be. I'd been dating the guy for three years, so I didn't take that for an answer. I said, 'just tell me what's wrong,' and he finally told me that some rich white guy wanted to take out his Black wife because she was going to divorce him, and he didn't want her to have anything."

"So, when Tony told you about this guy who he met, what did you say?" asks Hill.

"I didn't believe it," said Belinda. "I figured he'd met someone because we were on the outs." Belinda says she thought the whole thing about killing the rich guy's wife was his cover story for going to strip clubs or meeting up with another woman; she was sure Tony was hooking up with someone on the side. "I told him 'whatever, go do what you want to do.'"

In January 1987, a couple of months after Tony's first trip to Florida, Belinda says he went to Georgia and returned a couple days later. When she asked him how it went, he replied that they didn't have any luck because a big concrete retaining wall made it hard to sneak in the back. So, they tried to ring the doorbell, but no one answered.

"I said 'if you wanted to get a woman to answer the door, all you gotta do is take flowers to the door,'" Belinda says while reaching for a tissue. She looks over to Jo Ann McClinton, who is crying, and mouths the words, *I'm sorry.* Jo Ann simply looks down and leans into her husband's embrace.

Belinda has immunity from any prosecution, although she likely wouldn't need it. Georgia law says that a person must be a co-conspirator to be charged as a criminal accomplice; Belinda merely suggested the flowers—she never thought he'd actually do it. She may have been somewhat aware of Tony's crime, but she was not a participant in it—and awareness is not a crime in Georgia.

Belinda tells the court that when Tony returned from Atlanta again, he told her the job was done. She said she still didn't believe him—it was so far-fetched and out of character; Tony could be an asshole, but he wasn't a cold-blooded killer.

"He was angry that I didn't believe he wasn't cheating," she says. He told her he could prove it to her. He woke her up either late at night or early in the morning—she can't remember which, only that she grabbed her pillow and a blanket and got in the back seat of the car. She says she doesn't know where they drove, how long they drove, or where they ended up. She just knows that she woke up hungry to the aroma of bacon at a diner somewhere. She says she was annoyed because Tony wouldn't let her eat. She slid into a booth beside the window and people-watched while she sulked and craved eggs. Most of the customers wore tennis shoes, jeans, and T-shirts, but soon a guy walked in wearing a linen suit and leather docksider shoes, heading straight toward them. That's when Belinda says she finally realized none of it was a joke. "Tony did not know anybody in that upper class," she says. "He was country."

To reenact the scene in the diner, prosecutors have rolled an actual restaurant booth into the middle of the courtroom. The benches are faux wood with light red vinyl, flanking a white Formica table. Belinda steps down from the witness stand and directs Kellie Hill and Clint Rucker to sit on one side of the booth, playing Belinda and Tony. Belinda is the man. She walks into the pretend restaurant carrying a folded newspaper under her arm. As the man, she looks actor-Belinda in the eye and turns to actor-Tony and angrily says, "What is she doing here?"

Belinda, as the man, sits down at the booth and slides the newspaper across to actor-Tony while actor-Belinda looks out the window.

She describes Jim as a "pencil pusher. . . . I had more calluses on my hands then he did," she says. "Like he never had to work, like he was fed with a golden spoon. He didn't look like he belonged in the restaurant we were in."

She says the man left first and she and Tony left soon after. She can't remember anything about the car they were driving. She says while they drove away, she stared out the window and thought about how she'd get out of the relationship, away from Tony, as fast as she could. When they got back to Albemarle, Belinda says she moved out and got a job so she could save enough money to drive back to Texas.

For years, Tony would show up at her place in Texas—sometimes in his eighteen-wheeler, sometimes in his car. "He had to have his finger on me the whole time to keep me shut up," she says. She'd sleep with him, figuring that was the way to keep herself and her son Jimmy safe. At one point, she says, he threatened to kill her and kill himself. He'd set up a life insurance policy, and Jimmy would be their beneficiary. Another time, she says, Tony sent a black rose to her house to prove to her that she was being watched.

When Hill asks Belinda to identify the man who walked into the restaurant in Florida, she doesn't hesitate. "He's ruined many lives," she mutters before standing up from her seat on the witness stand and pointing to Jim. "He is right there," she says. "He can't even make eye contact."

When it's defense attorney Ed Garland's turn to question Belinda, her resolve begins to weaken. At sixty-four, Garland has perfected his craft and doesn't get rattled or wear kid gloves when he must push a witness. Years later, Garland will tell an *Atlanta Journal-Constitution* reporter that a trial is like war. "Whoever goes into it needs to go into it with that thought, with a huge amount of energy. You need to like the combat, and you need to be prepared for the ordeal."

But while Garland is prepared, energized, and ready to battle, Belinda is losing her cool.

Garland asks her if she's rehearsed her testimony with the prosecution, suggesting everything she says is scripted, including the whole drama of standing up and pointing to Jim. Belinda says yes, they've run through it all several times before, and then she gets defensive. She's tired and confused and gets lost in the older man's long winding questions. She spends the remainder of her long three hours on the stand sighing heavily, rolling her eyes, and gaveling her shellacked fingernail whenever she gets frustrated or longs to make a point. It's what the defense attorneys want—to see her unhinge.

Garland pushes on her earlier testimony about the trip she and Tony took to Florida to get the money.

"So, you can't say if you traveled one hour or twenty hours?" he asks incredulously.

"No," she says. She can't remember the car, whether they took secondary roads, stopped for lunch, crossed state lines, or crossed the country. Garland points out that she doesn't remember anything about that day but then can recall super specific details, like Jim's manicured hands and the soles of his shoes. It comes clear that the defense is suggesting Belinda only came forward after she learned of the *Extra!*

episode, or from seeing the other news coverage over the years on Court
TV, CNN, Fox, and others, not out of a desire to purge her soul, but to
protect herself and reap the substantial reward. She says she was never
in it for the money, but she'd take it now for all the bullshit she's had to
endure since coming forward.

"You understood you couldn't get the reward unless someone was convicted," says Garland. "You understood that, right?"

"I guess," sighs Belinda, rolling her eyes. "Whatever."

When she's fully rattled, Garland calmly asks, "When you were living
with Tony Harwood in the trailer, did he treat you in a way that it would
surprise you that he participated in an act of violence?"

Belinda can't follow his convoluted question and asks him to rephrase.

Garland waits a beat and says plainly, "Did Mr. Harwood beat you?"

There's a long pause while Belinda looks at him like a teenager about to
rage. "Yes," she says defiantly. "He laid hands on me." When he asks her
how often, she says, "It wasn't every week—just whenever he got mad. The
first year he was . . . you know how men do—they play their little game to
get the woman. After that they show their colors."

"Did he try to strangle you?" Garland asks.

Belinda looks away. "Do you want to know all the different ways?" she
lashes. When Garland doesn't answer, she says, "Yes, he has."

Garland is attempting to show that Belinda is a victim of domestic abuse
with an ax to grind against a violent man she spent years being afraid of.
He's trying to put as much distance between Jim and the long history of
drama between Tony and Belinda as he can.

When Garland suggests Belinda never actually met Jim Sullivan, she
blows: "I know what I saw and you can't take that away from me." Again,
she stands up and points. "He's right there," she says, almost yelling. "James
Vincent Sullivan." The whole courtroom is transfixed, and photographers
snap photos of her pointing, pointing, pointing.

Clint Rucker glances over at Jim, gazing down at his hands in his lap,
the only one in the courtroom not looking at Belinda.

CHAPTER 33

THE TRIAL, PART 2 (2006)

When court breaks for the weekend and starts up again on Monday, it's Tony's turn to take the stand. The prosecution's strategy is built around the fact that Tony likes being the center of attention, relishes that his photo is in the newspapers, that the cops come running to his jail cell anytime he wants to talk to them. "Tony is a narcissist and a liar," says Rucker, so the team uses that to their advantage. Pretrial, they'd send Sheila Ross to talk to him, knowing he would flirt with her, let his guard down, and tell her things to impress her. The team decides that Rucker, the only man on the prosecution team and thereby someone whose respect Tony will want, will be the one to question Tony at trial.

Tony walks into the courtroom wearing a dark gray blazer, a white dress shirt, and blue jeans. He has a long face with high cheekbones, sporting a freshly trimmed goatee, wire-rimmed glasses, and a short haircut. He looks well-groomed, like a community college professor or an insurance salesman. He has a deep pleasant radio voice and a rural North Carolina accent—he says "dubya" for W, "noth carolinah," and "yessar" for yes sir.

Rucker starts by throwing softballs—a "conciliatory examination," in legal-speak, where he asks Tony easy questions—his age (he turned fifty-five a few days ago), his hometown (Albemarle), education (ninth grade, later GED), number of siblings (three brothers and a sister), his profession (long-haul trucker). Rucker confirms for the jury that Tony is currently incarcerated and was originally charged with murder before he took a plea deal.

"Did you make a deal with state of Georgia?" Rucker asks.

"Yes sir," Tony responds.

"What did we—the State—agree to do?"

"You agreed to no further prosecution for twenty-year voluntary man-slaughter," says Tony.

"What did you agree to?"

"I agreed to testify."

"Will you answer each and every question posed to you?"

"Yes," says Tony, nodding and looking at the jury. "Without a doubt."

Rucker puts a picture of Lita on the screen and asks Tony if he'd ever laid eyes on her face other than today.

"Other than in the news, no," says Tony.

"Did you agree to participate in the murder of Lita Sullivan?" asks Rucker.

Tony scrunches his face and takes a long pause. "To be honest, I'd have to answer no. I didn't directly agree to murder Lita Sullivan."

"What did you agree to do?"

"The agreement was to 'take care of her.' My intention was never to participate."

"What do you think Sullivan meant when he said, 'take care of her?'"

"Well, I assumed that he meant to kill her," Tony says. "It meant either kill her or scare her, but you don't pay $25,000 to scare nobody."

Tony explains how he dropped off furniture at Jim's house in Florida in November 1986, how the workers he'd hired—he emphasizes that they were Black—had accidentally chipped the brown terra cotta floor tiles in Jim's foyer while moving the heavy piano. Tony says Jim got irate, but he wasn't about to let anyone abuse his workers so he told Jim to just file a claim and everything would get resolved. While they were filling out the paperwork on a little table inside Jim's foyer, Tony says Jim started complaining about his divorce, how his wife was going to take him for everything he had.

"And then he asked me if I knew anybody who could possibly take care of his problem," says Tony. "He was trying to feel me out." He says he thought Jim was just joking around. "I recognize shoe-shuffling and BS-ing when I hear it. I thought he was jiving me and . . . and I didn't take it serious."

That said, Tony says, "I told him, 'If you want this problem taken care of, it'd probably cost you around $25,000, half up front.'" Jim then drew a map of The Coaches, Lita's townhouse complex. Tony says he had no intention of ever going through with it, that taking the map was like "taking a flower from a Hare Krishna; you just take it and move on."

After he left Jim's he went home to Belinda, a woman he "worshipped the ground she walked on." He says he loved Belinda because she was beautiful, a lot of fun, a good mother, and someone who'd make any man proud. When Rucker asks how he feels about Belinda today, Tony pauses and says, "Well, the best way that I can answer that question that's been heavy on my heart is I'm glad she had more courage than I did." Rucker lets that float in the air and makes a mental note to go back to it.

He asks Tony if he ever hit Belinda, and he smiles and replies, "One time . . . I don't remember what started it, but she whacked me pretty good with her purse. It stung pretty good so I popped her upside the head with an open hand." He chuckles, a funny memory. That's when little Jimmy ran for the shotgun. He says he never hit her with his fist but adds, "I might've spanked her a time or two."

Tony says he realized Jim wasn't joking when he received $12,500 in the mail. The money arrived before Christmas—two certified checks that Tony held onto for a week before going to the bank to open two accounts—one for him and one for Belinda. Tony quit North American and blew the money paying bills, buying clothes, going on vacation. He put a down payment on a Buick Riviera for Belinda, and she bought him a diamond ring.

He says he and Jim talked by phone a few times—Jim had written his number on the back of the map. The hit, Tony says, was supposed to happen before Christmas. But Tony kept stringing it along and now tells the court he had no intention of going through with it. Rucker lets that go for now and pivots to the Florida trip to collect the money. The booth is still sitting in the middle of the courtroom, and Rucker asks Tony to come down from the witness stand to show the court where everyone was sitting. Tony directs Kellie Hill to the Belinda spot, while he sits down next to her in the Tony spot. He has Rucker sit across from them as Jim. It's the same setup Belinda gave, but Tony says the money changed hands in the restroom, where Jim retrieved an envelope full of cash from his sock. When Jim handed him the money, Tony says, "I told him I didn't kill his wife, and Jim said, 'Well, someone did.'"

Tony then tells the court his Tracy the Stripper, John the Bartender story. He says he'd asked his longtime friend Tracy if she knew anyone who would take on the job of shooting a rich guy's wife. He gave her some money—can't remember how much—and she found John, the bouncer at the strip club, to take the job. Tony says he changed his mind and wanted to call it off, but by then John had spent the cash and was eager to go through with it. So, says Tony, on January 13, the three of them—Tony, John, and Tracy—drive through the night to Atlanta.

"My intentions were to go down and meet Lita and tell her what was going on, maybe get some money on that end of the deal." When Rucker asks him to clarify, he says he was going to tell Lita that Jim had given him $12,500 to have her killed and see if she'd be interested in paying him to make it go away. In other words, he was going to shake her down for some cash. But that never happened. Instead, says Tony, they drove to the condo early in the morning, like 5:30 a.m. It was still dark. It was cold so he and Tracy stayed in the car with the heat and radio running while John went and knocked on the door. Of course, no one answered. John returned to the car and Tony drove to a payphone to let Jim know there was no answer. He also asked Jim for another $2,000 for the hassle. Jim said no. That's when they checked into the HoJo's.

Earlier, a GBI handwriting expert had confirmed under oath that "Johnny Furr" and other information scrawled on the Howard Johnson hotel registration matched the slanty all-caps handwriting of Tony

Harwood. Tony admits that he registered at the hotel, paid cash, and wrote down a fake name and address.

After getting some rest at the HoJo's, they drove back to North Carolina. Two days later, John and Tony returned to Atlanta, leaving just before midnight on January 15. Tony says he never thought John would go through with it, and he assumed they'd just go to some strip bars and party it up. They were driving a white Toyota, which Tony says must have been John's. When they arrived in the early morning of January 16, they had breakfast and, after some pancakes and eggs, they went to the florist around the corner.

Tony says he bought the roses while John waited in the car.

They drove to the townhouse complex on Slaton Road. John took the flower box while Tony stayed idling in the car. A couple minutes later, Tony says he heard two shots, maybe "a heartbeat" between them. Rucker asks him to tap the table to demonstrate and Tony does. Bang. Bang. The dull thud reverberates throughout the silent courtroom.

"Do it again," says Rucker, and Tony obliges.

Bang. Heartbeat. Bang.

Soon after the shots, Tony says, John came hauling around the corner and jumped in the passenger seat. He had blood spatters on his face. Tony floored it, made several turns through the morning traffic, and instructed John to toss the gun out the window before they got onto the interstate heading north.

They pulled off at the Suwanee rest area, and Tony called Jim collect. "When he answered, I said 'Merry Christmas' and that was the end of it," Tony says.

Private investigator Pat McKenna is sitting in the gallery right next to Jo Ann. "I almost lost my shit right there," he tells me later. "It just flashed. I thought every year for the rest of the McClintons' lives when they hear people saying, 'Merry Christmas,' it's going to trigger this memory."

Up until this point, Rucker has listened to Tony's answers without putting much pressure on the details. He wants Tony to feel safe and comfortable, to let him think everyone's buying his story. Judge Goger calls a recess, and they break for lunch.

"When we come back from lunch, all of a sudden I flip the script and start treating Tony as though he is the worst human being on Earth," says Rucker. He's ready to push on Tony's lies and inconsistencies. He knows Tony yearns to be likable, wants the jury to understand him, believe him. Rucker reminds the jury that the story about Tracy and John the Bartender didn't come forward until Tony had been incarcerated for five years, and that the whole idea that Tony was trying to stop it seems ludicrous.

"So, according to your testimony, you tried to undo it, right? After you hired a hitman, you were going to warn Lita?" says Rucker.

"Yessir."

"Why didn't you just call her? Say, 'Girl, run! Your husband is trying to kill you!?'"

"I never thought about it," says Tony.

"Why didn't you call the police?"

"I dunno."

"Could it be that you never had any intent but to do exactly what James Sullivan hired you to do, which was to 'take care' of his problem?"

"I never believed it would happen."

Rucker shakes his head. "Would you admit that that story is unbelievable?" he asks, exasperated. Tony says no, he would not admit that.

Rucker asks him to look the jury members in the eyes and tell them he wasn't Lita's killer. Tony turns, takes off his glasses, and looks at the jury. "I did not shoot and kill Lita Sullivan." But Rucker's not done.

"Did you call the family to tell them what you know?" he asks. "Tell the GBI, FBI, or any authorities what you knew? Did you tell anyone prior to your arrest?"

"No, I was afraid to," Tony says. He says he didn't want to lose Belinda, feared losing his freedom, and was afraid that no one would believe him. He says he pled guilty to manslaughter out of fear, not guilt.

"All those fears came true, didn't they?" says Rucker with a sigh. "You lost Belinda, you lost your freedom, and nobody believes you."

When it's the defense's turn to question Tony, Ed Garland stands up. "We have no questions for this witness," he says. Tony's field trip to court is over. He hangs up the borrowed blazer and returns to prison.

❖

GBI special agent John Lang takes the stand and recounts meeting Belinda and the taped phone calls between her and Tony. He describes how he found the incriminating North American Van Lines bill of lading—the moving contract that connects Jim and Tony, how Tony said, "I've been waiting for you boys," when they showed up to arrest him. He says despite every effort of police and investigators to comb Albemarle banks for cashier's checks or any trace of money changing hands, no evidence exists that Jim paid Tony anything. He confirms that, to this day, Tony's accomplices remain unidentified. The investigation, he says, is still open.

This is music to the defense attorneys' ears. While the case is about whether or not Jim is guilty, it's largely been the Belinda-and-Tony show, and it's easy for Ed Garland and Don Samuel to discredit them as unreliable witnesses.

In his closing argument, defense attorney Don Samuel says, "The prosecution says, 'we didn't have enough evidence until we got Harwood.' If you don't have enough and you add zero, you don't have enough." He then quotes Jack Sparrow from *Pirates of the Caribbean*: "'I am a dishonest man, and a dishonest man can always be trusted to be dishonest.'" He argues that Jim's life depends on the kaleidoscopic stories of a couple of money-motivated opportunists. In his statement at the start of the trial, he'd called Tony a "snowflake" for never telling the same story twice. "I should've said 'maniacal, pathological sociopath murderer,'" he says. "That would've been more accurate."

But prosecutor Clint Rucker steers it back to the real issue. It matters naught if Tony changes his story a million times over. The evidence presented during the trial is clear. Jim Sullivan paid a stranger to murder his wife and he did it for one reason only: pure, unadulterated greed.

Everyone stands as the jury is dismissed to begin deliberation. The courtroom is a disaster, a battleground strewn with the tools of war. Bits of the now disassembled restaurant booth rest against the wall, along with posters of photo exhibits, easel pads, and wonky limbs of easels not put away properly. The defense and prosecution tables are strewn with file folders, overflowing binders, half-empty coffee cups, and empty plastic water bottles.

All pretenses of tidy have fallen by the wayside.

CHAPTER 34

THE VERDICT (MARCH 2006)

The jury takes just four hours to deliberate. When the jury members file back into the courtroom, Jim leans in, red-faced, jaw clenching. It's March 10, 2006, ten days after the trial began.

Jim is charged with five crimes: malice murder, felony murder, two counts of aggravated assault, and burglary. The gallery is full of the McClinton family, their friends and lawyers, the FBI agents, U.S. Attorney Bill McKinnon, Brad Moores, Pat McKenna, and DA Paul Howard, who'd vowed to see this case to the end. The press waits, pens poised. All of Atlanta is holding its breath.

"You've reached a decision?" asks Judge Goger.

"We have, your honor," says the jury forewoman. The judge nods at her to continue. "We the jury unanimously find beyond a reasonable doubt the existence of the following statutory aggravating circumstance: James Vincent Sullivan caused or directed another to commit the murder of Lita McClinton Sullivan."

On the count of malice murder, reads the jury foreperson, we find the defendant . . . guilty. Jim flinches and mouths something to himself, maybe a prayer. Someone whoops from the gallery and is admonished by the judge. A lawyer grips Jim's elbow as Jim's lips purse and his jaw tightens. His face reddens as the next four counts come in: Guilty. Guilty. Guilty. Guilty.

Jo Ann and Emory McClinton embrace and cry as the gallery erupts with hugs and tears and relief. It's finally, finally over.

❖

Jo Ann McClinton has a recurring dream where she and Lita are walking toward each other. Lita is smiling. Jo Ann is desperate to reach her, but she can't—Lita never gets any closer. When Jo Ann wakes up, she relives the anguish of never seeing her eldest child—again and again and again.

"You cannot understand what my family has gone through unless you've walked in these same shoes," Jo Ann tells the jury during the phase of the trial where Lita's family can read "impact statements" before the jury decides whether Jim should get the death penalty. Jo Ann's mouth twitches as she fights back tears. She's exhausted; she's had to wait nearly twenty years for justice, had to endure countless court battles, had to watch her former son-in-law enjoy his freedom and wealth, seemingly without regret.

She's faced more than seven thousand days of not talking to her daughter.

"I ask not for sympathy, I ask for justice for my daughter's killer," she says, looking directly at Jim.

Lita's cousin Yolanda reads a statement on behalf of several family members where she calls Lita a loving, caring humanitarian, "the stabilizing force and the foundation of our close-knit family." Another cousin recounts traveling to Jamaica with Lita after they graduated from college, how they sang Foreigner's *I Want to Know What Love Is* at the top of their lungs. Lita's aunt says the world lost a vital, intelligent, and vivacious young woman, and Valencia, whose statement is read by a family friend because she still finds it too painful, says her sister missed the births of her two sons, as well as her fortieth and fiftieth birthdays. "I am not the same person I was."

Valencia's son Harrison Wiener, just nineteen, gets on the stand and says that although he was born six months after Lita's murder, he feels the loss, the impact of her death on the family, even two decades later.

"I see the pain of my Aunt Lita's death in the eyes of the people closest to me," he says. "I see it every Thanksgiving every Christmas and every family gathering, and I've seen it every year since I can remember."

Jim's own younger brother Frank Sullivan comes down from Boston to give a statement, not in support of his brother but against. The defense objects, saying Frank himself admitted that he and his parents never even knew Jim had married Lita, and therefore couldn't be allowed to read an impact statement, a privilege afforded only to family. The judge reluctantly sustains the objection, but that doesn't stop Frank from reading his statement to the press outside the courtroom.

"It is a great shame that I have to admit that James Sullivan is my brother," he reads, in the same quiet Bostonian accent as Jim. "James's behavior is not a reflection of the household that we grew up in. My parents lived for their children and created a comfortable nurturing happy home." He tells reporters that, if given the chance, he'd tell his older brother, "For the first time in your life, stand up and tell the truth. Admit to the McClinton family what you did to their daughter. Do you have any idea the pain and suffering you brought to our parents and your children?"

The only people who speak on Jim's behalf are two priests and a lawyer. A Jesuit priest from Holy Cross, Jim's alma mater, says Jim gave half a million dollars in endowments over the years. An Atlanta trial lawyer testifies that he came to court every day in 1992 (to demonstrate that he didn't run from that trial), and another priest testifies that he visits Jim often in prison. They pray together and Jim talks about Nana. He writes her long letters and says that she "is his life." The priest admits, when asked, that Jim never speaks about his four children.

The defense asks for mercy and appeals to the jury's compassion. Ed Garland says, "Whatever sentence you choose, he will die in one of Georgia's state prisons. It is not necessary that you put poison into this man's veins."

When Jim comes to court for the final time, on March 14, 2006, he looks like an old, angry man. He's already been found guilty; now, he will find out if the jury will put him to death. The prosecution and defense tables are now clear of papers and laptops. The booth and broken easels are gone, posters put away, evidence vanished—no longer needed.

"This is unlike a situation where a jury comes back and returns a verdict of guilty or not guilty," says Judge Goger. "This is going to be a verdict that will deal with the punishment, the sentence. Let's respect that. This process does not need to hear any sort of outburst. Please respect that. All right, bring in the jury."

Everyone stands as the jury files in.

It happens quickly. The forewoman holds the paper with shaking hands and reads, "We, the jury, unanimously fix the sentence at life imprisonment without the possibility of parole." Jim, leaning on the table, shows no reaction. His life has been spared, but he will never live outside of prison again. Emory McClinton, sandwiched between his wife and Pat McKenna, squeezes Jo Ann's arm and she responds with a quick smile void of joy; there's nothing joyful about any of this. Emory whispers to McKenna and pats his arm too. They've been through so much together.

"Would Mr. Sullivan like to say anything before the sentence is imposed?" asks Judge Goger, looking over his glasses at Jim.

"No. Thank you," says Jim quietly. His hands shake as he slides his little tube of Vaseline back into his yellow file folder.

In September, six months after the verdict, a Fulton County Superior Court judge will deny Jim's attorneys' request for a new trial. He appeals. Finally, in 2008, the Georgia Supreme Court denies that appeal, exhausting all of Jim's efforts to walk free.

CHAPTER 35

WHERE'S THE MONEY?

Despite winning the wrongful death judgment in civil court, the McClinton family never received a dime from Jim Sullivan, nor did their lawyers.

As a refresher: in 1994, a jury concluded Jim was guilty of orchestrating Lita's death and awarded Lita's estate $4 million. Jim appealed in 1997 and won on a technicality; he successfully argued that the wrongful death suit had been filed after the two-year Florida statute of limitations had expired. The McClintons' lawyers counter appealed. They argued that when they filed the case in 1992, they were abiding by Georgia's statute of limitations, which was five years—and that since the murder occurred in Georgia, the court should follow Georgia law. Finally, in 1999, after Jim had already vanished, the Florida Supreme Court reversed its judgment and reinstated the original award to the McClintons, plus interest.

To be clear, the McClinton family has never been interested in Jim's money, they just didn't want him to have it. Today, Jo Ann wants nothing to do with it. But the McClintons' lawyers held hard to the effort as a matter of principle. It's money a jury awarded to the family—a debt Jim should've been forced to pay. It burned everyone that Jim had managed to squirrel it out of reach.

DEB MILLER LANDAU

"We wanted to have it taken from him," says Pat McKenna. "Because money meant more to him than human lives. It meant more to him than his own family."

Of course, whether James Sullivan has any money left is up for debate, but many people believe he does. When he was arrested, the FBI's legal attaché in Thailand found records showing Jim had worked with a Palm Beach lawyer to stash away his remaining funds in offshore accounts, which he shielded from debtors through a trust in Lichtenstein. But searching for money in offshore accounts is difficult and expensive. McKenna even refinanced his house to pay for an investigator to go to Lichtenstein, but the investigator ended up getting arrested for harassing a banker, and the whole thing went nowhere. In 2003, David Boone filed a lawsuit against the US branch of Swiss Bank, Julius Bear, and the Palm Beach lawyer who, he alleged, funneled cash to Jim in Thailand. The complaint included multiple counts of fraudulent transfer of funds, federal money laundering, and others. The lawsuit alleged that by helping Jim hide his money while he was a fugitive, the bank defrauded the McClintons. The case was ultimately dismissed, as were several others over the years as Jim's defense team fought for his freedom. A judge is often reluctant to take money away from someone under criminal prosecution because they need some way to pay for their defense.

Although the money trail went cold after Jim's conviction, it's not entirely frozen. In 2018, lawyers Moores and Kupfer won a case in Florida circuit court to lift the twenty-year statute of limitations on the civil court judgment (which, with interest, has ballooned to an estimated $17.5 million). When Boone and Moores died in 2018 and 2020, respectively, it seemed any attempt to find the money also died. But that's not quite true.

❖

After he left the Sullivan case, special agent John Kingston went on to cover white-collar financial crimes for the FBI, busting wealthy criminals for money laundering, embezzlement, and fraud. He frequently worked with the Department of Justice and the Office of International Affairs and has a good handle on the intense complexities of international banking laws. When we met, he asked me a thousand questions about the status of the wrongful death judgment and the whereabouts of Jim's funds. It sparked a convoluted game of telephone tag and revealed to me that I was in way over my head.

In November 2022, I met with retired appellate attorney Richard Kupfer in Florida. Like everyone else I spoke to for this project, Rick was surprised to hear from me, but also intrigued. Rick, now retired, arranged for us to meet at a fellow attorney's West Palm Beach law office, where he hauled a massive box of files out of his trunk and plunked it in the middle of a conference table. Rick is fit, tidy, with a Florida tan, glistening white teeth, and bright blue eyes. He's into outer space, travels around the country looking through telescopes and following lunar and solar events. Along with maintaining excellent files, he followed the 2006 trial and kept an interest in the case. He helped me tremendously by explaining the details when I was drowning in legalese. When we met, he explained that the civil judgment had to be renewed every seven years to stay valid. The last renewal was in 2016—which Jim, from prison, tried to fight. But the renewal succeeded. My math concluded that the next renewal would be just months away.

"So, who's handling the renewal now?" I ask Rick.

"Good question," he says, looking me in the eye, thinking. "I don't know."

We reached out to Boone's former law partner, Bill Stone. While Stone certainly knew about the case, he didn't have much to do with litigating it—that was David and another attorney named Simone Siex Boone, who happened to also be David's widow. Stone told me that Simone, now retired, is still handling the renewal and was recently in the office digging through files. I immediately called her.

"We've tried several different ways of trying to collect on the judgment and have been unsuccessful every time," she explained, clearly weary after decades of disappointment in their inability to track down Jim's assets. "Most of the places that we have chased the money to are places that are very protective of their banking clients. So, you just can't get to it. And that's the biggest issue—it's not so much where it is, but how do you get to it."

She's vowed to continue renewing the judgment. She said the 2016 renewal was extended for ten years, so the next renewal will be up in 2026, at which point Jim will be eighty-five. As long as there is an open judgment, as long as they keep renewing the judgment, any money Jim has will need to go toward paying it off. If the judgment were to lapse before his death, Nana, Jim's fourth wife, would be Jim's likely beneficiary. Because of this, it behooves her to say nothing, and she hasn't. Over the years, lawyers have deposed Nana and her daughters, but they've remained tight-lipped and have denied knowing anything about Jim's past, or his assets.

CHAPTER 36

A TRUCKER
AND A MILLIONAIRE
(2023)

When Tony Harwood pulls up in an old beige pickup truck and parks beside my minivan at Albemarle's City Lake Park in early 2023, he's been out of prison for almost five years. My heart is racing. I wave awkwardly and see the shadow of a tiny person in the passenger seat. I breathe a little sigh of relief knowing he's brought his girlfriend, a woman he'd previously described as "a hoarder," "alcoholic," "schizophrenic," and "bipolar," a woman suffering from emphysema and myriad other ailments. I know from our past phone calls that he's been living with her on and off, between bouts of her kicking him out or him leaving because he can't stand the chaos. I guess this means they're back together.

The first time he called me after months of my trying to find him, he was living in his truck. "You would not believe what I'm going through right now," he said. He was between jobs, trying to find an affordable rental, getting squirrely living in the cab of his truck. "This is probably the worst time in my life." He paused. "Other than January the 16th, 1987."

I was taken aback that he brought it up so quickly. I thought I'd have to pry any discussion of that day out of his big felon hands, but he went on to tell me how his once-close family is now fractured and suffering with their own troubles and ailments. They mostly ignored Tony's letters from prison. "They are totally convinced that I actually pulled the trigger," he said.

I found it confusing—even after all this time, after twenty years behind bars, Tony is sticking to the story that he didn't shoot Lita?

"Lemme tell you this, the day, January the 16th, when that man pulled that trigger, I stopped living," he'd told me the first time we spoke on the phone. "I prayed every day from that day forth that God would take this burden off my chest. When they arrested me in '98, it was a relief. I was so glad it was finally coming to a head."

On that same call, he asked my astrological sign and whether I was single. He also wanted money, a dedicated private investigator, a metal detector (to go look for the gun), Georgia criminal law books, and assurances that I wouldn't throw him under the bus. I told him journalistic integrity meant I couldn't pay him for his story, but maybe Pat McKenna and I could turn over some stones if it ever came to that. He vanished for a while and then emailed again. It seemed more than anything—more than money or stuff or investigative ability—he wanted the world to know that he wasn't a cold-blooded killer.

❖

When Tony gets out of the pickup, I feel a little disappointed. In my mind, he's a giant. But now, at seventy-two, he's stooped from chronic back problems and is clearly a shrunken version of what he once was. He wears a black leather cowboy hat, an oversized black winter coat, blue jeans, and black running shoes with Velcro straps.

He eyes my van: "What, you don't know your colors?" he says.

I had mistakenly described the minivan as black when it was dark gray. I laugh nervously, mutter something about how it was dark when I picked up the car, but he's already walking over to help his girlfriend out of the passenger side of the truck. She is tiny, frail. She's just gotten out of the hospital, has deep purple bruises on her arms from IVs, and carries a little oxygen tank in a hot pink tote. It's so cold, I suggest we go to a coffee shop, but they're not getting back in the car. He nods toward my minivan.

"Oh, yeah, in the van? OK," I say. I slide the side door open, and the girlfriend climbs into the back seat, Tony takes the passenger seat, and I return to the driver's side. Together, we look out at the lake, and he starts talking about long-haul trucking, how today's drivers don't know shit, how wind impacts drive time, how he's a pro. His hands are thick, strong paddles. A silver ring with a carved red scorpion hugs his ring finger. An old Timex Indiglo watch clings to his wrist. He fiddles with the lid to his plastic bottle of 7-Up. Maybe he's nervous too.

We spend a long time talking about trucking, the cold temperatures, the recent death of Lisa Marie Presley, the downsides of Albemarle, the meth problems. Tony and his girlfriend met in the second grade but only really got to know each other when Tony got out of prison in 2018. They insist Kamala Harris is evil and the Chinese are conspiring to kill pets by injecting poison into dog food.

Finally, he's ready to talk about the murder, the event that put him in prison for twenty years—the event that has us sitting here together in a desolate park in the middle of nowhere.

Despite the three distinct composite drawings from eyewitness descriptions, he says, "There weren't never three people." He doesn't know why the composites don't look like anyone and disagrees that the one of the shooter resembles him. I want to pull the composite up and hold it next to him, but don't want to freak him out. Later, I study it and think, it sure could be him, it looks an awful lot like him. But it's also just a sketch from more than thirty-five years ago—and it may not be him, too.

He bought the roses, he says, and has no idea why the clerk described him with a scruffy beard and mustache and unruly brown hair. He mentions several times that Randall Benson, the florist, was gay by way of explanation. When I ask what that has to do with anything, he says Benson lied because he had AIDS and was dying. Benson did die at the age of forty-one, in 2002, but whether he was sick in 1987 would've been completely unknowable to Tony. But regardless, Tony's idea that Benson would lie to police because he was dying makes no sense anyway. There are so many head-scratching nonsensical moments like this with Tony, red herrings swimming in every direction. I find myself repeatedly lured into these murky mental estuaries where I lose sight of the shore.

When I ask him about Tracy the Stripper, he tells me he'd known her from decades ago in Texas; she used to date a friend of his and was a top-less dancer before hanging up her dancing shoes and becoming a lesbian. He says he reconnected with her in the months before the murder while she was working at the Palace. He told her he needed to find someone to do a hit, basically a subcontractor. He gave her $1,500. She found John the Bartender, who was ready to jump in and murder a woman he didn't know for the price of a few grams of cocaine.

"Why would John do it?" I ask.

"He thought we was going to go in business killing people," Tony says.

But, I say, you were the one who took the money from Jim, you bought the flowers and drove to the condo—twice. You orchestrated the whole thing. None of this would have happened if not for you. Surely, I think, he must admit that.

But no, Tony reminds me that he never thought John would go through with it, basically the same story he testified to at Jim's trial. It's both inter-esting and crazy, the way he distances himself from responsibility. He says, sure he took the money from Jim, but it was Tracy who hired the hitman, and John who did the shooting. His theory is that the cops never went after John because they couldn't tie him to Jim. They needed Tony to take the fall because he was the only one connected to Jim.

A lot of our conversation in the minivan bounces around. I have to be careful how hard I press him. I feel like I'm roasting a marshmallow; every time I think I'm getting close to a nicely browned morsel, the whole thing suddenly bursts into flames. Occasionally, Tony gets out to smoke a ciga-rette in the cold—I won't let him smoke in the car, partially because there's a big NO SMOKING sign embedded in the dash, but mostly because there's a woman with an oxygen tank in the back seat. In these few moments the girlfriend and I are alone, she tells me about her life. She's been in and out of abusive relationships her whole life. A few months after Tony got out of prison, he showed up on her doorstep and just sort of moved in. They're on the outs, she says; he's sleeping on the couch.

When they drive away that day, I stop the recorder and look out at the lake. I'm exhausted, burnt out on little sleep, the long, winding conversation, and the afterburn of adrenaline. Maybe this John guy *did* do the shooting and, if so, he got away with murder. Why didn't Tony bring up the whole stripper-bartender story until a good five years after his arrest? If it was Tony, why, after doing his twenty years in fourteen different prisons, is he so adamant it wasn't him? Wouldn't he be better off just keeping his mouth shut and fading quietly into old age? If it wasn't Tony, why didn't investigators find the real shooter? Why, after so much investigative muscle and manpower, does this piece remain unsolved?

I look down and see that Tony's left his green 7-Up cap on the floor of the car. For a second I think maybe I should bag it for DNA but then chuckle at myself; of course, it makes no sense. I check my phone; after nearly three hours, I have several texts from my friend in Atlanta. *Are you OK? Where are you? Are you ALIVE? Call me!*

❖

I learn later when I am going through the GBI case file on Tony Harwood and James Sullivan that investigators did indeed find John the Bartender, still living in Matthews, North Carolina. GBI agents interviewed him several times over the years and spoke with his probation officer, his acquaintances, and the Palace's former owner. John managed the Palace for three years—from fall 1986 till spring 1989, so the timing was right. He was fired for theft before being arrested and sent to federal prison in 1990 for bank and mail fraud. He was a gun guy; at the time of his arrest, FBI agents seized several firearms, but none of them matched the gun that killed Lita.

One could argue that John somewhat resembled the driver in the composite photos but looked nothing like the drawing of the shooter. John was a big guy, around six feet tall, 240 pounds, with a receding hairline and glasses. He would've been in his mid-thirties in 1987. He had three fingers missing from his left hand, due to a construction accident in 1986, a year before Lita's murder. He'd repeatedly told investigators he couldn't remember Tracy and didn't know Tony or anything about the murder. Nothing—other than the fact that he'd worked at the Palace—ever tied him to the crime.

I'd asked Tony on one of our many phone calls what he and John talked about in the car. After all, they'd driven together between North Carolina and Atlanta at least twice, but he says they didn't really talk about anything.

"What was there to talk about?" Tony says.

"I don't know," I said. "Life? Women? Strippers? Drugs? The fact that you were going to go kill a woman?" Then I asked him about John's messed-up hand.

"His what? Messed up neck?" Tony asked.

"No, HAND," I said. "Apparently he had a pretty significant injury on one of his hands."

"I wouldn't know," said Tony. "I don't know nothing about him."

I find it hard to believe that Tony, a talker, drove in silence with a guy on such a long road trip. I also find it strange he wouldn't notice that the guy he'd hired to kill Lita, a guy with whom he'd spent at least twenty hours in a car and several hours at the HoJo's, was missing three fingers.

Investigators also found Tracy, who did work for a time as a dancer at the Palace, but she quit working there two years before the murder. She said she knew Tony a long time ago, that she'd dated a friend of his in Texas, but that was a lifetime ago. She said she knew nothing about the crime or why he would implicate her. She knew of a bouncer at the Palace named John, a volatile individual who liked to dominate women—he was once arrested for assaulting a dancer—and who kept a gun behind a cabinet at the bar. But she said she'd never considered him a friend and would certainly never broker a deal between him and Tony. She also testified to all this via video during Jim's 2006 trial.

Tracy died in 2022. John, now in his seventies, still lives in Matthews, not far from the old Palace bar.

❖

Prosecutor Clint Rucker doesn't believe for a second that Tony wasn't the triggerman.

"If there was a 'John the Bartender' out there . . . between all the resources that are available to law enforcement, believe me, they'd have found his ass," he told me recently, adding that it's not uncommon for even the most hardened criminals to deny responsibility for crimes because to do otherwise would be admitting to an unfathomable level of depravity. "It's hard to finally look a person in the eye and say, 'Yeah, I shot her in the head. I shot an unarmed woman in the head for money,'" said Rucker. "And Tony Harwood is such a narcissist, he would never admit to being a monster."

Rucker reminds me of a pivotal moment in the trial when Lita's neighbor Bob Christenson was on the stand. Bob's eyewitness description had been the basis for the composite drawing of the shooter. When Tony was arrested in 1998, the cops put him in a physical lineup and brought Bob in, but he couldn't pick out the man he saw deliver flowers eleven years earlier. At trial, Rucker made a risky move and showed Bob a Harwood family photo taken around the time of the murder—risky because prosecutors generally don't ask witnesses a question unless they are certain of the answer.

"Are there any facial features or characteristics of the white males in the photo that resemble the man you saw outside the home of Lita on January 16, 1987?" Rucker asked Bob on the stand.

"Yes," said Bob. Rucker handed him the pointer stick and asked him to say who. Bob immediately pointed to a man kneeling in the first row.

"Would it surprise you to know that that man was Tony Harwood?" Rucker asked. Before Bob could answer, Judge Goger sustained a defense objection, but the cat was out of the bag.

Reflecting on it now, Rucker says, "It's one of my favorite moments in my professional career, you know, a real Perry Mason moment."

Rucker interviewed several jurors after the trial and recalls one of them saying that even without Tony's and Belinda's testimony, they would've found Jim guilty. They said the calls and Christenson's identification of Tony in that family photo would've been enough.

Former FBI agent John Kingston has a theory that the accomplices were Tony's brothers. After all, he said, the driver and flower buyer had an uncanny resemblance to two other Harwoods. This may explain why Tony was so tight-lipped about his accomplices, why he didn't bring up the bartender—potentially just a foil—until years after his arrest. Investigators did interview the brothers—one was in prison for molesting his stepdaughter—but nothing tied them to the murder either.

Special Agent John Lang says maybe Tony wasn't the triggerman, but if not, why not give authorities all the details—why keep it cagey and vague? Were Tony and John too coked up at the time to remember the details? Did they spend the hours driving to and from Atlanta pit-stopping to snort lines? Lang says no one knows the truth except Tony.

"He knows exactly what happened, without a doubt," Lang told me. "That's between him and God."

But ultimately maybe it doesn't matter who pulled the trigger. Tony orchestrated the whole thing and spent twenty years migrating through fourteen different Georgia prisons. Today, he takes whatever trucking jobs he can get and struggles to make ends meet. He called me once, excited because the husband of an old family friend had died and Tony got to keep his clothes. Of his hundred or so friends on Facebook, many are bikini-clad women, likely bots. He posts a lot about forgiveness, including this quote: "Forgive others, not because they deserve forgiveness, but because you deserve peace." It's hard to know if this refers to him or everyone else. At the root of almost every story in his life is the belief that everyone has thrown him under the bus, that everyone's a liar, including Belinda, Tracy, the prosecutors, defense attorneys, Agent

Lang, his own lawyers, the eyewitnesses, the florist. He'll probably say that I'm a liar too.

But Tony was always just a conduit, a pawn. The real culprit is James Vincent Sullivan, who today sits behind bars at the Augusta State Medical Prison (ASMP), a facility that houses inmates with severe medical cases or who require specialized treatment. A prisoner's health-care information is private, and my open records requests for information about Jim's life in prison were denied. I wanted to know who visited him and when, whether he partakes in programs, or has had any altercations with other inmates. But the only thing they'll tell me is that he's had visitors, which I believe is likely singular, likely Nana—the woman he married in Thailand. Don Samuel told me that she'd contacted their office at the height of COVID-19 asking to get Jim out, but Samuel never replied. "What was the point?" he said. "The answer was 'No.'"

In Georgia, an inmate needs to put you on their visitation list before you can visit. I wrote to Jim several times, offering him an invitation to tell his side of the story, but he never replied.

Jim arrived at ASMP in 2021, after dozens of prison moves. Like many prisons in Georgia, ASMP is plagued with problems. News reports tell of violence among inmates, corrupt corrections officers, ineffective leadership, inadequate staffing, and a serious backlog of requests for medical care. I can only imagine what life is like for Jim, confined to a cement cell with only a single sink, a toilet, and the weight of his thoughts. Does he long to stretch out in the 17,000 square feet of Casa Eleda? Does he recall the labels of his fine wine collection in Costa Rica? Does he dream of smoking cigars overlooking the bay in Thailand? Can he remember the faces of his children? Does he wonder what happened to Coco, the dog? Finally, does he dream of Lita when he closes his eyes, imagine her big, bright smile and the golden way she made people feel—until he wakes up and remembers what he did?

Unlike most prisoners in the Georgia prison system, Jim grew up a privileged white man. He came from a loving family and had a stellar education, a windfall of inheritance, and a chance at living a big, meaningful life. Maybe he would've been better off without these privileges; maybe then he would've learned how to love.

Jim will never again play tennis, walk the beach, drive a Rolls, or breathe the crisp air of freedom. At eighty-two, he is down to 119 pounds, a diminished version of an already small person. One day, he too will die—and no one will send flowers.

EPILOGUE
RACE, POWER, PRIVILEGE

I spoke to dozens of people while researching this book and of most—if not all—I asked this one question: What did race have to do with this story? I wanted to know if thoughts had changed in the decades since Lita's murder, especially as our country continues to reckon with its history of white supremacy. Most of the white people I interviewed said they believed racism had little to do with the case, or they struggled to articulate how it did. But *every* Black person I asked said, yes, *of course* race mattered.

"Race underlies everything we do in this society. Once you become knowledgeable about these issues you realize that everything you do relates to the color of your skin," Emory McClinton once told me. He and Jo Ann had encouraged their children to see people as individuals, not to judge them by whatever group they belonged to. But, he said, if racism isn't slapping you in the face, it's always lingering in the background. For Black people, he said, injustice is a duplicitous ghost that appears in many forms and requires constant vigilance. In marrying Jim, Lita had let her guard down.

Former prosecutor Clint Rucker believes Jim was attracted to Lita because he got off on the idea he was getting away with something. "I think that his attraction to her was because of her skin color," says Rucker. "From the times of slavery, that's what we are talking about—this forbidden attraction between two statuses of people."

Jim treated Lita like a trophy, a showpiece, a thing. He believed she should've been thankful for his adoration, happy that he allowed her to wear the jewelry he bought her but kept under lock and key, and grateful to live in his mansion. Her feelings and needs didn't matter because they weren't of value to him. When their lust for each other began to wane, he found his thrills elsewhere, often with other women of color. He thought Lita should just shut up and put up with that too.

"I thought there was a real devaluation of her as a person," says Rucker. "Sullivan was so much older than Lita. He had lived. He had been married previously. Here's this chance to taste the forbidden fruit. But when I get tired, I'm going to kick you to the curb." He says Suki was just a replacement, a new flavor of forbidden fruit.

"He had a thing about minority women," says Yvette Miller, the longtime appeals court judge and former Miss Macon who thought of Lita as a sister. "But he felt like they were inferior."

Former GBI agent John Lang, who'd shared with me naked photos of Jim wearing his house-arrest ankle bracelet with Black prostitutes at Casa Eleda, says he doesn't think this case was about race; Jim just had a thing for women of color.

❖

Winfield Ward Murray, a lawyer and federal immigration judge, teaches a Race & Law class at Morehouse College. In it, he examines the Bill of Rights, specifically looking at discrepancies in bail. The Eighth Amendment, which protects defendants against cruel and unusual punishment and excessive bail, also favors the wealthy and white. In his class, he uses James Sullivan as an example of a man who was a prime murder suspect for almost twenty years but continued to slip through because he could afford bail and high-priced lawyers. It's a privilege afforded to the rich, especially white people. The NAACP says 34 percent of the nation's prison population is Black, despite Black people accounting for less than 14 percent of the general population. Black Americans are incarcerated at more than five times the rate of white people, which means they get issued bail more frequently, and often at higher rates than their white counterparts, even when they're charged with the same crime.

"When Blacks are unable to afford bail they have little choice but to languish in prison while they await trial," says Murray. "This is before they are ever convicted of a crime. This only exacerbates the strain on Black families mentally, emotionally, and of course economically."

He also talks about how white criminals are treated differently throughout the criminal justice system when the victims are Black and the defendant is white or perceived to have wealth and power. For example, he says, in the Charleston church massacre where nine Black people were killed during bible study in 2015, at the time the largest mass shooting at a place of worship in US history, police offered the shooter, twenty-one-year-old Dylann Roof, a McDonald's burger on the way to jail. During the bond hearing, the judge in the case, who had a history of uttering racial slurs, made a plea asking everyone in the courtroom to consider that Roof's family were victims too. It sparked outrage in the community but underscored a historical tendency to give white people the benefit of the doubt when they're accused of crimes—again, a consideration rarely given to Black defendants.

Did Jim get away with murder for nearly twenty years because he was rich? Because he was white? Would he have gotten away with it so long if Lita were white? Would anyone (including me) have given the story attention if they were uneducated white people or poor Black people?

In 2018, Murray wrote in *Atlanta* magazine that although his city seems a bastion of open-mindedness compared to the rest of the South, "Atlanta is not a bubble. Atlanta, as it turns out, is inextricably linked to Georgia—and to America. The racism that permeates our society can be found everywhere."

❖

Ancient oaks and magnolia trees cloak the forty-eight acres of Atlanta's Oakland Cemetery in a dozen shades of green. More than 70,000 people are buried here—from bankers and philanthropists to governors and Pulitzer Prize-winning writers. Margaret Mitchell rests here, along with Kenny Rogers and Maynard Jackson. It used to be that the dead were divided—Confederate soldiers rest together in a rectangle-shaped section of the cemetery across the path from Jewish Hill. The African American Burial Grounds sit surrounded by a vast potter's field. Some gravestones are so old the names and dates are indecipherable, as though the slate and granite are dissolving into the earth like the bodies beneath them. It's an interesting thing to think about—all these opposing forces of Atlanta's history coalescing in the boundaryless earth below.

Recently, I ventured through the maze of the cemetery to find the McClinton family plot, where Lita's ashes are interred in a white marble columbarium. I sat down on the marble bench that faces a large, powerful bronze sculpture titled "Duo," by Mexican sculptor Victor Salmones. It depicts two people, one being held lovingly by another. On the ground before it, a plaque reads: *In loving memory of Dearest Lita, the giver—whose inner beauty was blinding.* It felt exceedingly intimate to be sitting there, listening to the birds in the trees, the MARTA trains humming in the background, a jet zooming by overhead. It was early spring, still mild; soon everything would bloom and burst into life and the air would be heavy with heat. The rest of the McClintons will end up here too one day, including Harrison Wiener, who was an unborn baby in Valencia's womb when his Aunt Lita was killed. Growing up, Harrison loved hearing stories about the aunt he never met. Today, Harrison is in his late thirties, married with a child of his own. When I sent him the video footage of him giving his impact statement at Jim's 2006 trial, he struggled to watch it—it's still too painful to carry all the anguish his family has gone through.

Ingrid Marable, Poppy's daughter, who was the three-year-old hiding in the upstairs closet when Lita was shot, is now a strong woman in her early forties. "When I was young, I remember wanting a new godmother because I wanted to have someone here on earth who loved me like Mama

Lita loved me," she told me. "I wish I could have grown up with her in my life. But I have always felt her presence watching over me."

Lita's death sent reverberations through generations. There's something about her story that made lawyers spend their careers helping her family, compelled hardened cops to shed tears at her vindication. She meant so much to Detective Welcome Harris that she was mentioned in his obituary. Every single person I spoke with for this story remembered it well, had held onto details they could've long forgotten. Whether they knew her or not, people cared about Lita, wanted to feel her presence even when she was gone. That stayed deep inside me too as I moved across the country, built a family, and grew to an age Lita would never be. My old box of files, filled with yellowing papers that carry the work of hundreds of police, agents, lawyers, and reporters, is joined now by gigabytes of digital files and a million hand-scrawled notes. I realize now why I never got rid of it: every time I look, I see something new.

❖

So many people were impacted by Lita's life and death but there is no one for whom the ache is deeper than Lita's family.

Emory McClinton Sr. passed away in December 2023 at age ninety, with Jo Ann, his wife of more than seventy years, at his side. In his long life, as a father and a fighter, he had opened so many minds, including my own. I imagine he's up there somewhere, free from pain, dancing with his eldest daughter.

When I visited Jo Ann before Emory passed, she told me she has a recurring vision of Lita wearing a blue sundress walking in the garden with her dog Ashley Wilkes at their old house on East Lake. I felt a palpable shift as Jo Ann drifted away for a moment, out of the room into a happier time, watching her eldest daughter sashay through the garden. She said she could see it, clear as day.

"I don't know why it's important," she said. "But it is."

A NOTE ON SOURCES

E very single moment, conversation, and detail in this book came from source materials or live interviews—on the odd occasion, I added some minor details to animate or recreate scenes. I found much of my information in court documents, transcripts, police reports, investigative files, and the records graciously lent to me by former FBI special agent John Kingston and lawyer Rick Kupfer. I leaned on the hard work of reporters from the *Atlanta Journal-Constitution*, the *Macon Telegraph, Palm Beach Post*, and *Sun Sentinel*, among others. I pulled in details from my original *Atlanta* magazine article, "Social Disgraces," and from two books: *The Palm Beach Murder* by Marion Collins (St. Martin's True Crime Library) and *Deadly Roses: The Twenty Year Curse* by Marvin Marable. Some of my information came from television shows, including *America's Most Wanted, Dateline, Dominick Dunne's Power, Privilege & Justice, 48 Hours, FBI: Criminal Pursuit*, BET's 2019 docudrama *Murder in the Thirst*, and, most recently, Oxygen Network's *Real Murders of Atlanta*.

I'm grateful for the Freedom of Information Act, MuckRock, and all the people who chase down FOIA requests. Thank you to all the keepers of the past, specifically Robin Gay at the Georgia Bureau of Investigation, the staff at the National Archives in Atlanta, Holly Smith at Spelman College, the Atlanta Police Department, and the staff at the Fulton County Courthouse.

A NOTE ON STYLE

Throughout this book, we have chosen to capitalize the word "Black" when referring to Black people to reflect contemporary style norms.

ACKNOWLEDGMENTS

From the moment we first met, I knew my editor Jessica Case was a woman on my wavelength. Thanks to Jessica and Julia Romero, copyeditor Victoria Rose, proofreader Stephanie Marshall Ward, designer Maria Fernandez, and all the folks at Pegasus for making this book come to life. Thanks to my agent Rick Richter, and Caroline Marsiglia at Aevitas Creative Management, for believing in the project from the start. To Jill Cox-Cordova, my sensitivity reader turned friend—you are a wonder.

I'm forever grateful to *Atlanta* magazine's Scott Freeman for first assigning me this story in 2004 and for his unwavering belief in my writing, then and now.

To all the folks who started as strangers and who, over phone calls, emails, or in-person visits, became friends. This generous tribe includes the incomparable Patrick McKenna, Richard Kupfer, Clint Rucker, Don Samuel, Winfield Ward Murray, Yvette Miller, Ingrid Marable, Bill McKinnon, Chris Harvey, Simone Siex Boone, Vickie Rogers, the late Brad Moores, David Boone, and John Connolly. My true partners in crime include FBI agent John Kingston, GBI agent John Lang, and FBI agents Todd Letcher and Mike Greene. Special thanks to the late Bill Montgomery from the *Atlanta Journal-Constitution*, and to Frank Cerabino and Jane Musgrave from the *Palm Beach Post*.

To Tony Harwood—thank you for sharing your side.

To my family—especially mum Barbara Kroon, dad Bill Miller, and sister Karen Magelund, for being early readers and lifelong believers. To my boys Cash and Ryder for always cheering me on, even when I was drowning. Thank you for reminding me we can truly do anything.

To Jennifer Hyde for her incredible cinematic eye, beautiful bonfires, and spare bedroom in Atlanta. I literally couldn't have done this without you. To all the Atlanta crew for the love and support.

To the fabulous Lit Ladies, for brainstorming, early encouragement, and review of so many drafts: Chloe, Eileen, Heidi, Kaarin, and to Elizabeth Rusch for bringing us all together.

To Fiona Mayhill for always knowing who I am, even when I forget sometimes. To Talie Smith for the daily walks and wide-open heart. To the Euchre Bitches—Heidi, Lisa, Brooke—for the endless enthusiasm, and to super reader Chris Kyle for editing between costume changes at Mardi Gras. Thanks to early readers Emily Culbert and Jan Dunham, and to Matt H. King for the author photos. Thank you, all.

Finally, my heartfelt gratitude to the McClinton family, specifically Jo Ann McClinton, the late Emory McClinton, Valencia McClinton, and Harrison Wiener. Jo Ann, thank you for your trust. I hope I did you proud.